The Value of Debt in Building Wealth

The Value of Debt in Building Wealth

*Creating Your Glide Path
to a Healthy Financial L.I.F.E.*

Thomas J. Anderson

WILEY

Published by John Wiley & Sons, Inc., Hoboken, New Jersey.
Published simultaneously in Canada.

For general information on our other products and services or for technical support, please contact our
Customer Care Department within the United States at (800) 762-2974, outside the United States at
(317) 572-3993 or fax (317) 572-4002.

Wiley publishes in a variety of print and electronic formats and by print-on-demand. Some material
included with standard print versions of this book may not be included in e-books or in
print-on-demand. If this book refers to media such as a CD or DVD that is not included in the
version you purchased, you may download this material at http://booksupport.wiley.com. For more
information about Wiley products, visit www.wiley.com.

Library of Congress Cataloging-in-Publication Data:

Names: Anderson, Thomas J. (Certified investment management analyst)
Title: The value of debt in building wealth / Thomas J. Anderson.
Description: Hoboken : Wiley, 2017. | Includes bibliographical references and
    index. | Description based on print version record and CIP data provided
    by publisher; resource not viewed.
Identifiers: LCCN 2016046388 (print) | LCCN 2016058654 (ebook) | ISBN
    9781119049258 (pdf) | ISBN 9781119049265 (epub) | ISBN 9781119049296
    (hardback)
Subjects: LCSH: Debt. | Loans, Personal. | Finance, Personal. | BISAC:
    BUSINESS & ECONOMICS / Personal Finance / Money Management.
Classification: LCC HG3701 (print) | LCC HG3701 .A635 2017 (ebook) | DDC
    332.024/02—dc23
LC record available at https://lccn.loc.gov/2016058654

Cover Design: Wiley

Printed in the United States of America

10 9 8 7 6 5 4 3 2 1

FOR ROWAN, RORY & REID

I love YOU more ;-)

Contents

Foreword

L ike many Americans, I have a complicated history with debt. In my 20s living in New York City, I spent more than I could afford, borrowing to fill the gap and running up my credit card. I was living above my means, digging myself into a hole of debt with no experience of knowing how hard it would be to climb out.

I couldn't get out of it on my own. Eventually, I met my future wife, and after we married, she pulled me out of my debt with her savings—not a great way to start a marriage.

Debt also helped me build my wealth. In the mid-2000s, when my wife and I bought our house, we took out the largest mortgage we could afford. What's more, the mortgage we took out was interest only. We had no plans to pay off our mortgage and we never have. Today, the house is worth more than twice as much as it was when we bought it (at least according to Zillow). And that money we saved by not paying down any principal on our mortgage, roughly $8,400 a year, or $96,600 by now has gone, in part, toward renovating the house. We have a new kitchen and a finished basement. Without that savings, we also likely wouldn't have felt comfortable maxing out our 401(k)s and contributing to our kids' college savings accounts.

I'm not sure exactly where I got the idea that it was OK to take out a huge mortgage and go for a home loan that—at least at the time—other people were saying was too risky. But I know at least some of the courage to do so came from Tom Anderson and the conversations we have had over the years, often late at night when we should have been talking politics or sports. We are fellow finance geeks.

A quick disclaimer: I have known Tom Anderson for more than 20 years. We met in college, became quick friends, and have stayed friends ever since.

As unbiased as I can be, Tom is one of the most insightful and original thinkers among the financial planners I have known. And having been a personal finance and investing reporter for a good portion of my career, I have known many.

What you have here is a powerful tool to increase your wealth, lower your stress about your money, and create a happy future. Do the worksheets; they are great. Like me, you may not get all passing grades, but what you will get is a sense of what direction to go and how to get there. And I certainly got a lot more confidence I could get where I wanted to be.

Most personal finance books are really works of pop psychology—a bag of tricks to make you feel better about your finances, not actually improve them. Paying off your lowest balance credit card, for instance, instead of your lowest rate credit card, may make you feel better about your finances, but in the long run it will actually make you poorer. And, as Tom shows in this book, having no mortgage or debt might make you feel better, but it may also cut off your best path to wealth.

Tom lays out how to move into a better financial position without needing any tricks.

Tom does make one point in the book I would quibble with: He says that stock market valuations are so high, and the prospects for growth are so low, that U.S. markets in general are likely to disappoint. I have a more optimistic view of U.S. market growth. But we always engage in friendly debate and, in the end, he is right—none of us knows the future. Even if interest rates stay low for longer than expected and stock market returns are better than expected, that makes now an even better time to follow Tom's advice on how to convert debt into equity on your own personal balance sheet.

What you have in front of you is a true gift: A powerful guide to your financial future at the exact right time in history when the advice it has to give is most likely to generate the biggest reward. Use it wisely.

Stephen Gandel
Deputy Digital Editor, *Fortune* Magazine
September 30, 2016

Acknowledgments

I t is with deep and sincere gratitude that I want to recognize the
Museum of Science and Industry in Chicago. While standing at an
exhibit on the Fibonacci sequence, the golden ratio and balance in
art, life, music and nature, a wave of inspiration came over me. It took
much longer than I would have anticipated to take the initial inspiration
and turn it into a specific and actionable plan, but it never would have
happened without that special trip to the museum. I also want to thank
the Adler Planetarium, which serves as a constant source of inspiration.
I am a finance nerd who knows virtually nothing about art or science, but
the museums of Chicago are my temples—my life would be incomplete
without you.

The seeds that were planted at the Museum of Science and Industry
would not have had soil in which they could grow had it not been
for my time at Washington University, the University of Chicago, and
brief time at the University of Pennsylvania and London School of
Economics/City University. Thank you so much for your contributions
to this book and to the broader field of finance. In particular, I want to
recognize Dr. Mahendra Gupta and Dr. Anjan Thakor at Washington

University for the incredible unwavering support for the vision and mission of this platform.

Sticking with the theme, the seed needed water, sun, and fertilizer to grow. The initial version would not have been possible without Jordan S. Gruber, who once again helped me structure my initial ideas. He magically brings order and structure to my crazy, random thoughts. Robyn Lawrence then refined it and gave the book the shape it has today. I love working with you.

I also want to recognize Paul Mulvaney, Daniel Eckert, Adam Browne, Brian Fagan, Ed Lomasney, Chris Merker, Doug Neuman, Tyler Olson, Chris Janus, and Nathan Swanson. You are dear friends who challenge me and tolerate endless debate and discussion on these ideas and most anything else that one could possibly care to argue. Duncan MacPherson, I enjoy exchanging ideas with you and you deliver an incredible service to financial advisors throughout the world. I am very grateful to my dear friend, Stephen Gandel, for his contributing the foreword. I appreciate your kind words and look forward to many more late night discussions—and to policing the bets in the book.

To the whole Supernova crew, this would not be possible without you and your support. Jani Anderson, Jeff Finn, Kishore Gangwani, Jim Guthrie, Mike Jackson, Jayruz Limfueco, Jun Lin, Lauren Kurtz, Ted Nims, Bill Slater, Jenny Sun, Brandon Swinton, Dongsheng Wu, Kevin Zhang, Yanan Zhang, and David Zylstra, zero days are work days when I'm with you. I love our shared vision for the future. Working together, I believe we can release people from the burdens of oppressive debt and break the paycheck-to-paycheck cycle and that we truly can empower people to live their best life possible. Thank you to Rob Knapp and Tao Huang not only for your roles on the team, but also for being guiding forces in my life.

Special recognition to the following members of the team: Julie Schmidt, Jaramee Finn, Fred Rose, and Ryan Segal had direct, significant and indelible contributions to this book. I have collaborated with Randy Kurtz since we were roommates in London. The research presented in Chapter 5 with respect to the merits of a diversified portfolio and the probabilities of success is all based on his work. His passion toward integrated, comprehensive, holistic wealth management advice motivates me every day. Bryan Goettel had a truly heroic role in shepherding this project and its many iterations through an extraordinarily busy 2015 and 2016.

Emmons Patzer, your OWE concept continues to be a foundation upon which I build every day. Thank you for being such a great mentor and a continued fountain of ideas. Along with Emmons, Bill King, Steve Vanourny, Eliot Protsch, Mahendra Gupta, David Lessing, Chris Reichert, and Scott Wolfrum have served as an outstanding group of advisors. You are truly an amazing group of thought leaders.

Once our plant grew out of control, skilled readers and editors came and made it pretty again. I would like to thank Erica Arnold, Christina Boris, Mark Fortier, Nicholas Kane, Ari Meltzer, Jennie Minessale, Matt Murray, Maureen O'Brien, Emily Schmidt, and Margaret Shepard. Kelly DiNardo, you are a talent and have a gift. Thank you for the candor and for the encouragement to say it like I see it.

Rafe Sagalyn, Brandon Coward, and the team at ICM are outstanding agents that continue to facilitate a great platform. I appreciate your advice and guidance.

Congratulations to the newly married Tula Weis! You continue to be my North Star. This project took me a while longer than I hoped, and you have no idea how much I appreciate your patience and support. Thank you to Jeremy Chia, Gayathri Govindarajan, Cheryl Ferguson, Mike Henton and the rest of the Wiley team—I sincerely appreciate your editorial skills. David Knuth, I sincerely appreciate your editorial help as well as your assistance in reviewing the math. Any remaining mistakes are my own.

Allison Parker, I can't thank you enough; your contributions and support mean more to me than you will ever know.

Darla, Kerry, Jo, Jon, Julie, Stacey, Pen, Damian, Oui, Johanna, you are part of my family and I love you dearly. Mom and Marty, Britt and Steve, Dad—thanks for the unconditional love and encouragement—especially through a crazy 2015/2016. Sarah, you are a wonderful mother to our beautiful children and I appreciate all that you have done to make this book possible.

Rowan, Rory, and Reid—this book is truly dedicated to you. Should anything happen to me, I hope you will keep this beside you as my guiding advice. I want you to enjoy the present, be prepared for emergencies, and be on track for the future. Debt can be a powerful tool to help you in so many ways—but you have to use it responsibly. I hope this book can serve as a glide path to help you navigate life throughout the many different phases, curve balls, and ups and downs that we all experience. And, if you wake up and find you are 60 years old and you still need more advice, I hope you will turn back to my last book. This way, I will always be by your side.

About the Author

Tom **Anderson** is the founder and CEO of Supernova Companies, a financial technology company that provides a comprehensive platform focused on managing both sides of an individual's balance sheet.

Tom is a *New York Times* bestselling author and nationally renowned financial planning expert. While traditional wealth management focuses primarily on client assets, Tom challenges conventional wisdom by demonstrating the value in evaluating individuals' complete financial picture. He has trained more than 10,000 financial advisors nationwide on how to implement his balanced, holistic wealth management strategies.

While he was Executive Director of Morgan Stanley Wealth Management, Tom was recognized as one of the top 40 advisors under 40 years old by *On Wall Street* Magazine. Throughout his career he has been named multiple times by *Barron's* Magazine as one of America's Top 1,200 advisors: State by State. His first book, *The Value of Debt*, is a *New York Times* and *USA Today* bestseller and was named the #2 business book of 2013 by WealthManagement.com. His second book, *The Value of Debt in Retirement*, has been featured in the *New York Times*, *USA Today*, *Forbes*, the *Washington Post*, CNBC, Fox Business, and Bloomberg.

Tom has his M.B.A. from the University of Chicago and a B.S.B.A. from Washington University in St. Louis, where he achieved a double major in finance and international business. During his undergraduate years, Tom studied abroad extensively, participating in programs at the London School of Economics and the Cass Business School at City University London, and he spent a year at ESCP Europe on their Madrid campus. In 2002, he attended the University of Pennsylvania Wharton School of Business, obtaining the title of Certified Investment Management Analyst (CIMA®), sponsored by the Investment Management Consultants Association (IMCA). Additionally, Tom has earned the Chartered Retirement Planning Counselor^{SM} (CRPC®) designation through the College for Financial Planning.

Prior to his career in private wealth management, Tom worked in investment banking in New York. He is fluent in Spanish and has lived and worked in Spain and Mexico. His extensive academic studies at some of the top schools in finance and economics, international experiences, and institutional background deliver a unique perspective on global markets.

Tom lives in downtown Chicago with his three children and his beautiful Goldendoodle, Harry, who is named after one of Tom's greatest influences, Nobel Prize–winning economist Harry Markowitz.

About Supernova Companies

Supernova is a new way of thinking about your world, challenging conventional wisdom yet representing Theory Implemented™. What began as an education company evolved to a comprehensive platform that centers on the effective management of both sides of the balance sheet and the delivery of balanced, integrated, holistic wealth management services.

The mission of Supernova Companies is to empower individuals to live their best life possible. We believe that the path to financial freedon happens through the effective management of both assets and liabilities, working together as part of a common plan and a bigger picture.

Supernova believes that by managing your life in an interconnected and holistic way, you will have a better chance of living a balanced life where you can not only enjoy the present, but also are prepared for the future and the curve balls life sends all of us along the way.

In the short term, we assist borrowers with refinancing to debt that has lower rates and better terms, striving to save consumers tens of billions per year in unnecessary interest expense.

The long-term vision of Supernova is to Revolutionize Debt™ by making the world safer for savers and to lower costs for borrowers. Supernova envisions a future where people throughout the world have access to borrowing money at rates lower than most governments and companies. Rather than having many loans, borrowers will have a loan—a single lending solution for all of their needs.

Through this process, Supernova envisions a world where interest rates start at zero percent for all borrowers, where there are zero inefficiencies, and where all people will have the biggest pie possible. A world where there is zero risk in the financial system and where you are more concerned about your grocery store having food on the shelf than you are concerned about a financial crisis, recession, or depression.

Supernova: knowledge empowering life.
SupernovaCompanies.com

Introduction

"The best preparation for tomorrow is doing your best today."
—H. Jackson Brown Jr.

There is considerable value to using debt in building wealth. Not credit card debt. Not payday loans. I'm talking about the right debt, positioned the right way and used in a thoughtful, balanced way throughout your life. Like chocolate, coffee, or red wine—a little bit can be a good thing, when handled responsibly.

The goal of this book is to illustrate what a balanced and comprehensive path may look like throughout the time that you are accumulating wealth. I will demonstrate the power of debt and compare it to conventional wisdom. The goal is to empower you to make better and more informed decisions. After all, as I will prove to you, the decisions you make with respect to debt are likely to be the biggest financial decisions you will make in your life.

My books *The Value of Debt* and *The Value of Debt in Retirement* were critically acclaimed because they sparked new ways of thinking that helped wealthy people work both sides of their balance sheets—just as corporations do—to become even wealthier. I understand that people are not companies, but that doesn't mean we can't learn from their ideas.

I wrote my first books as guides for people who have $1 million or more in assets, and back then I was pretty sure that people needed a net worth of at least $500,000 to implement my concepts.

A funny thing happened. People with much less money started playing with the concept of a strategic debt philosophy—and it worked. I realized these are not just concepts that make rich people richer. When used responsibly, debt can help anyone with discipline and the right disposition build enough wealth to live the life they want and put themselves on the path to retiring comfortably and productively.

If the very phrase "intelligent use of strategic debt" sounds heretical to you, you're not alone. The concept of "good debt" shows up as counterintuitive and even disruptive in a world that scolds us for taking on personal debt. We're blasted with horror stories about people who get buried in oppressive, high-interest debt (unfortunately all too easy to do, especially when you're young and inexperienced). And we've all taken in the popular advice about becoming debt-free as the first step to financial freedom.

This is unfortunate. Debt is a powerful tool that corporate financial officers have understood since capitalism was born. Savvy use of debt provides liquidity and flexibility, allowing smart companies to jump on opportunities and ride out emergencies. Why wouldn't smart investors who are building wealth do the same?

For the past two decades, many people have learned (and benefited) from Dave Ramsey and Suze Orman's advice. These financial authors have helped many people get out of debt, especially out of the oppressive type of debt I agree should be eliminated. However, they often assume people are irresponsible and almost scold them. I approach things a little differently—I give you the credit you deserve. I assume you are disciplined, smart, and rational.

I will provide a glide path for your financial journey. Glide paths are traditionally buoy lanes for ships and runway lights for airplanes. They are crucial for success and survivability. If captains and pilots don't stay within their confines, they could crash. Glide paths set a course and provide necessary boundaries. This book, your financial glide path, will help you set your course and provide you the necessary boundaries to get you on track for a comfortable life and secure retirement.

This book isn't for people who accumulate wealth to acquire more things. I believe happiness comes from relationships, experiences, and giving back, not things. I believe things and trying to acquire them can become a trap.

Living simply is, simply, more satisfying. I was born and raised in the Midwest, and I learned that early on. I know that no matter how much I amass, someone will always be richer than me. In my business, I see far too many people who have $5 million comparing themselves with people who have $15 million and people with $15 million comparing themselves with people who have $50 million. It goes on and on, exponentially upping the ante and limiting their ability to enjoy life's real blessings.

This book is for people who want to build wealth so they can pay for education and experiences that will enhance their lives and those of their family members, protect them in emergencies, help them seize opportunities, and allow them to retire comfortably and productively. It's for people who understand that they can't buy the good life but who value liquidity and flexibility as important tools to create and maintain it.

My ideas aren't for everyone. I will suggest that you live in the smallest house you can manage rather than the largest one you can afford. I'll show you why renting can be smarter than buying a home, especially early in your financial life. I'll ask you to give up on buying the latest-model BMW and to think long and hard before jetting off to Tulum. I'll ask you to buy less and do less than you can afford. That's not the American Dream, but it's a foundational pillar when using strategic debt to build wealth. Don't even think about using debt as a tool to build wealth if you can't follow this rule.

You must be willing to live below your means if you want to build liquidity and investments. You need a financial ecosystem that could survive a crash like 2008 or, as is my prediction, something worse. You need a mind that's open to debt as a tool that can work for you as well as against you and a team of financial and legal advisors who think along these same lines.

On your glide path to financial security, working both sides of your balance sheet can give you the liquidity and financial flexibility to lift off and land with ease, elegance, and grace. If you think you have what it takes, take the wheel of your financial life and steer it into the prosperity you deserve.[1]

Endnotes

1. Author's note: The information in this chapter is to be considered in a holistic way as a part of the book and not to be considered on a stand-alone basis. This includes, but is not limited to, the discussion of the risks of each of these ideas as well as all of the disclaimers throughout the book. The material is presented with a goal of encouraging thoughtful conversation and rigorous debate on the risks and potential benefits of the concepts between you and your advisors based on your unique situation, risk tolerance, and goals.

Chapter 1

The Traditional Glide Path

"It does take great maturity to understand that the opinion we are arguing for is merely the hypothesis we favor, necessarily imperfect, probably transitory, which only very limited minds can declare to be a certainty or a truth."

—Milan Kundera

In the traditional financial glide path, debt adds no value. It should be eliminated as fast as possible. Doing so is financially responsible, will increase security, save money, reduce stress, and put you on a better path to financial freedom. In this view, you typically hear:

- Debt is bad.
- You should be debt free when you retire.

- Debt creates anxiety, stress, and pressure.
- Having debt causes you to "waste money on interest."
- All things equal, you would rather not have debt.
- Debt increases risk in your life.
- Being debt free is less risky than having debt.

I'm going to prove to you that this is not true. Together, we're going to rid ourselves of the anti-debt hysteria and explore a better, balanced way.

In a Perfect World, No Debt!
But Our World Isn't Perfect

Debt is risky, and, in a perfect world, we would all rather avoid risk. The problem is that we do not live in a perfect world.

In their Nobel Prize–winning economic theorem, Franco Modigliani and Merton Miller hypothesize that capital structure (how much debt a company has) doesn't matter in a perfect world, but we don't live in one.[1] In our imperfect world, how much debt companies carry matters quite a bit. Companies carry debt because it works for their bottom line even though they likely have the resources or could raise money to pay for things in cash.

People, on the other hand, do not have this luxury. Our ability to buy things is limited to our income, assets, and use of debt. *No one would need debt if we could rent everything we want and need, under terms and conditions we find desirable, and at a cost equal to what it would cost to borrow money to buy.* In this perfect world, most people would be neutral to renting versus buying—and renting would often make more sense.[2] You don't buy a car and house for a one-week vacation in Hawaii. You rent because the terms and conditions are much better than buying. This same concept could apply to everything in your life, but it doesn't for a combination of financial and emotional reasons.

In our imperfect world, many people use debt to buy things they could not otherwise afford with cash they have on hand, including houses, cars, education, or investing in their small business.[3] As a result, many—if not most—people choose to take on debt early in life and spend their lives trying to pay it down. Is this a good strategy? Should people borrow money? If so, how much should they borrow? How fast should it be paid down? How does buying compare to the alternatives?

HOUSTON—WE HAVE A PROBLEM!

The vast majority of us use debt as a tool at some point in our lives and race to pay it off because we perceive it adds little to no value and adds stress to our lives. At the same time, most people desire to ultimately retire, yet are not on track for retirement. Is it possible that we can find balance in this tug of war between paying off debt and being on track for retirement?

A survey of college graduates who make more than $50,000 per year indicates:[4]

- 93 percent plan to retire by age 75 (and 86 percent before age 70).
- 85 percent of those surveyed either have debt or plan to use debt at some point in their life.
- 93 percent want to retire debt free.
- Only 27 percent think it is even possible that having debt in retirement is a good idea.
- 73 percent say that debt increases stress.
- 96 percent would choose to not have debt if they had the choice.
- 50 percent do not feel on track for retirement, and studies indicate that as many as 90 percent of Americans fail tests for meeting future retirement needs.[5]

You Owe a Debt to Your Future Self

Whether or not debt is bad or debt is good depends on your resources relative to your needs. If you can afford to pay cash for something, then paying cash might be a great idea. But whether or not you can afford it is just one part of a much bigger picture: *If you want to retire, you owe a debt to your future self.*

If you are 100 percent confident that retirement isn't an issue for you, then you have a lot of flexibility and could consider the potential benefits of paying cash for everything. However, most of us have to work and save in order to retire. I, for one, do not have enough money to retire tomorrow with the lifestyle I would like to live. For those of us in this situation, we have a dual mandate—we need to reduce our debt and save for retirement.

If you are like me, you want to enjoy the journey along the way, too. I want to see the world and live in a house big enough to host parties. I'm happiest by a campfire and I don't need anything extravagant, but I like doing some crazy things from time to time. If we want to also enjoy life, it's actually a tri-mandate!

Around most kitchen tables, a conversation begins whenever extra money comes in (perhaps a bonus or a raise). Should we pay down debt? Should we buy that thing we've had our eye on? Should we save toward retirement? Should that savings be in our retirement plan or in our investment account? And if we invest it, what should it be invested in? Maybe we should get that new house after all.

I've studied finance my entire life. There are about a million articles telling me how to invest my money, predicting the future (and generally being wrong), and feeding me financial news 24/7. Why do I feel like we are always guessing on these important decisions? What about my debt? How much should I have, and how should it be structured? Why does everybody tell me to get rid of it? I only have so much money; if debt is bad how do I handle my tri-mandate of saving, enjoying life, and paying down debt?

So how can I be responsible, have the things I want, enjoy life, yet save toward the future, be on track to retire, reduce anxiety, and increase flexibility? I value flexibility and hate being trapped; I want freedom. Will being debt free give me freedom? Or is there another way?

Break the Paycheck-to-Paycheck Cycle

Money flows into every household like water through a hose. When all is well, it flows freely and abundantly. But a kink in the hose (loss of a job, a serious medical condition, even a natural disaster) could stop the flow. If you haven't been storing water in cisterns, you and your family will be parched and in peril.

Too many Americans are in exactly that position. According to one survey, 76 percent of Americans live paycheck to paycheck, fewer than one in four has enough money saved to cover at least six months of expenses, and 27 percent have no savings at all.[6] A separate survey found that 46 percent of Americans have less than $800 in savings.[7] The estimated collective savings gap for working households 25–64 is estimated to be between $6.8 trillion and $14 trillion. Two-thirds of working households age 55 to 64 have not saved more than one year's worth of salary.[8] The well is not deep enough to sustain them through a crisis.

Is it possible the conventional wisdom that debt is bad has contributed to our savings gap? I believe our anti-debt mentality is contributing to the fact that we are dramatically under saved and ill prepared for crisis. I believe it's time to consider a new glide path and to break this cycle.

I believe there is a better, balanced, and simple way to accumulate wealth by using both sides of your balance sheet—your assets and your debts.

Companies Embrace Balance

Every successful company in the world has a chief financial officer (CFO) who looks holistically at the company's finances to maximize resources and profits. You and your family are not a company, and I understand that there are important differences. But a CFO's raison d'être is to do well financially, and we can learn some important, broad lessons from CFOs as we establish our personal, financial glide path. I believe one of the important tips we can take from CFOs is how they work both sides of the balance sheet to design and implement an overall debt philosophy and establish lines of credit as part of a holistic picture.

Structuring the right amount of debt in the right way is critical because too much risk could bankrupt the company and too little debt could leave it vulnerable. Once they've found their formulas, most CFOs keep fairly constant debt ratios from year to year.[9] Every corporation in the world uses debt as a tool to fund operations and leverage opportunities, and you and your family should, too.

WHO NEEDS AN AAA RATING?

Only two companies in the United States issue AAA bonds.[10] AAA bonds mean a company has the highest possible credit rating and generally the least amount of debt.

Pick a large company you admire, and chances are high that its bonds do not have the highest credit rating. Make no mistake, this is a proactive choice by the CFOs and they are well aware that they do not have the highest rating. These companies could easily choose to be AAA, but they don't see the value in having the highest credit rating.

They've chosen to embrace the liquidity, flexibility, and tax benefits associated with debt. At the same time, they make sure they don't have too much debt so that they take on too much risk.

Most Fortune 500 companies find a balanced middle ground between being debt free and having too much debt.

There's an incredible disconnect between how companies and individuals look at debt: Almost all successful companies use debt as a tool to provide liquidity and a cushion for emergencies and opportunities, but very few individuals and families are even willing to think about this strategy. Individuals and families tend to either have too much debt or want to pay off all of their debt as soon as they can. In our new financial glide path, we'll take a CFO-like approach and work both sides of our balance sheet.

The Power of Savings

We need to frame questions about debt, savings, and balance against the fact that compounding matters to long-term investment returns. Table 1.1 shows that to retire with $1 million, you can choose to save any of the following:

- $360 a month at age 20 (with a total of $194,400 saved and invested);
- $700 a month at age 30 (with a total of $294,000 saved and invested);
- $1,435 at age 40 (with a total of $430,500 saved and invested);

Table 1.1 Summary of Savings Rate to Accumulate $1 million by 65

Age	Amount Saved & Invested	Total # Payments	Total Saved & Invested	Percentage of Total Saved and Invested Compared to Person Starting at Age 60
20	$360/month	540	$194,400	23%
30	$700/month	420	$294,000	34%
40	$1,435/month	300	$430,500	50%
50	$3,421/month	180	$615,780	72%
60	$14,261/month	60	$855,660	N.A.

- $3,421 at age 50 (with a total of $615,780 saved and invested); or
- $14,261 at age 60 (with a total of $855,660 saved and invested).

Assuming a 6-percent rate of return, each of these approaches yields $1 million at age 65. But what's particularly interesting is the person who starts at 20 invests $194,400, or about 77 percent less than the person who starts saving at 60 and invests $855,660. This is the difference compounding makes. And I believe we are so anxious to pay down debt that it can come at a cost of deferring our long-term savings and that this cost is significant when we finally direct money to savings. We do not give our money time to grow for us.

THE DIFFERENCE COMPOUNDING MAKES

Jennifer and Josh are both savers and investors. Jennifer starts saving and investing at age 20 and saves $2,000 a year until she's 29—a total of $20,000. Josh starts saving and investing the same amount, $2,000 a year, when he's 30 and does so until he's 65—a total of $70,000. They both invest in a diversified portfolio of equities and receive an average 8-percent return over the entire period of time that their money is invested. Who will have more money in retirement at age 65?

At age 65, Jennifer will have about $463,000; Josh will have about $375,000—$88,000 less. This is because Jennifer reaped the benefits of earlier compounding.

Starting early makes an enormous difference![11]

A New Glide Path: Debt Adds Value

Considering that while we would rather not have debt but that it is often a necessary tool, let's reframe the "Debt is Bad" attitude:

Debt adds value, and when used in a balanced way, has a positive effect on people's lives.

Let's test this theory. Imagine there are two households, the Nadas and the Steadys. They live in a magical world with no taxes or inflation, interest rates never change, and investment returns are certain. This world is also magical in that banks will let people borrow however much they want for homes. Let's also imagine the following:

They both start at 35 years old.
They start with zero assets.
They both make $120,000 per year and never make a penny more or a penny less.
If they invest money they earn a rate of return of 6 percent.
If they borrow money they can borrow at 3 percent.
Their house appreciates by a rate of 2 percent per year.
They both save $15,000 per year ($1,250 per month).
They never move.

Imagine they both purchase a house when they are 35 years old for $300,000, 100 percent financed. Therefore, they both have a $300,000 mortgage. With a 30-year amortization, this has a house payment of about $1,250 per month, which is covered from their cash flow, not their savings.

For how much they have in common, it turns out they do have one big difference between them: Their attitudes about debt. The Nadas want to get rid of it as fast as possible. The Steadys are OK with it as long as they build up their savings. The Nadas direct all of their savings to paying off the house. The Steadys never pay down a penny extra on their house and build up their savings. Let's look at their lives at 65.

They both have a house worth approximately $550,000. They never intend to move, they have to live somewhere, and they both live in a house of the exact same value so the value of the house isn't relevant.

The Nadas paid off their house in 142 months, or in a bit under 12 years. They have owned their home free and clear since they were 47. At this point, they redirect their $2,500 per month savings toward retirement. This is their $1,250 former house payment + $1,250 monthly savings (monthly savings = $15,000 per year / 12 months). At retirement, they would own their house and have about $1 million.

The Nadas followed the traditional glide path with a conventional "Debt is Bad" attitude. But questions remain: Are the Nadas able to accomplish their retirement objectives? Was this plan optimal?

While $1 million sounds like a lot, they were making $10,000 per month and used to spending $7,500 per month. If they have a 6-percent return on their investments, they will receive a monthly income of about $5,000 per month (6 percent × $1 million / 12). According to conventional wisdom they "did everything right" but will have to take a pay cut of about $2,500 per month.

The Steadys took a different approach. They made the minimum $1,250 per month payment on their mortgage. They directed the additional $1,250 into savings, which grew to approximately $1,250,000. They paid off their mortgage the day they retired. So they not only own their own house, but have $250,000 more than the Nadas. At 6 percent per year, their income is $75,000, which is $6,250 per month. This is about $1,250 per month better than the Nadas, but $1,250 shy of where they would like to be. Perhaps their expenses change a little so maybe this is all right and maybe the Steadys are OK.

Let me introduce you to a third family, the Radicals. They are on a new glide path and take an entirely different approach to debt: They never pay it down.

The Radicals only pay interest on their mortgage, which is $750 per month (3 percent × $300,000 = $9,000 per year, or $750 per month). They take the rest of their money, about $1,750 per month, and contribute it to savings for the same 30-year period. Everybody worries about the Radicals because everybody knows that on the day they retire they have a $300,000 mortgage—but their savings have grown to $1.75 million. On the day they retire, the Radicals could pay off their mortgage and still have $200,000 more than the Steadys and $450,000 more than the Nadas!

> Same people, same lives, same investment returns, just different decisions with debt. Vastly different outcomes!

But these are the Radicals, so what if they left their $1.75 million invested and kept the mortgage forever? At the same 6-percent return, they would have a monthly income of $8,750. They would still have to make the $750 interest payment on their mortgage leaving them with $8,000 per month in income. This is more than the $7,500 they were spending when they were working. *The Radicals' monthly income increases during retirement.*

What about inheritance?

If the Nadas don't change their spending habits, they are on track to run out of money in 18 years.

If the Steadys don't change their spending habits, they are on track to run out of money in about 30 years.

If the Radicals don't change their spending habits, they are on track to have about $2.5 million when they are 105 years old.

And the Radicals' kids? Sure, they'll inherit debt—$300,000 worth of it—but they are inheriting far more in assets and are easily able to repay that debt and still have more money than the Nadas or the Steadys. Would you rather inherit $2 million of assets and $300,000 of debt, for a net of $1.7 million, or $500,000 with no debt?

The math proves the *"Debt is Bad" belief is false and that "Debt Adds Value" is true.* This short story summarizes *The Value of Debt* and *The Value of Debt in Retirement,* my earlier works.

The problem is, simply saying "Debt adds value" is generally unsatisfactory for many reasons:

- The assumptions are too broad and unrealistic; it doesn't represent the real world. This leads to more questions than answers and a lot of debate.
- It is unlikely to be right; the actual results will be dramatically different.
- It isn't dynamic. It doesn't reflect the changes we experience throughout life.

- It isn't specific or actionable. It doesn't provide a glide path or insight into the appropriate amount of debt to carry throughout life.

Because of the dynamic nature of our lives and the world in which we live, we need something more.

Finding Your Glide Path

In our current world order, most people have high levels of debt early in life and race to be debt free by the time they retire. Along the way, they experience stress, anxiety, and financial insecurity. Is there a better way? To find out, I set out to design a more fluid, dynamic formula using the following building blocks:

Core Tenets

People's preferences: In a perfect world, we could rent everything we want and need with the terms, conditions, and price we desire. However, we do not live in a perfect world.
For financial reasons or personal preferences, most consumers choose to use debt at some point in their lives. Most choose debt reluctantly. They do not like debt and want to be debt free. Most consumers want to retire.

People's reality: Most consumers are not on track for retirement and/or have anxiety about having enough money for retirement.

- Many people feel stress and anxiety about money in general.
- Many live paycheck to paycheck.
- Money is one of the leading causes of fights in relationships.
- Most do not have the freedom and flexibility they would like.

Companies: The vast majority of companies choose to embrace debt. There are far more AA-rated than AAA-rated companies, and more A-rated than AA-rated companies.[12] A lower rating is a proactive choice, a strategy to embrace debt.

Math: Compounding interest is powerful. The longer money is working for you, the bigger difference it makes.

Finance: In their Nobel Prize–winning theory, Modigliani and Miller said that in a perfect world, debt does not matter.[13] Because we do not live in a perfect world, capital structure (how much debt companies have) matters.

In his Nobel Prize–winning theory, Harry Markowitz said that one of the biggest determining factors in your rate of return is your capital structure—how much debt you have.[14]

Strategic debt philosophy: There are different types of debt. Some are bad, and some can be good.

If you are ahead of your goals, you don't need debt. If you are behind on your goals, debt can be a powerful tool. This is because:

- It is a mathematical fact that debt can reduce risk.
- It is a mathematical fact that debt can reduce taxes.
- It is a mathematical fact that debt can increase return.[15]

The Need for Specific, Actionable Advice

One day I was walking through the airport and somebody stopped me and said: "Hey! You're the guy who wrote that book about debt! How much debt should I have?" When I share this story, people chuckle. It's a great question, but how could I provide him with specific information, on the spot, that would be relevant to his life? He was not looking for me to pull out my fancy calculator and give him an answer to how much value debt could create. He was looking for an actionable plan and a path.

When I do media interviews, reporters show little interest in what people who already have money should do. The vast majority of us are still trying to make our money in the first place. There is tremendous demand for ideas about what people who are accumulating money should do at each phase of their life. People want to understand the potential benefits and risks of taking on debt—oh, and please make it very simple and easy to understand!

In my other books, I've said that debt ratios between 15 percent and 35 percent may be optimal over the long term.[16] In these works,

I illustrate that this range is more conservative than most companies use, and that debt ratios of 33 percent may reduce risk, lower your taxes, and increase your returns. However, these ranges are based on individuals who have already accumulated considerable assets. They do not accommodate early accumulators.

For example, using the debt ratios in my previous works, if you wanted to buy a $500,000 house with a $400,000 mortgage, you would have to accumulate about $700,000 in assets first. Similarly, if you want to purchase a $250,000 house with a $200,000 mortgage, you would need to first acquire $350,000 in assets.

While this is possible, it is extremely unlikely for most people. The reality is most people will take on a higher level of debt early in life to buy the house. Then they are faced with juggling how to pay down debt, save for retirement, and enjoy life. Many young accumulators also have other debt, like student loans, credit card debt, car loans, or all of the above. They need to add this to the equation and figure out how and when to pay down their different types of debt. We need a balanced approach that is flexible so it can evolve with us throughout our lives.

It is my belief that in our anti-debt world, most people are taking on too much debt too early in life and paying down that debt too aggressively. As a result, they are not saving until later in life. I believe this strategy is a considerable cost to society and that there is a better, more balanced path.

We can embrace a sensible, balanced approach to debt throughout our lives—an approach that mimics the balance exhibited in nature, art, architecture, music, and even our own bodies. This balanced approach will reduce stress, increase financial security and flexibility, and increase the probability of a secure retirement. Used appropriately, strategic debt is not a waste of money, but rather, an opportunity to increase the likelihood you will be able to accomplish your goals in the short, medium, and long term.

What follows is a new glide path, what I consider a balanced approach that looks at the four phases of L.I.F.E.:

Launch. When your net worth is low and/or you are truly just getting started

Independence. When you have accumulated a small nest egg

Freedom. When you have a medium nest egg

Equilibrium: When you have a large nest egg, are living a balanced life, and are preparing to retire

We'll examine these phases as interconnected, a baton passing from one hand to the next in the relay of life. As the size of your nest egg changes, the debt ratios change. However, each has similar balance. Similarly, each phase of your financial life involves a different base amount and objectives but builds off the same inspiration. We'll consider both sides of the balance sheet. We'll look at tools to address the variances and differences in our lives. We'll keep the ideas big picture and approachable and let you turn to the guides, appendices, and online resources for more in-depth details. The goal is not to force a fit, but to consider new parameters, new buoy lights to inspire you to find YOUR glide path.[17]

Endnotes

1. See the concepts of weighted average cost of capital and the Modigliani-Miller Theorem: F. Modigliani and M. Miller, "The Cost of Capital, Corporation Finance, and the Theory of Investment," *American Economic Review* 48, no. 3 (1958); F. Modigliani and M. Miller, "Corporate Income Taxes and the Cost of Capital: A Correction," *American Economic Review* 53, no. 3 (1963).

2. This is not an impossibility. For example, if housing is a great investment that maintains its value after depreciation, then investors should be willing to buy houses and rent them at a low rate to consumers, capturing not only the rental income, but also the appreciation of the asset as their total return. Rental rates could in fact be lower than purchasing rates. This in fact happens in many markets today, within and outside of housing.

3. Note that many consumers' desire to own is not limited to assets that we perceive to be likely to go up in value over time. Consumers also want to own items that are more likely to go down in value such as cars, boats, clothing, and intangible assets such as education (which theoretically leads to higher productivity and wages, a positive trade-off, or better future opportunity).

4. Results based on survey conducted by Supernova Companies in December 2015. The survey featured 394 respondents who met the following criteria: age 21–60, minimum of college degree, and annual income of at least $50,000. Full results are available here: https://www.surveymonkey.com/results/SM-KCDY3XGJ/.

5. Nari Rhee, "The Retirement Crisis: Is it Worse than We Think?" *National Institute on Retirement Security* (June 2013). http://www.nirsonline.org/storage/nirs/documents/Retirement%20Savings%20Crisis/retirementsavingscrisis_final.pdf.

6. Angela Johnson, "76% of Americans are living paycheck-to-paycheck." *CNN Money* (June 24, 2013). http://money.cnn.com/2013/06/24/pf/emergency-savings/.

7. Ibid.

8. Rhee, "The Retirement Crisis."

9. This is a central theme of Thomas J. Anderson, *The Value of Debt* (Hoboken, NJ: John Wiley & Sons, 2013). In particular, Chapter 3 goes into extensive detail on corporate debt ratios. For those who would like detail, see endnote 3 from Chapter 3 of *The Value of Debt*.

10. Lucinda Shen, "Now There Are Only Two U.S. Companies With the Highest Credit Rating," *Fortune* (April 26, 2016), http://fortune.com/2016/04/26/exxonmobil-sp-downgrade-aaa/.

11. The case studies presented are for educational and illustrative purposes only and cannot guarantee that the reader will achieve similar results. Your results may vary significantly and factors such as the market, personal effort, and many others will cause results to vary. All of the case studies throughout the book are hypothetical and not intended to demonstrate the performance of any specific security, product, or investment strategy. Opinions formulated by the author are intended to stimulate discussion.

12. This potentially excludes some big insurers and some government-affiliated organizations. Arguably all large companies have different forms of short-term debt such as accounts payable, accrued payroll, and so on, and all have lines of credit to facilitate short-term differences in payables and receivables. The number of AAA, AA, and A companies will, of course, change over time. The concept, which is a key driver, is expressed well in this piece from Karen Berman and Joe Knight, "When Is Debt Good?" *Harvard Business Review* (July 15, 2009), https://hbr.org/2009/07/when-is-debt-good.

13. See the concepts of weighted average cost of capital and the Modigliani-Miller Theorem: Modigliani and Miller, "The Cost of Capital, Corporation Finance, and the Theory of Investment," and Modigliani and Miller, "Corporate Income Taxes and the Cost of Capital."

14. Modern Portfolio Theory was developed and explained by Harry Markowitz in his paper "Portfolio Selection," published in 1952 by the *Journal of Finance*. Markowitz was awarded the Nobel Prize in Economic Sciences

in 1990 largely based on this essay and his 1959 book, *Portfolio Selection: Efficient Diversification*.

15. These three facts are the basis of the book *The Value of Debt in Retirement*, by Thomas J. Anderson (Hoboken, NJ: John Wiley & Sons, 2015).

16. For more detail on the optimal debt ratio and how I came up with my target range for individuals, I encourage you to check out Chapter 3 of Anderson, *The Value of Debt*.

17. Author's Note: The information in this chapter is to be considered in a holistic way as a part of the book and not to be considered on a stand-alone basis. This includes, but is not limited to, the discussion of the risks of each of these ideas, as well as all of the disclaimers throughout the book. The material is presented with a goal of encouraging thoughtful conversation and rigorous debate on the risks and potential benefits of the concepts between you and your advisors based on your unique situation, risk tolerance, and goals.

Chapter 2

Foundational Facts

"An investment in knowledge pays the best interest."
—Benjamin Franklin

G lide paths, like runway lights for airplanes, set a course and provide necessary boundaries. The runway is different at each airport so the lights are helpful markers for the plane. When it comes to personal finance, I have my own markers. I consider these foundational facts for your financial journey, the boundaries to keep us on course:

1. All debt is not equal: There are different types of debt.
2. Your rate of return for paying down debt is exactly equal to your after-tax cost of debt.
3. Sh*t happens—Value liquidity.
4. Yes, you can—save.

5. Compounding matters to the upside *and* downside.
6. The past is the past. Focus on the future.
7. Behavioral economics matters.

All Debt Is Not Equal: Oppressive, Working, and Enriching Debt

Before we even begin our quest to explore another path, we have to cover an essential ground rule: There are different kinds of debt. The different types of debt can be seen in Table 2.1.

Debt has a bad name, and I blame *oppressive debt*. It should be avoided at all costs. It is characterized by high interest rates, amortization schedules, and typically no tax deductibility. It is what most people think of more generally when they think of debt. It makes you poorer in real time, and it's hard to get out from under once it starts building up.

Amortizing debt

Amortizing debt is debt that is paid off with a fixed payment schedule over a period of time.

I consider anything with a rate higher than inflation plus 6 percent to be oppressive debt—the trans-fat of debt. In the United States in

Table 2.1 Oppressive, Working, Enriching Debt: You OWE It to Yourself to Understand the Differences

Type	Examples	Sources	Impact
Oppressive debt	Payday loans, credit card balances	Loan sharks, credit card companies	Oppresses debt holders and makes them continually poorer
Working debt	Mortgages, small business loans, low-cost student debt	Mortgage lenders, SBA loans	Has a real cost but enables things that might not otherwise be possible
Enriching debt	Debt that you choose to have but could pay off at any time	Mortgages or low-cost securities-based loans	May increase return, reduce taxes, and actually reduce risk

late 2016, this would be any debt that has an interest expense over approximately 8 percent and certainly anything with a rate over 10 percent. If you have this type of debt, pay it off. This is not the type of debt I am talking about. Oppressive debt doesn't allow you to work both sides of the balance sheet.

If you have a mortgage, student loan, or small business loan, you are using *working debt*. Generally, this is debt tied to a specific purpose and has a lower rate—typically under inflation plus 6 percent and ideally closer to inflation on an after-tax basis. In the United States in late 2016, this would be debt that generally has an after-tax cost between 2 percent and 8 percent. The Steadys in Chapter 1 used working debt for their mortgage.

Enriching debt is debt that you choose to have yet could pay off at any time.[1] It's at a very low interest rate, perhaps close to the rate of inflation, and you also have the money in the bank to pay it off. This type of debt may allow you to capture the spread, meaning over time you may have the opportunity to make more money on an investment than it costs to borrow the money.

For example, if you're paying 3 percent on a loan that enables you to leave investments that are earning 6 percent intact, you're actually earning 3 percent. Consider the Radicals from Chapter 1, who kept a mortgage when they retired even though they could pay it off at any time.

INTEREST RATES AND THE CURRENT ECONOMIC ENVIRONMENT

Interest rates, on their own, are neither good nor bad. They are a function of the economy at any given time. I am not only mindful that interest rates are at generational lows, but also that they are likely to change significantly over the next 5, 10, 20, and 50 years. Further, these concepts transcend the world, and different countries have different interest rates.

Moving forward in the book, I will simply use absolute numbers that represent the interest-rate environment in late 2016 in the United States.

Paying Down Debt Gives You a Return Equal to Your After-Tax Cost of That Debt

How does this work? If you pay down credit card debt at 19 percent, you get a 19-percent return. If you pay down a small business loan at 8 percent, you get an 8-percent rate of return. Paying down a fully tax-deductible mortgage at an interest rate of 3 or 4 percent, however, gives you a rate of return of only 2 or 3 percent. In some instances, due to a combination of low rates and tax benefits, paying down student debt could give you an after-tax return of zero!

This is a stunningly simple fact that many people fail to consider with respect to debt. If you feel that your investments have a high chance of doing better than your after-tax cost of debt, then there can be value to having the debt. If you feel that your investments are likely to do worse than your after-tax cost of debt, then you might want to consider paying down debt.

The key here is the time horizon. Your time horizon is the rest of your life—and potentially longer if you have family you are trying to take care of. This isn't a question of beating the cost of debt every minute, hour, day, week, year, or even every three or five years. It is a question of beating it on average and throughout time. If you believe there is a reasonable chance the cost of debt is below what you might average in returns over the next 10 years or longer, then there may be value to debt. If not, then you should consider paying down that debt.

Looked at through this lens debt becomes more interesting. There can be times you might want to consider higher debt ratios and there might be times you want to consider lower debt ratios. Unfortunately, most people are overconfident and borrow too much in good times and are quick to eliminate debt in bad times. We will discuss these strategies in more detail later but for now, remember that paying down debt gives you a rate of return equal to your after-tax cost of that debt.

Sh*t Happens—Value Liquidity

Cash is a form of insurance. Companies often have both accessible amounts of cash and outstanding debt. The cash almost always has a rate of return less than the cost of debt, thereby earning a negative spread. Why don't they just use the cash to pay off their debt? Because having cash and debt enables the company to better run both offense and defense with a range of outcomes in mind. Apple is a company many people, including me, admire. They have billions and billions of dollars in cash. They also have billions of dollars in debt.[2] They do it strategically because they value the liquidity, flexibility, and tax benefits associated with the debt. This is an essential concept for individuals as well.[3]

Many of us are familiar with life insurance. I have some so there's money for my kids if I die. This is good for them, but doesn't do a lot for me as I'll be dead. I hope my passing is a low-probability event, yet many young professionals buy insurance to protect against this risk. I'm not against this—I'm a client—but it's interesting so many of us pay a lot of money to protect against a relatively low-probability event.

A higher probability event is that at some point in life you could be unemployed, in an accident, made homeless by a disaster, decide to move, or have a health scare. Bad things can happen to all of us. Access to cash can help.

Consider Diana and Terry. Terry is in a rush to pay off all of his debt. He has a $500,000 house and a $400,000 mortgage. He directs all of his cash and savings toward paying down his loan and eventually gets it down to $300,000. Terry loses his job. He can't access any of the money in his home unless he sells it. And he doesn't have any income or cash to pay the mortgage.

Diana values liquidity. She puts $100,000 down on her house but directs all of her cash and savings toward building up $100,000 in cash—cash that she just holds in a money market, savings account, checking account, or under her mattress. Just cash. When the crisis hits, Diana has $100,000 accessible, which she uses toward covering bills and supporting the family. She has flexibility if she needs to move and is in a position to evaluate her choices and make her next job choice prudently. Diana can survive.[4]

Never underestimate the power of liquidity. Having $10,000 to $50,000 of liquidity increases your ability to survive shocks. Having $50,000 to $100,000 of liquidity enables you to potentially thrive through shocks. Having $1 million or more of liquidity is a powerful place that relatively few people reach.

Too often people say, "Well you can just use your home equity line of credit." Maybe. A home equity line of credit (HELOC) is a very powerful tool I recommend everybody carefully consider. If there is no cost to set it up and no cost to having it open, then it can be a great standby emergency fund. If it has a lot of costs associated with it, you may want to think twice.

Many people were surprised during the financial crisis of 2008 when HELOCs were reduced or revoked.[5] They thought they had a safety net, but it was yanked out from under them when they needed it most. If you feel comfortable putting your safety net in the hands of a bank credit committee, consider this an option. If you like to control your destiny independent of others, cash is king. *In a perfect world, you should have both cash and a HELOC.* We will talk about how much cash as we move through the different phases of L.I.F.E. later in the book.

BLIZZARDS HAPPEN

When I was in business school, my professor told us about a famous case involving the CEO of a manufacturing company with a plant in Boston. On the Wednesday before Thanksgiving, the CEO left the office just as heavy snow began to fall. On Monday, he and his employees returned to work and found that snowfall from the holiday blizzard had caved in the plant's roof. All the equipment inside was destroyed, and the plant wouldn't operate for weeks, maybe months. It was a disaster.

The professor asked us whose fault we thought this was. What do you think?

Most students' initial reaction was to blame Mother Nature—how could anyone predict an act of God? The students considered the blizzard an *exogenous* event, or one that developed from external factors. No one could foresee a snowfall of such magnitude!

However, the blizzard was actually an *endogenous* shock, one that should have been in their base case assumptions. It snows in Boston! Why didn't the company have a snow removal service? And why did it have a flat roof—inappropriate for the climate—in the first place? The CEO should have been better prepared.

Disasters happen—in Mother Nature and in your life. Taking into account any shock or disaster you can think of—and even those you can't—is imperative when building a long-term financial plan.

LIFE WILL NOT GO ACCORDING TO YOUR PLAN

Life sends us curve balls. Consider that:

- You could be unemployed for at least six months.
- You might need to move—across the street or across the country.
- You could have a rock-star career—and then get sidelined.
- You could be forced to take a pay cut.
- You could have a health scare.
- A family member could need help.
- An investment opportunity could pop up.
- An investment could go bad.
- You could fall in love, changing your world completely.
- You could fall out of love, changing your world completely.

While those are events that could happen, the following are events that will happen with virtually 100 percent certainty:

- Natural disasters will strike.
- Stock markets will crash.
- Recessions will happen.
- Wars will break out.

Stress test your financial plan, considering every possibility from personal loss of a primary income stream to global runaway inflation. Liquidity—cash—can get you through more things than you can imagine. Liquidity has gotten people through crises since money was invented. Not being prepared for shocks in your personal financial ecosystem triggers a range of problems from late fees and penalties to damaged credit and questionable survival. And, of course, the worry, stress, anxiety, and distraction associated with financial distress take a toll on your relationships and physical and mental health.

To assess your risk of experiencing financial distress, ask yourself the following questions:

- Are you a single- or dual-income household?
- How stable or volatile is your income stream or streams?
- How likely is it that you (or your spouse) will lose your job for any reason?
- If you (or your spouse) lose your job, how long would it take to replace that income?
- How likely is a severe recession or other financial crisis to directly impact your job(s) and income stream(s)?
- How would a severe recession or depression impact you and your family?
- How much of a cushion do you have in reserve? How accessible or liquid is it?
- How likely are you to be affected by uninsurable or uninsured natural disasters?
- Could others who rely on your income have extreme financial needs?

Yes, You Can—Save

Saving is hard for a lot of people. Trust me, if you are saving less than 5 percent, I get it. I once lived paycheck to paycheck and with a lot of debt. I had a great job but $5,000 on my credit card and $0 in my checking account. If you are in this camp, I offer some tools to help you out of this trap as we move forward through the different phases of L.I.F.E. After all, paying off debt is a form of savings and, as I discussed above, your rate of return in paying off debt is exactly equal to your after-tax cost of debt.

How much should we save? My ideal target is at least 15 percent. You will find that saving at 20 percent gives you more freedom, flexibility, and less anxiety. You need to save at least 10 percent or you need to plan to work for a very long time. On the flip side, unless you expect a very short career (such as a professional athlete), then I see little value to saving more than 30 percent of your income. We want to find the balance and enjoy life, too.

If you are not at this savings level today, then I will outline a glide path to gradually ramp to this level. But you are wealthier than you think. If you make more than $54,000 a year, you bring in more than half the households in the United States.[6] If you make more than 50 percent of the people in your community, there's no reason that you cannot save 10 to 20 percent of your income. This savings rate is the foundation to your glide path. If you make more than half of all Americans but aren't willing to adopt a glide path to move to where you save at least 10 percent of your income, then put this book down right now.

What counts as savings? I define savings as contributions that improve your net worth. You can improve your net worth by increasing your assets or reducing your debt. So in addition to normal savings from cash flow, I also count retirement plan contributions, employer matches, and payments toward principal on outstanding debt (not interest!).

For example, Emily and Rob make $100,000 per year. They save $10,000 to their 401(k) and get a 4-percent match from their employer, making their retirement savings $14,000. If they also save $5,000 into their checking account, and pay down $5,000 of principal on debt, their total savings would be $24,000, or 24 percent of their income.

A couple of important clarifying points:

1. As we move forward, I will assume a savings rate of 15 percent. If you have a high level of debt (especially student debt or credit card debt), then it may take more time or a higher savings rate to accomplish the glide path.
2. I encourage you to exclude car payments as a part of savings. For example, you have a $30,000 car loan for five years at 5 percent and are making a monthly payment of around $566. Some of that payment is going to principal and some is going to interest. One could argue that by paying down the car you are reducing

debt and increasing your net worth. The problem is that the car is also depreciating and it will be worth less in the future. To factor in the principal payment, you would also need to factor in the depreciation to look at the net savings. If you understand what this means and it sounds like how you would like to approach things, then I'm comfortable if you include the principal payment net of depreciation in your savings figure. However, if you want a simpler, straightforward, conservative, and easy approach, then I recommend you exclude your car payment(s) from the formula, even if you are paying some toward principal.

---

5 + 5 = 16

Many companies match the contributions that employees make to their retirement plans. For example, if you save 5 percent, your company may put in 3 percent for a total of 8 percent. If you and your spouse are fortunate to have this and each save 5 percent of your income, you will be on track for a 16-percent savings rate.

Compounding Matters—For the Upside and the Downside

Compounding matters in both the upside and the downside. In other words, the financial decisions you make have the potential to exponentially help you, but they can also exponentially hurt. This is an essential pillar to *The Value of Debt*. Let's start by looking at the bright side of compounding and then I will share a personal story about the dark side of compounding.

Consider the following story illustrating the bright side. A farm worker responds to an ad seeking someone to do heavy manual labor during the long, hot days of August. The ad says, "Name your own fee." The worker proposes the following: "For the first day, to demonstrate my good will to you and show you how hard I work, you can pay me one penny. Starting the second day, and every day after that, I ask that you double the amount I was paid the previous day. The second day I will get two more pennies on top of the first penny for the first day, and the third day I will get four more pennies added to what I've already been paid, and so on. I start with just a penny a day, and all you have to do is double that penny every day for the next 30 days, and we'll be done. Sounds pretty good, right?"

You're a smart boss and decide to check the math. Because of the power of compounding interest, by the end of August, you would owe your employee 2,147,383,647 pennies, or almost $21.5 million (see Table 2.2). Everyone in the accumulation phase should understand that power.

Compounding Lessons and Hard Knocks

Like most people, I've made good and bad financial decisions. Perhaps the most amazing one I've ever made was to invest in my employers' 401(k) retirement savings plans. I started working at 21. I made small contributions—about $2,000 to $3,000 per year. As my income grew, I directed more to my retirement plans. I estimate that I have been saving about $15,000 per year for the past 15 years (15 × 15 = $225,000) plus about $15,000 during my earliest career for a total of about $240,000 saved. The total value of my retirement savings is about $425,000.

If I keep saving $15,000 per year for the next 30 years (through age 70) and average a 6-percent rate of return, I'm on track to accumulate $3.6 million. And this doesn't include employer contributions, which is good news because they're becoming less common.

If I had taken the money as income instead of savings, I estimate I would have about $144,000 instead of the $425,000 I have now. I would have lost nearly $300,000 that I've earned through growth, tax savings, and employer contributions.

Now, if telling you that I have $425,000 in retirement savings sounds like bragging, let me tell you the dark side of this story. If you look at how much I've saved (about $240,000) and compare it to the value of the portfolio (about $425,000), my rate of return has not been that amazing—especially because my return includes some of the match,

Table 2.2   The Power of Compounding Interest

Day	# of Pennies Added	Total Owed
1	1	$ 0.01
2	2	$ 0.03
3	4	$ 0.07
4	8	$ 0.15
5	16	$ 0.31
6	32	$ 0.63
7	64	$ 1.27
8	128	$ 2.55
9	256	$ 5.11
10	512	$ 10.23
11	1,024	$ 20.47
12	2,048	$ 40.95
13	4,096	$ 81.91
14	8,192	$ 163.83
15	16,384	$ 327.67
16	32,768	$ 655.35
17	65,536	$ 1,310.71
18	131,072	$ 2,621.43
19	262,144	$ 5,242.87
20	524,288	$ 10,485.75
21	1,048,576	$ 20,971.51
22	2,097,152	$ 41,943.03
23	4,194,304	$ 83,886.07
24	8,388,608	$ 167,772.15
25	16,777,216	$ 335,544.31
26	33,554,432	$ 671,088.63
27	67,108,864	$ 1,342,177.27
28	134,217,728	$ 2,684,354.55
29	268,435,456	$ 5,368,709.11
30	536,870,912	$10,737,418.23
31	1,073,741,824	$21,473,836.47

or contribution, I received from my employers. Here's why: At a very young age, I got my portfolio to $100,000 pretty fast. Impressed with my accomplishment, I thought:

I have $100,000. I'm an amazing investor.

If I save $15,000 per year for the next 45 years with a 12-percent rate of return, then I will have $21 million when I'm 70.

Driven partially by my own greed and the encouragement of an equally naive friend, I invested the $100,000 very aggressively. I thought, *I'm young. I have time. I can be risky!* That didn't work out so well. My $100,000 promptly became $50,000. I lost half of my money and about three years' worth of savings. Worse, when your assets fall by 50 percent, you have to go up 100 percent just to get back to even. Sure, I was saving so my account continued to grow, but I would have made those savings anyway.

I got so excited about the power of compounding on the upside that I didn't consider the power of compounding on the downside. I wish I had understood the following: If my ridiculous assumptions about where compounding could take me were true, I had to be prepared for that power to turn against me. Based on those assumptions, *every dollar I lost at that young age is the equivalent of losing about 164 future dollars.* From that perspective, my $50,000 loss actually cost me $8.2 million.

Don't make the mistake I made: Excessive risk is no way to build wealth. Small ups and downs are normal and a natural, healthy part of investing. Huge downs are devastating. Here's what I learned:

- If you're ahead in the 9th, don't play the 10th.
- If you have time on your side, you don't need to take big risks.
- If you don't have time on your side, you can't afford to take big risks.
- Believe me, you don't have to go through a big down more than once to understand the lesson.

The Past Is the Past; Focus on the Future

Whenever I'm tempted to do a forensic accounting of my exact contributions and matches to my savings to determine my rate of return for the past 15 years, I stop myself. What exactly will that tell me, and what will I do with that information?

Too many people focus on where the money came from (inheritance, earnings, real estate, etc.), what their net worth used to be, or what rate of return they have earned. Your spending, habits, and returns from the past are all irrelevant. You can't change anything in the past. You can do things to change your future, and that's where you should focus.

When considering the future, keep two things in mind:

- Nobody knows the future. It will probably be balanced with good and bad.
- We are not entitled to anything.

Too many people think they or others know the future. Nobody knows what the price of oil, gold, or a Coke will be in two years, let alone 5 or 10 years—not you, not the talking head on TV, not the economist in the newspaper.

There is a fundamental difference between those who think they know and those who know they don't know. Those who know they don't know are prepared. You can't predict a crisis, a natural disaster, or a bear market. The only way to be prepared for an unknown future is to have enough liquidity.

I have seen too many people who believe bad things won't happen to them. They are protected by their education, health, wealth, family, or title. They believe it will be easy to get a new job and overcome obstacles. If you feel this way, good for you. This confident attitude makes it easier to overcome obstacles. But you can't pay your bills with confidence so tread cautiously. Many of my friends who felt entitled have been greatly disappointed. No one knows the future and no one is entitled to anything.

Behavioral Economics Matters

Economics typically starts with the assumption that you are disciplined and rational. The problem is we set a plan and then life comes along with a bright, shiny object to distract us.

My ideas present a potentially slippery slope. I will show you ways to minimize your house payments so you can increase your savings, but if you blow the money you save on your mortgage you will be unprepared for crises at best, unable to retire or enjoy life at worst.

Consider Jeremy. He wants to buy a home with a $300,000, 15-year amortizing mortgage at 3 percent. His monthly payment would be a little more than $2,000 per month. He realizes he is likely to live in the property for only five years and instead chooses a five-year, interest-only loan at 4 percent for a monthly payment of about $1,000 per month. Jeremy gets to live in the same house, but he has $1,000 per month cash flow difference. *I assume if you could afford to make the $2,000 per month payment but choose to make the $1,000 a month payment the extra $1,000 per month goes toward increasing savings or reducing other debt—NOT to spending.*

Too often, people don't do this. If they have an extra $1,000 per month of cash flow, they spend it. I assume you are able to handle the power of these ideas. This is a big assumption. If you are prone to spending money and are unable to save extra cash, then you will need to consider alternatives. Amortized mortgages are effectively a forced savings program. Before implementing my ideas, ask yourself if you can handle the responsibility and discipline they require.[7]

Endnotes

1. An important note on the term *enriching*: The *Merriam-Webster Dictionary* defines the verb "enrich" as "to make (someone) rich or richer; to improve the quality of (something); to make (something) better; to improve the usefulness or quality of (something) by adding something to it." (See www.merriam-webster.com/dictionary/enrich.) I want to be clear, by embracing these concepts and considering adding a strategic debt component to your finances, your life, there are no guarantees. There are absolutely risks involved, so please, do not mistake the term "enriching" as a guarantee of success. Don't forget the important key point: This is debt you have the money to pay off. You've made an educated, conscious decision to take on this debt. You can read more about the concept of Enriching Debt in *The Value of Debt in Retirement*, by Thomas J. Anderson (Hoboken, NJ: Wiley, 2015).
2. Apple Inc. (2015). *Annual Report 2015*. Retrieved from http://investor.apple.com/sec.cfm?view=all.
3. Tax laws are complex and subject to change. Tax information contained in this presentation is general and not exhaustive by nature. It is not intended or written to be used, and cannot be used, by any taxpayer for the purpose of avoiding U.S. federal tax laws. This material was not intended or written to be used for the purpose of avoiding tax penalties that may be imposed on the taxpayer. Individuals are encouraged to consult their tax and legal advisors (a) before establishing a retirement plan or account, and (b) regarding any potential tax, ERISA, and related consequences of any investments made under such plan or account. These materials and any statements contained herein should not be construed as tax or legal advice. Tax advice must come from your tax advisor.

4. The case studies presented are for educational and illustrative purposes only and cannot guarantee that the reader will achieve similar results. Your results may vary significantly and factors such as the market, personal effort, and many others will cause results to vary. All of the case studies throughout the book are hypothetical and not intended to demonstrate the performance of any specific security, product, or investment strategy. Opinions formulated by the author are intended to stimulate discussion.

5. FDIC, Financial Institution Letter (June 26, 2008), https://www.fdic.gov/news/news/financial/2008/fil08058.pdf.

6. http://www2.census.gov/programs-surveys/demo/tables/p60/252/table1.pdf.

7. Author's Note: The information in this chapter is to be considered in a holistic way as a part of the book and not to be considered on a stand-alone basis. This includes, but is not limited to, the discussion of the risks of each of these ideas as well as all of the disclaimers throughout the book. The material is presented with a goal of encouraging thoughtful conversation and rigorous debate on the risks and potential benefits of the concepts between you and your advisors based on your unique situation, risk tolerance, and goals.

Chapter 3

A Balanced Path
to L.I.F.E.

"The definition of insanity is doing the same thing over and over and expecting different results."

—Albert Einstein

W hether traveling by boat, plane, car, or train, there are markers to determine where you are and beacons to help navigate the path where you want to go. We all stand at different milestone markers of our financial journey and we all need beacons to set the glide path going forward.

Whether you have a lot of assets, are just getting started, or are even behind, you can have balance. Let's take a look at the four phases of your financial L.I.F.E.

1. **Launch.** In this phase, you are just starting to build your wealth with an emphasis on reducing oppressive debt and building up a savings reserve. Your net worth is less than 50 percent of your gross annual pretax income (if your income varies, use the most conservative estimate).
2. **Independence.** You have a small nest egg and many people consider buying a home or taking on some working debt. Your net worth is between 50 percent and two times your gross annual pretax income.
3. **Freedom.** Your net worth is between two and five times your gross annual pretax income. You are at the point where you can safely and confidently take advantage of the debt strategies I discuss here and reap the benefits of your financial decisions.
4. **Equilibrium.** Your net worth is greater than five times your gross annual pretax income. You have a healthy, accessible cushion of cash in reserve. You are saving and enjoying life. You're likely on track to retire with a comfortable amount of money to cover your expenses and enjoy life.

I'm going to present the phases in two chapters. I group Launch and Independence together because they involve a lot of questions about getting started, managing student debt, breaking the paycheck-to-paycheck cycle, and buying a house. If you are able to successfully move past the Independence phase, you likely have a net worth greater than approximately 60 percent of the United States and will be on track for a successful retirement.[1]

I group the Freedom and Equilibrium phases in a separate chapter because they are breakthrough levels where you have built up enough assets that allow you to truly make strategic choices with respect to debt, your balance sheet, and the optimal path forward.

People who are fortunate enough to be in this zone have clearly done something right. That said, I will prove there is an optimal way to balance debt throughout your life. I will show you a path that will materially increase the chances you will be on track for a successful retirement and able to balance the tri-mandate of saving, paying down debt, and enjoying the present.

HOW TO CALCULATE YOUR NET WORTH

To calculate your net worth, add up all your assets and all your liabilities and subtract liabilities from assets.

Assets	Liabilities
Home: $250,000	Mortgage: $150,000
Investments: $40,000	Student loan: $40,000
Retirement savings: $80,000	
Total: $370,000	Total: $190,000

Net Worth: $370,000 Assets − $190,000 Liabilities (Debts) = $180,000

Total assets include:

- Market value of all publicly held securities, cash, and investments across account structures (taxable, tax-deferred). For example, if you have $2,000 in a savings account, $3,000 in a checking account, $5,000 in an IRA, $10,000 in a 401(k), and $10,000 of stock that you inherited, you would have a total of $2,000 + $3,000 + $5,000 + $10,000 + $10,000 = $30,000.
- Vehicles at 80 percent of Kelly Blue Book trade-in value (liquidity discount)
- Real estate at a price that could be received in 90 days less a 6 percent commission
- Art, jewelry, antiques, collectibles (worth more than $5,000), valued at price items would receive at auction tomorrow less 10 percent commission. Things worth less than $5,000 have nominal value and should be excluded.
- Partnerships and closely held businesses valued at a 15 percent discount to comparable, publicly traded companies, plus an additional 20 percent liquidity discount. For example, if you have a closely held business that is worth $1 million based on similar publicly traded companies, you would typically discount that value by 15 percent for being small and another 20 percent for being illiquid (difficult to sell). $1 million × (1 − 15 percent) × (1 − 20 percent) = $680,000.

- If you have shares in a start-up company or other speculative venture use the value at which you could internally sell your vested shares back to the company.

Total debt includes:

- Face value of all mortgages, loans, debts. This includes student debt, credit card debt, debt to family members or friends, pay-day loans, and home equity lines of credit. It is everything you owe everybody.
- Tax obligations due in the next 24 months that have not been reserved or withheld
- Current value of future tax obligations that you believe should be included
- Current value of all contractual obligations that cannot be completely covered by income (lease payments, long-term rentals)

Total assets − Total debts = Net worth

To figure out where you are in the four phases, divide your net worth by your gross household income. Gross income is how much you are paid—the top line—before taxes, before savings, before health care and before all of the other expenses that come out of our paychecks. Here are some quick examples:

Launch: Net worth is less than 50 percent of gross annual pretax income

- You make $60,000 and are worth less than $30,000.
- You make $150,000 and are worth less than $75,000.
- You make $300,000 and are worth less than $150,000.

Independence: Net worth is between 50 percent and two times your gross annual pretax income

- You make $60,000 and are worth between $30,000 and $120,000.
- You make $150,000 and are worth between $75,000 and $300,000.
- You make $300,000 and are worth between $150,000 and $600,000.

Freedom: Net worth is between two and five times your gross annual pretax income

- You make $60,000 and are worth between $120,000 and $300,000.
- You make $150,000 and are worth between $300,000 and $750,000.
- You make $300,000 and are worth between $600,000 and $1,500,000.

Equilibrium: Net worth is greater than five times your gross annual pretax income

- You make $60,000 and are worth more than $300,000.
- You make $150,000 and are worth more than $750,000.
- You make $300,000 and are worth more than $1,500,000.

I encourage you to review all of these phases because this is the foundation of the process. From here, we can build a framework for balance customized to you, your goals, your life, and the circumstances you find yourself in at any given point in time. Chances are very low that your life looks exactly like any of the following examples so I will discuss how to tailor the process to where you are and where you want to be.

Within each phase we lay out a prioritization of goals. I like to think of money coming into a household like water through a hose. We need to make choices on where we want to direct that hose, which plants we want to water and in what order. Once one plant is watered, we move on to the next one. Sometimes when we water plants, we may water one for a while, move on to some others, and then come back to a particularly thirsty tree to top it off. The same concept applies here. Sometimes we will focus on a few objectives, then come back to top things off. Once you complete all the steps from one phase, you can move on to the next.

I encourage you to utilize the interactive tools and worksheets from the different phases on our website, valueofdebt.com.

Phase 1: Launch!

When your net worth is less than 50 percent of your gross annual income, you want to take as many steps as possible to *avoid taking on any new debt*. To be clear, I mean all debt. If your net worth is less than 50 percent of your gross annual income, debt can be the evil force that causes bad things to happen in your life. Many of those in the anti-debt camp are typically giving advice to this segment of the population and, in many cases, their advice is solid.

I have found that a heavy concentration of debt horror stories generally have at least two of the following three things in common:

1. The individual's net worth was less than 50 percent of their gross annual income.
2. The individual had oppressive debt.
3. Crisis of some type struck the household and the individual did not have the liquidity or savings to ride out the storm.

Learn from others and avoid a similar fate. If you are in the Launch phase, I need you to survive and to move forward. I want you to eliminate oppressive debt and build up liquidity and flexibility.

Step 0: No oppressive debt. Eliminate all credit card debt and/or debt with an interest rate higher than 10 percent. As money comes in, pay down debt and don't add to your debt. Remember, your rate of return on paying down this debt is exactly equal to the cost of that debt. If you have credit card debt at 15 percent, you are getting a guaranteed return of 15 percent by paying down this debt. I know of no other investment that delivers these types of guaranteed returns.

Step 1: Build a cash reserve equal to one month's income. When you're living paycheck to paycheck, it's easy to get caught up in payday loans and other oppressive debt. You need a reserve in your checking account. If you have oppressive debt and zero balance in your checking account, you are running your life on fumes. Bankruptcy—or worse, your survivability—could be on the line. Bottom line: Do everything in your power to keep oppressive debt at zero and build a one-month reserve as fast as you possibly can.

Step 2: Introduce retirement savings. Because of the power of compounding interest, you want to build a retirement base as early as you can. Target a level equal to one-month's income. Ideally this is in a tax-deferred plan such as an IRA or a company-sponsored retirement plan like a 401(k).

I want to be clear on the order: First, have zero oppressive debt and a one-month cash reserve. Second, start building up retirement savings.

Step 3: Grow your cash reserve. The goal is to add two additional months of cash reserve, so you have three months of liquid, accessible cash for emergencies. Now you have oil in the engine and gas in the tank. You have broken the paycheck-to-paycheck lifestyle. Starting your retirement savings is essential, but I'd rather you have enough liquidity to survive. Once you have a total of three months' savings plus a base of one month of retirement savings, your liquidity, flexibility, and survivability increase materially.

To me, one of the most important accomplishments of this phase is the likely impact on your future behavior. All of the best savers I know avoid oppressive debt and have a cash reserve. Zero in their checking account isn't zero, it is when they hit the lower limit of where they feel comfortable, typically at least a three-month reserve. Once you get comfortable holding cash and not having oppressive debt, you will have a strong foundation from which you can build the rest of your savings.

A Case Study

Jason and Amy make $96,000 per year. Their monthly income is about $8,000 per month. They have $5,000 on their credit card, $2,000 in their checking account, $3,000 in their savings account, and $15,000 in their 401(k). Table 3.1 shows where they are and compares it to a balanced path. They could use the glide path to guide their decisions.

The table suggests Jason and Amy reprioritize, and they consider:

1. Reducing their oppressive debt; it is $5,000 too high.
2. Building up cash in their checking account by $6,000.
3. Deemphasizing/pausing from adding to their retirement plan. To be clear, they should NOT take funds from their retirement plan. Table 3.1 simply suggests this bucket might be overwatered. The best way to get it in balance will be to grow everything else around it.
4. Building up cash in their savings account by an additional $13,000.

This is a pretty common situation in which people have a strong early start to retirement savings but also have credit card debt and limited cash

Table 3.1   A Sample Balanced Path—Launch!

Goal/Bucket	Formula	A Balanced Path	Where They Are	Gap
No oppressive debt (No debt at a rate higher than 10 percent)	0	$ 0	$5,000 on the credit card at 20 percent	–$ 5,000
Build a one-month cash reserve (checking account)	Monthly income × 1	$ 8,000	$ 2,000	–$ 6,000
Start a retirement plan. Build to a balance of one month's income	Monthly income × 1	$ 8,000	$15,000	$ 7,000
Continue building cash savings until you have an additional two months' reserve (savings account)	Monthly income × 2	$16,000	$ 3,000	–$13,000

savings. If this is you, I'm thrilled you've started saving for retirement early, but I'm concerned you do not have enough liquidity to handle the curve balls life sends.

WHY NOT JUST BORROW FROM MY 401(K) IF I NEED CASH?

Although this can be a way to help address an immediate financial need, it comes with a number of negative consequences and risks. While perhaps it could be used in an absolute emergency, doing so needs to be weighed against the costs and risks and evaluated against bankruptcy and various asset protection strategies. This should be a worst-case plan, not a base-case plan. Personally, I cannot come up with an example of where borrowing from a retirement plan would be better than having the cash reserves to ride out a storm.

Here's how I suggest Jason and Amy change things. Let's assume they are saving 12 percent, all in their 401(k). Their employer matches 3 percent of the first 3 percent of their contribution. They could consider the following action steps:

1. Reduce their 401(k) savings to 3 percent. This lets them take advantage of the match (free money!), but gives them more take-home pay to even out their balance sheet.
2. Direct all other savings to eliminating oppressive debt.
3. Build up cash reserves in checking first, then in savings.
4. Continue this process until each bucket reaches its goal.

They should try to accomplish these goals over a three- to five-year period. If they try to do it in less than three years, the change would be too radical and nudge them off course. I would further advise that they target building toward an 18 percent savings rate. They could do this by increasing their savings by 1 percent per year for the next three years. They would be saving 15 percent plus their employer match of 3 percent, for a total of 18 percent.[2]

If you aren't saving at 15 percent, you should build to that rate over time. Here is a good trick to get there: Take 15 percent less your current savings rate/5. For example, if you are saving at 5 percent, then 15 percent less 5 percent = 10 percent. 10 percent/5 = 2 percent. You could consider increasing your savings by 2 percent per year for the next five years, gradually working toward 15 percent.

EMPLOYER MATCH IS IMPORTANT—BUT IT ISN'T EVERYTHING

If you are fortunate to have a match from your employer in your retirement plan, it is very valuable. At the same time, so is money in your checking account. I would hate if you missed out on a match from your employer; it is free money. I would also be devastated if you needed money for an emergency and didn't have it. The above is a framework to establish goals. You need to balance these two items. One is not more valuable than the other. The decision of how much to save and where to direct that savings needs balance. I want you to have money for retirement and money for emergencies.

Application

1. Write down your gross pretax annual household income = _____
2. Divide the number by 12 = _____

For example, if your household makes $60,000 per year, you would write down $5,000. If your household makes $120,000, you would write down $10,000.

Using your monthly income as a base figure, we can start to build a customized plan and a glide path. Together, we will create a table with a suggestion for what a balanced path can look like. Then we can fill in where you are at this point in your life. The final step will be to look at the gap between the balanced path and where you are right now. If you are higher in a certain area, then I suggest you de-emphasize adding to that bucket. If you are lower in a certain area, then you will want to focus on building to the target zone.

It is important that you look at each step sequentially, like a video game: You have to clear level one in order to get to level two. This is true for the phases and the steps within a phase. Once a step is full, check it off and move on to the next step or phase.

We all learn at different paces and in different ways. Being familiar with how to use these tables will be key to moving forward in the other phases so Table 3.2 includes more commentary on how the process works. If it is still confusing, I recommend you read through the material one time, focusing on the examples, and then come back and try it with your personal life.

Table 3.3 is for you to use so we can determine a specific action plan. I recommend you begin with the column that says Balanced Path first. This will give you the glide path for what each goal should look like. As you fill in where you are, start at the top and work down. For example, the goal is zero oppressive debt. If you have $10,000 on

Table 3.2 Instructions (Assume annual income of $60,000 and monthly income of $5,000)

Goal/Bucket	Formula	A Balanced Path	Where You Are	Gap
No oppressive debt (No debt at a rate over 10 percent)	0	0	Write down the total amount of oppressive debt you have—debt like credit card debt.	The difference between the balanced path and where you are.
Cash reserve, build to a one-month reserve (checking account)	Monthly income × 1	Write down your monthly income × 1. For example, $5,000	If you have at least one-month reserve in checking, write that number down. If it is lower, write that number down.	Write down the difference between the goal and what you have.
Start a retirement plan. Build to a balance of one month's income	Monthly income × 1	Write down your monthly income × 1. For example, $5,000	Write down the total balance of your retirement plans.	Write down the difference between the goal and what you have.
Continue building cash savings until you have an additional two months' reserve (savings account)	Monthly income × 2	Write down your monthly income × 2. For example, $10,000	Write down the total of your checking and savings, less the one-month reserve above.	Write down the difference between the goal and what you have.

43

Table 3.3 Blank Phase 1: Launch!

Step/Goal/Bucket	Formula	A Balanced Path	Where You Are	Gap
No oppressive debt (No debt at a rate over 10 percent)	0	**0**		
Cash reserve, build to a one–month reserve (checking account)	Monthly income × 1			
Start a retirement plan. Build to a balance of one month's income	Monthly income × 1			
Continue building cash savings until you have an additional two months' reserve (savings account)	Monthly income × 2			

your credit card then you would write zero in the balanced path, $10,000 where you are and $0 − $10,000 in the gap column = (−$10,000). This gap of $10,000 means that you are $10,000 too high, you have $10,000 too much oppressive debt. If this is the case, I suggest you deemphasize other goals and focus on paying down credit card debt.

As you fill out the table, try not to get discouraged about any existing gaps you have. Remember, it is not helpful to look at the past. Know that much of America is right where you are, and many are likely worse off than you. Focus on the future and you can have a successful Launch.

There is one complicating trick to this phase: I am separating your checking and savings accounts. I want you to have a three-month total reserve so you break the paycheck-to-paycheck cycle. I think it is important to separate the money and use your checking account for expenses and a savings account for emergencies. I find it helpful to separate the two, but if you disagree you can look at those two steps as interconnected goals and focus on the total in the two accounts.

The bigger point is that too many people over emphasize retirement savings early and risk having too little in cash while they also have oppressive debt. This is the cycle that I want you to break.

When your household income is more than $50,000 and you have no oppressive debt, a retirement plan with a balance of at least one month's income, and three months' cash reserve, congratulations are in order. You are ahead of approximately 40 percent of Americans.[3] You're much less likely to live paycheck to paycheck again. You can consider buying a home or making those major purchases. And, if you can accomplish this and establish an excellent credit score, your financial future is bright.

Frequently Asked Questions

My goal is to make the advice throughout this book specific and actionable. With that in mind, let's address some of the more common questions that come up during this phase that warrant more discussion:

- What about student debt?
- Should I rent or buy my house?
- What if I already own a house?
- What if I do not have a match from my employer?

What about Student Debt?

Many people find themselves with student debt and are trying to balance building up savings, paying down debt, and enjoying life. If you have student debt, it is essential that your savings rate be at least 15 percent, and ideally, closer to 20 percent of your income. Although this might sound high, remember, I count the principal payment toward your debt as part of your savings rate. It is also important to know I would recommend against saving more than 30 percent—if you are newly out of school this is a prime time to enjoy life! Therefore, 15 percent to 30 percent should be your markers in the channel.

If you are not saving at this level, use the trick I outlined earlier to work toward a 15 percent goal over the next three to five years: 15 percent target—your current savings rate/5. For example, if you are saving 5 percent, then 15 percent − 5 percent = 10 percent/5 years means that you should add 2 percent per year to your savings and gradually ramp toward the 15 percent rate.

Jenny makes $40,000 a year. I suggest she save $6,000 to $12,000 per year. If she saves less than that, say $2,000, then I would suggest that she increase her savings by 2 percent per year for the next five years. If Jenny

Table 3.4   Ramping Up Savings

Time	Income	Savings	Savings Step Up	Total Savings	Total Annual Savings	Income after Savings
Year 0	$40,000	5%	0%	5%	$2,000	$38,000
Year 1	$44,000	5%	2%	7%	$3,080	$40,920
Year 2	$48,000	7%	2%	9%	$4,320	$43,680
Year 3	$52,000	9%	2%	11%	$5,720	$46,280
Year 4	$56,000	11%	2%	13%	$7,280	$48,720
Year 5	$60,000	13%	2%	15%	$9,000	$51,000

gets raises and not only keeps her savings percentage constant, but also adds to it, she's on a very powerful glide path. Table 3.4 shows what her life could look like in a few short years.

If you are under 25 years old, I think it is fine to start with a 5 percent savings rate and to gradually increase it toward 15 percent over the next five years. The trade-off may be that you have to work longer, but trust me—mid 20s is a once-in-a-lifetime experience that is to be enjoyed to its fullest. If you can avoid oppressive debt and get through the Launch phase, covering the minimum payments on student debt, you are doing great.

If you are older than 25, it is never too late to get started. If Jenny is 30 and making $60,000 today and saving 5 percent, then the same rules would apply. She'd bump up her savings by 2 percent each year until she gets to the 15 percent objective. Table 3.5 shows what this could look like.

Table 3.5   Ramping Up Savings—Higher Income

Time	Income	Savings	Savings Step Up	Total Annual Savings	Total Annual Savings	Income after Savings
Year 0	$60,000	5%	0%	5%	$ 3,000	$57,000
Year 1	$65,000	5%	2%	7%	$ 4,550	$60,450
Year 2	$70,000	7%	2%	9%	$ 6,300	$63,700
Year 3	$75,000	9%	2%	11%	$ 8,250	$66,750
Year 4	$80,000	11%	2%	13%	$10,400	$69,600
Year 5	$85,000	13%	2%	15%	$12,750	$72,250

I assume Jenny receives raises. I have no idea what those raises will actually look like. But, as an educated young professional, I assume her income will go up early in her career. Importantly, if it does not, we will see that 15 percent will keep her on track and that she will be able to replace her income in retirement.

Now that we are saving, let's look at debt. When should we pay down the debt? How much should we pay down? How does the debt fit into the rest of the Launch plan?

If the after-tax interest expense on the student debt is over 8 percent, then I want you to reduce it as quickly as possible. For example, if some of your student debt hit your credit card, pay that off. While I want you to pay it off quickly, have cash for an emergency first.

BEWARE OF THE STUDENT DEBT LIQUIDITY TRAP!

Typically, once you pay down your student loan it is a one-way liquidity trip—you can't get that money back. I would hate to see you pay down $5,000 on student debt and then lose your job.

I want you to get rid of your high-cost debt but I also want to make sure that you can ride out a storm. As we talked about in Chapter 2, sh*t happens—and it definitely happens early in life and it will happen to you. Nothing will get you through a crisis like cash.

I'm going to say it again. Drop your anxiety about your debt. Or at least be as concerned about your cash. You can't have debt and live paycheck to paycheck or you are screwed in a crisis. I hate debt over 8 percent, but I hate not having a cash reserve even more.

Honestly, when I wrote this book I decided that step zero is zero oppressive debt, but that decision was with great debate and hesitation. I still can't decide if the most important first step is to have at least a one-month cash reserve or zero oppressive debt. You need to balance these thoughts and make your own decision on what is most important. But the race is to get to zero oppressive debt and have a cash reserve.

If the after-tax cost of debt is between 5 percent and 8 percent, then I suggest once you eliminate oppressive debt, around 30 percent of your savings should go toward reducing the student debt and around 70 percent toward filling up the buckets in order in the Launch phase.

If the after-tax interest expense of your student debt is under 5 percent, then don't pay more than the minimum payment until you build up your checking, savings, and retirement accounts and be sure you are taking advantage of an employer match (if you are lucky to have one).

The only exception to these guides would be if for some reason the math falls below the minimum payment due. You always need to make the minimum payment. Also, I want to be sure you are taking advantage of your employer match. For most people, they should make the minimum payment on their student debt, take advantage of their employer match (nothing more), and build up cash reserves. Table 3.6 summarizes these ideas.

Let's look at a few examples. Remember Jason and Amy? Let's assume that in addition to their balance sheet from the previous example (p. 40) they also have $30,000 of student debt at 7 percent with a 10-year repayment plan. Their required monthly payment would be about $350. I would encourage Jason and Amy to always make the minimum payment of $350 on their student debt and to make the 3 percent contribution to their retirement plan to get the match. All additional savings should go to pay off their credit card debt.

Remember, Jason and Amy are saving at a rate of 12 percent. Once their credit card has been paid off, I suggest they keep making the 3 percent savings to their retirement plan. With the remaining 9 percent, they have about $8,500 per year of additional money directed toward

Table 3.6 Not All Student Debt Is Equal

After-Tax Rate	Goal
>8%	Pay off quickly—especially if you have a cash reserve. Pay off quickly but balance with building up cash if your cash reserve is low.
5% to 8%	Pay off in a balanced approach.
<5%	Pay off as slowly as possible.
	Always Make the Minimum Payment!

savings. I would direct about $2,500 toward student debt and about $6,000 toward building up cash.

If Jason and Amy have a higher rate for their student debt, I would suggest they pay it off more quickly, perhaps directing 80 percent or more of the savings to reducing the debt.

If Jason and Amy have a lower interest rate, under 5 percent, I would deprioritize paying down the debt. In this case, I would encourage them to just make the minimum payment of $350 per month and to move to the Independence phase once they fill the buckets from the Launch phase.

You might note that (1) the pretax and post-tax savings of Jason and Amy may not be apples to apples and (2) I said they could count the principal payment toward their savings rates. If you are the type of person that is asking these questions, then good for you! These guide posts should serve as wide markers in the channel and you are prepared to steer your own course. If you are not into this level of detail, then hopefully the beacons serve as targets for which you can aim.

Should I Rent or Buy My House?

When you're in the Launch phase, I think you should strongly consider renting. Home ownership presents too much risk relative to your resources. *Until your net worth is more than 50 percent of your annual income, I strongly advise you to wait to buy a house or make any major purchases.*

If you already own a home but your net worth is less than 50 percent of your annual income, you will find value in jumping to the charts in the Independence phase. The only exceptions to my preference for renting include:

- The rent-versus-buy math for your market is strongly in favor of buying.
- You plan on being in the house for more than five years and ideally more than seven years.
- You have an accurate assessment of deferred maintenance issues and/or are able to handle repairs yourself.

For example, if you are in a small metropolitan market, enjoy doing home improvement projects, and anticipate you will be in the home for more than five years, then it could make sense to own. If you live in a major metropolitan market, do not like doing home improvement projects, and anticipate being in the property for less than five years, the data will likely lean heavily toward renting.

People who purchase or already own a home during this phase tend to believe:

1. Things won't go wrong:
   a. With their job. Their income will be consistent and growing.
   b. With their house. Repairs will be nominal in cost and scope.
   c. With their family. There will be no illnesses or emergencies.
2. That home price appreciation will be significant.
3. They will not move soon. Moving has considerable costs that may eat into appreciation and may require savings.

Our society encourages too many people to buy homes too early in life because they believe home ownership is a path to financial freedom. My recommendation for you and your family is that until you have no oppressive debt and savings equal to at least 50 percent of your income, home ownership is too risky and should generally be off the table.

People are so quick to want to buy because they think they are wasting money on rent. There are two problems with this:

1. Many of these same people will have life insurance, medical insurance, car insurance, and fire insurance to protect them from all sorts of emergencies. In my opinion nothing protects you like money in the bank. At this stage you do not have enough liquidity to afford the risk of home ownership. Renting is a form of insurance.
2. This is assuming the rent-versus-buy math is strongly in favor of buying. When you own a house you have to cover interest expense, taxes, and maintenance as well as depreciation. When you fully factor in the cost of ownership and compare it to renting you should be willing to pay a slight premium to have access to your money.

From a big picture, instead of thinking that renting is wasting money on rent, consider thinking that buying is wasting money on interest expense and taxes *and* taking more risk. It is simply too early for you to take on the risk of homeownership. For more detail on why the concept of "wasting money on rent" simply isn't true see the Resource Guide.

What if I Already Own a House?

If you own a house and either have oppressive debt or have not built up cash reserves or retirement savings, *immediately deemphasize paying down your mortgage* and focus on the following:[4]

1. Eliminate oppressive debt.
2. Contribute to your 401(k) at a level to maximize your match.
3. Build up cash savings so you are not living or at risk of living paycheck to paycheck.

Focus on the "insurance value" of liquidity. If you pay down more money on your house, it will not change the value of your house. You need more liquidity to ride out a storm, not more equity in your home. You also do not have enough retirement assets to be on track. Paying down the house is much less important than building up assets and liquidity.

What if I Do Not Have a Match from My Employer?

If you do not have a match from your employer, you may want to consider the following:

1. Eliminate oppressive debt.
2. Determine your total level of savings. If it is less than 15 percent, then try to get it there within three to five years.
3. Consider directing 40 percent of your savings to retirement and 60 percent toward your checking/savings account.

For example, if you make $100,000 and are saving 10 percent or $10,000 a year and you do not have a match from your employer. I suggest directing $4,000 (or 40 percent) toward your retirement accounts and $6,000 or (60 percent) toward your cash and checking. Continue at these ratios until you build up a one-month reserve in retirement and a three-month reserve in your savings. When you hit the one-month goal in retirement start directing all of it toward building up your savings.

Phase 2: Independence

When you graduate from the Launch phase you have no oppressive debt, the equivalent of three month's income in savings, and one month in retirement. In the Independence phase your net worth is more than 50 percent of your annual income and less than two times your gross annual pretax income. We will begin the same way as we did in the Launch phase, but we will consider three scenarios: You do not own a house, you would like to buy a house, you already own a house. Start by doing the following:

1. Write down your gross annual pretax household income = _____

2. Divide the number by 12 = _____

Scenario 1: You Do Not Own a House

Continuing to expand on the same framework we used in the Launch phase we get the following steps:

Step 0: Zero oppressive debt. While it may seem a bit repetitive, it is worth repeating. No oppressive debt. Not now. Not ever.

Step 1: Build a three-month cash reserve in your checking account. Three months' reserve in a checking account is a good level of "oil in the engine" to cover surprise expenses. With the three-month reserve in your savings account, you'll have six months of cash reserve, which gives you greater ability to ride out many storms.

Step 2: Build your retirement savings. Work towards saving six times your monthly income.

Step 3: Establish a big life changes fund. Many people want to own a home. Others want to get married and have a big wedding. Still others want to go to graduate school or change careers. I suggest building a nine-month cash reserve in your savings account for these kinds of purchases.

Meet Steve and Kevin. They rent and plan to continue renting for a while. They make $90,000 a year and save $15,000 each year. They have $15,000 in checking, $5,000 in savings, $75,000 in retirement, and $25,000 in some mutual funds. They recently went on a trip and are carrying $5,000 on their credit card but want to pay it off from savings over the next couple of months. Table 3.7 provides a sketch of where they are and of what a balanced path could look like with these goals.

Table 3.7 A Sample Balanced Path—Independence, No House

Goal/Bucket	Formula	A Balanced Path	Where You Are	Gap
No oppressive debt (No debt at a rate over 10 percent)	0	$ 0	$ 5,000	$ 5,000
Cash reserve, checking account	Monthly income × 3	$22,500	$15,000	−$ 7,500
Cash reserve, savings account	Monthly income × 3	$22,500	$ 5,000	−$17,500
Retirement investing	Monthly income × 6	$45,000	$75,000	$30,000
Big life changes	Monthly income × 9	$67,500	$25,000	−$42,500

With their annual income of $90,000, their monthly income to use for the table is $7,500.

I would suggest that Steve and Kevin need to eliminate that credit card debt quickly. They are ahead on retirement and behind in building up their cash reserves and big life changes bucket. Therefore, I would encourage them to first eliminate the credit card debt, deemphasize retirement savings (but always be sure they are taking full advantage of

Table 3.8 A Blank Balanced Path Worksheet—Phase 2: Independence, No House

Goal/Bucket	Formula	A Balanced Path	Where You Are	Gap
No oppressive debt (No debt at a rate over 10 percent)	0	**0**		
Cash reserve, checking account	Monthly income × 3			
Cash reserve, savings account	Monthly income × 3			
Retirement investing	Monthly income × 6			
Big life changes	Monthly income × 9			

their employer's match), build up checking, build up savings, and then build up their big life changes bucket.

Table 3.8 provides a tool to sketch out what a balanced path could look like with these goals. Feel free to combine checking and savings into one bucket.

THE DIFFERENCE BETWEEN SAVING AND INVESTING

Savings and investing are not the same things.

When you save, you set aside money for a specific goal within a specific time period.

When you invest, you have longer-term objectives and may or may not need the money along the way. It might be for retirement or for some unforeseen event 10 years from now. You need to put your money into different accounts based on your needs.

If you need it in less than 5 years, put it all into savings.

If you need it in more than 10 years, invest it.

If you need it in 5 to 10 years, carefully weigh the risk of loss versus the potential gain. The closer you are to 10 years, the more you may be comfortable with some risk. The closer you are to 5 years, the safer it should be.

LESSON LEARNED: FOCUS ON SAVING

Once I broke the paycheck-to-paycheck cycle and changed my lifestyle, my savings grew considerably. In 2001, I started saving more than I spent each month. I was young and single and had a good job. The "tech wreck" began. A company that had recently traded at $250 per share fell to $100 per share. There were 10 other stories like this. This was my chance! I promptly scooped up shares.

Well, the stock fell to $75. Great time to buy more, I thought. If the shares hit $150, I will double my money.

The stock fell to $30. But I thought this company was a "toll keeper" that would make money as long as the Internet grew—and I was sure the Internet would grow. I backed up the truck and bought more.

The stock fell to $4. I didn't buy more. I was afraid—and poor again.

I met a girl. We fell in love. We decided to get married. I needed money for a ring, a wedding, and a new house. I sold my stock. Fortunately, it had bounced higher than $4, but it was still far below what I paid for it.

What happened? I didn't understand the difference between savings and investing. Today that stock is at $90. With enough time, my investments may have actually worked out, but that wasn't my timeline; I needed to sell it earlier.

I invested money when I didn't have the luxury of time and should have been saving instead. While it sounds incredibly boring, during this phase you need to focus on saving rather than investing. Establish a base retirement account and, trust me, keep it as safe and boring as possible.

Scenario 2: You Would Like to Purchase a House

Brandon and Teresa are in the Independence phase and want to buy a house. They make $60,000, or $5,000 per month. They have:

- $0 oppressive debt
- $15,000 in their checking account
- $15,000 cash reserve in their savings account
- $30,000 in retirement savings
- $45,000 in their big life changes fund

That equals $105,000 net worth.

Let's assume they want to buy a $240,000 house. In this example, their income is approximately equal to the median income and their home purchase is approximately equal to the average (median) home purchase price.[5] If Brandon and Teresa use their down payment savings of $45,000, they need a mortgage for $195,000.

Table 3.9   A Balanced Path Worksheet—Phase 2: Independence, Buying a House

Goal/Bucket	Formula	A Balanced Path	Where They Are	Gap
No oppressive debt (No debt at a rate over 10 percent)	0	$ 0	$ 0	$0
Cash reserve, checking account	Monthly income × 3	$ 15,000	$ 15,000	$0
Cash reserve, savings account	Monthly income × 3	$ 15,000	$ 15,000	$0
Retirement investments	Monthly income × 6	$ 30,000	$ 30,000	$0
House equity (you put the money down on the house)	Monthly income × 9	$ 45,000	$ 45,000	$0
Equity in long-term investments (house and retirement)	Monthly income × 15	$ 75,000	$ 75,000	$0
Net worth	Monthly income × 21	$105,000	$105,000	$0
Mortgage	Monthly income × 39	$195,000	$195,000	$0
Total assets	Monthly income × 60	$300,000	$300,000	$0

Table 3.9 shows what Brandon and Teresa's financial life could look like.

Note the $195,000 mortgage divided by the $240,000 purchase price equals 81 percent loan-to-value. We will get into more detail on mortgages later, but many loans require a 20 percent down payment. If Brandon and Teresa have to dip into their savings to get the mortgage to 80 percent, that's fine. It is okay to dip into your savings from time to time; that's what it's there for. At the same time, if you use that reserve, it is essential you immediately build it back up to get back in balance.

Recall our notes on calculating your net worth. Table 3.10 shows how buying the house changes both sides of Brandon and Teresa's balance sheet.

Table 3.10   Balance Sheet after Home Purchase

Assets	Amount	Liabilities	Amount
Checking account	$ 15,000	Oppressive debt	$ 0
Savings account	$ 15,000		
Retirement investments	$ 30,000		
Home	$240,000	Mortgage	$195,000
Total assets	**$300,000**	**Total liabilities**	**$195,000**
Net worth	**$105,000**		

Notice the debt ratio is $195,000/$300,000 or 65 percent. This level of debt is too high long term and needs to be reduced. Long term, I would like to see their debt ratio closer to 35 percent and falling. There are two ways for Brandon and Teresa to reduce their debt ratio: Grow assets or pay down debt. At this point in their life, the best thing for Brandon and Teresa is to focus on growing their assets, not on paying down this low-cost, working debt.

WHAT ABOUT DEBT-TO-INCOME RATIOS?

The vast majority of articles I have seen start out by looking at debt to income and things like payment coverage ratios. While it is important to consider these viewpoints, the L.I.F.E. process incorporates balanced ratios that include both income and assets and looks at them in an interconnected, holistic way.

It is true that lower-interest-rate environments may enable somebody to buy slightly more house than I suggest, and higher-interest-rate environments may make this process more challenging. Rather than use low-interest rates to buy more home, I prefer you are prudent and buy less house than you might be able to afford. You should direct the excess money to building up liquidity and savings. *The best way to feel rich is to live in a less expensive home than you can afford.*

A Case Study of Dual Income, No Kids

Bryan and Kate are married with dual incomes, have no kids, and live in Chicago. They are in their late 30s and have been renting since college. They make $180,000, or $15,000 per month, and would like to move into a house and start a family. Table 3.11 shows what their financial picture looks like.

Bryan and Kate are following a balanced path, so how much home might they consider? For now, I want to focus on the balance between assets and liabilities and income, independent of interest rates. If Bryan and Kate purchase a house worth $750,000, their assets would be $950,000 and their liabilities would be $600,000, as shown in Table 3.12.

Application

As we did in Phase 1, use Table 3.13 to compare where you are to what a balanced path might look like with these goals. As a reminder, start by filling in the answers to the suggested balanced path. Then fill in where you are, starting at the top and working down. The gap is the difference between where you are and what a balanced path represents.

Table 3.11   Dual Income, No Kids Ready to Buy a Home

Goal/Bucket	Formula	A Balanced Path	Where They Are	Gap
No oppressive debt (No debt at a rate over 10 percent)	0	$ 0	$ 0	$ 0
Cash reserve, checking account	Monthly income × 3	$ 45,000	$ 50,000	$ 5,000
Cash reserve, savings account	Monthly income × 3	$ 45,000	$ 50,000	$ 5,000
Retirement savings	Monthly income × 6	$ 90,000	$100,000	$10,000
Big life changes/ House savings	Monthly income × 9	$135,000	$150,000	$15,000
Net worth	Monthly income × 21	$315,000	$350,000	$35,000

Table 3.12 Dual Income No Kids after Purchasing a Home

Goal/Bucket	Formula	A Balanced Path	Where They Are	Gap
No oppressive debt (No debt at a rate over 10 percent)	0	$ 0	$ 0	$ 0
Cash reserve, checking account	Monthly income × 3	$ 45,000	$ 50,000	$ 5,000
Cash reserve, savings account	Monthly income × 3	$ 45,000	$ 50,000	$ 5,000
Retirement savings	Monthly income × 6	$ 90,000	$ 100,000	$ 10,000
House equity (you put the money down on the house)	Monthly income × 9	$ 135,000	$ 150,000	$ 15,000
Equity in long-term investments (house and retirement)	Monthly income × 15	$ 225,000	$ 250,000	$ 25,000
Net worth	Monthly income × 21	$ 315,000	$ 350,000	$ 35,000
Mortgage	Monthly income × 39	$(585,000)	$(600,000)	$(15,000)
Total assets	Monthly income × 60	$ 900,000	$ 950,000	$ 50,000

This can give you a framework to consider, discuss, and apply to your personal situation.

Scenario 3: You Already Own a House

If you already own a house, the same concept applies. Fill out Table 3.13 and look at where you are relative to the recommended areas.

If your mortgage is under your monthly income × 39, that is OK, but I suggest you deemphasize paying down any more against your mortgage. Instead, money should go to building up the other areas such as cash, retirement savings, and the big life changes account. At this point, you still have many more changes to come and nothing helps more than having money at the ready.

Table 3.13   A Blank Balanced Path Worksheet—Phase 2: Independence, with a House

Goal/Bucket	Formula	A Balanced Path	Where You Are	Gap
No oppressive debt (No debt at a rate over 10 percent)	0	**0**		
Cash reserve, checking account	Monthly income × 3			
Cash reserve, savings account	Monthly income × 3			
Retirement savings	Monthly income × 6			
House equity	Monthly income × 9			
Net worth	Monthly income × 21			
Mortgage	Monthly income × 39			
Total assets	Monthly income × 60			

If your mortgage is higher than your monthly income × 39, then we need to check in with the other categories. If any other area is low, meaning it is under the suggested balanced path, then I suggest you build up those areas before you work toward paying down your mortgage. This is controversial. The "debt is bad" camp will tell you to reduce your debt by paying it down. My point is to reduce your debt ratio by building assets. In this phase of L.I.F.E., independent of your age, you need more assets, not less working debt.

Always remember, you can change your net worth by paying down debt or by building up assets. To be clear, I would rather that you direct future savings to the other categories until they are close to full/accomplishing their goals. I also would consider the list to be a prioritized list. I suggest you first build up your checking and savings and then your retirement. By the time you hit a net worth of 21 × your monthly income, you are ready to start to look at moving into the next phase.

LOWER YOUR DEBT RATIO BY BUILDING UP ASSETS

While you are in Phase 2, I strongly suggest you reduce your debt ratio by building up your assets rather than paying down your debt. This gives you a larger base of resources, which will increase your liquidity and flexibility and potentially enable you to capture the spread or earn a rate of return on your investments higher than your after-tax cost of debt.

If any other number is significantly out of line from the target, you want to deemphasize adding to that bucket and build up everything else around it so you're closer to balance.

I want to hammer home a few important points as we are still building our long-term foundation. Table 3.14 highlights a few of the differences between what so many people do and my specific recommendation.

Congratulations—if you are under 50 and you clear the Independence phase, saving at a rate of at least 15 percent, then it is likely that

Table 3.14 Recommendations for Dealing with Debt

Many People ...	My Recommendation
Have some oppressive debt	Get rid of it!
Do not have a three-month reserve in checking	Build up to it. It is okay to have debt and cash.
Do not have a three-month reserve in savings	Build up to it. You need reserves to get you through hard times.
Dramatically over- or undersave for retirement	Embrace a balanced approach early and keep the balance throughout your life.
Race to pay down debt	Consider not paying down working debt during this phase. Your net worth is still under twice your assets. Your debt ratio will fall by building up assets or by paying down debt. Your top priority is to build assets.

your net worth is not only near the top 40 percent of all Americans, but you are also likely to be on track for retirement.[6]

AVERAGE NET WORTH OF AMERICANS IN TOP 40 PERCENT

Half of all Americans under 44 years old have a net worth of less than $35,000, and half of Americans 45 to 54 years old have a net worth of less than $85,000. It doesn't take a fortune to have a net worth that lands you in the top 40 percent of Americans.

35 and younger: $33,477
35 to 44: $128,430
45 to 54: $228,708
55 to 64: $333,750

Source: USA Today (http://www.usatoday.com/story/money/personalfinance/2015/01/31/motley-fool-net-worth-age/22415229/)

Endnotes

1. Carmen DeNavas-Walt and Bernadette D. Proctor, *Income and Poverty in the United States: 2014* (September 2015), https://www.census.gov/content/dam/Census/library/publications/2015/demo/p60-252.pdf.
2. The case studies presented are for educational and illustrative purposes only and cannot guarantee that the reader will achieve similar results. Your results may vary significantly and factors such as the market, personal effort, and many others will cause results to vary. All of the case studies throughout the book are hypothetical and not intended to demonstrate the performance of any specific security, product, or investment strategy. Opinions formulated by the author are intended to stimulate discussion.
3. DeNavas-Walt and Proctor.
4. Your personal situation may be unique and the goal of this book is to encourage thoughtful conversation and debate on each of these concepts. Here I am assuming that you have a low-cost mortgage. Remember, your return on paying down debt is equal to your after-tax cost of debt. For example, if you have a mortgage at 5 percent and credit card debt at 20 percent, you should focus on

paying off your credit card debt first. All things being equal, one would rather have 5 percent debt than 20 percent debt. Once oppressive debt is eliminated, I suggest you build up more liquidity so that you can survive the shocks life sends all of us. And finally, building up a base of retirement assets early will increase the chances that you will be on track to retire. If you are on a high-cost mortgage, such as a high-interest-rate private mortgage, these ideas may not be as applicable.

5. https://ycharts.com/indicators/sales_price_of_existing_homes.

6. Author's Note: The information in this chapter is to be considered in a holistic way as a part of the book and not to be considered on a stand-alone basis. This includes, but is not limited to, the discussion of the risks of each of these ideas as well as all of the disclaimers throughout the book. The material is presented with a goal of encouraging thoughtful conversation and rigorous debate on the risks and potential benefits of the concepts between you and your advisors based on your unique situation, risk tolerance, and goals.

Chapter 4

Freedom and Equilibrium

"There is a better way to do it—find it."

—Thomas Edison

I n his bestselling book *Seven Habits of Highly Effective People*, Steven Covey urges readers to begin with the end in mind.[1] He writes that we first create things in our minds. When you build a home, he points out, you make detailed blueprints before a single nail is hammered. You make sure you've thought through every detail of your dream home before you break ground. I want to think about our finances this way as well. Once you have broken through the initial phases you have a strong foundation in place. From here we can "begin with the end in mind" where we can balance the tri-mandate of enjoying life, paying down debt, and being on track for retirement. Together, we can create a blueprint for your financial goals.

Now that you have made it through the Launch and Independence phases, you are on a balanced path. You have no oppressive debt, a liquid safety net and, possibly, your first home purchased. Now we consider the next steps: Enjoying life and preparing for retirement. In the Freedom and Equilibrium phases we'll work to reduce your debt ratio and build up assets.

Phase 3: Freedom

When your net worth is less than five times your annual income, you simply do not have enough money to retire. During this phase, you want to reduce your debt ratio, save toward retirement, and enjoy life.

I want you *to be able to be debt free.* If you have these resources and choose to pay off your debts, then good for you. If you understand the potential risks and benefits and embrace a strategic debt philosophy that works both sides of the balance sheet as companies do, then good for you. I want you to be thoughtful and balanced so you can embrace holistic strategies that minimize risk and maximize the probability of a comfortable retirement. I will prove to you that working both sides of the balance sheet and continuing to have debt during this phase will increase your path to financial freedom. First, let's establish the path and the plan.

Early in life and at the end of the Independence phase it's likely your debt ratio is high, potentially over 50 percent. Consider Brandon and Teresa, who we met in Chapter 3. Their debt ratio was 65 percent. Debt ratios above 50 percent depend on income and a lot of things going right. By the time you retire, we want your debt ratio well under 40 percent. So in this phase, we'll focus on reducing it from 65 to 40 percent. This is the next stop on our financial journey; the beacon we can follow on the horizon.

Your debt ratio can decrease by paying down debt *or* by building up assets. *In this phase we want to decrease your debt ratio by building up assets.* This creates a stronger base and allows more of your money to take advantage of the power of compounding. And, this puts you on track for retirement. As you start this phase, you have a significant unfunded liability—your retirement—that you need to be saving toward. We want to focus on building up assets more than paying down low-cost, tax-efficient debt.

A Case Study

Let's look back to the end of Independence and revisit Brandon and Teresa. Table 4.1 shows their debt ratio of 65 percent (195,000/300,000).

In nature, balance and ratios are very similar across both large and small objects. For example, the ratios that create the balance in a rose or sunflower has a lot in common with the balance, ratios, and proportions in a hurricane, which has a lot in common with the balance, ratios, and proportions of the Milky Way. The proportions are similar, but the units are different.[2] For example, you could measure the Milky Way in centimeters, but that isn't practical. Therefore, as we move to a bigger balance sheet, with different goals, we need to move to different and bigger base units.

The goal of this book is to provide a specific and actionable glide path for the different phases of L.I.F.E. The goal of the first two phases was to build a foundation of assets, which are built from savings, which come from income. In Launch and Independence, the base unit we started with was one month of gross pretax income.

If income was the star and centerpiece of the Launch and Independence phases, debt is the star and centerpiece of Freedom. The goal of the Freedom phase is to reduce your debt ratio. Since reducing debt is

Table 4.1 Brandon and Teresa Balance Sheet after Home Purchase

Assets	Amount	Liabilities	Amount
Checking account	$ 15,000	Oppressive debt	$ 0
Savings account	$ 15,000		
Retirement investments	$ 30,000		
Home	$240,000	Mortgage	$195,000
Total assets	**$300,000**	**Total liabilities**	**$195,000**
Net worth	**$105,000**		

the primary goal then we need a different base unit, one that relates specifically to your debt. Therefore, do the following:

1. Write down your total liabilities (your total outstanding debt) = _____

2. Divide this number by 8 = _____

This is your base unit for this phase.

Looking back at Brandon and Teresa, we remember that their only debt is their mortgage. Therefore, Brandon and Teresa would divide 195,000 by 8, which would give them a base unit of 24,375. Now while you may choose to be that precise, I prefer to round it to 24,000. You could also round it to 25,000. Again, think of this as wide channel markers more than hard-and-fast specific formulas.

Why are we dividing by eight? During this phase we are trying to reduce debt as a percentage of the total balance sheet so we start with debt as the target and build around it. The number eight is derived from something called the Fibonacci sequence. More details on this can be found in Appendix A: Phi Phound Me, or if you're curious on the math specifics then I would encourage you to visit valueofdebt.com. If you like the big picture, then stick with me on this formula while we go through the case study and you will see how it comes together.

It is worth noting that this phase is likely to represent 10 to 15 years or more in your life. Typically, income will change considerably for most households during this period. There may be promotions or raises, one person may stay at home, go back to work, and so on. By focusing on debt instead of income we look at how balanced our financial glide path is and discover beacons that can shine independent of the many other changes in life.

Table 4.2 shows where they are today.

A few things stand out with this table. Notice that cash is a combination of checking and savings in a single bucket. When we combine the two they are a sliver high. We have two new categories: Other and Long-term investments.

The Other category includes personal property such as equity in a car, wedding ring, and furniture in the house. People like to include the value of personal property, but they are of little consequence to our long-term economic analysis, so don't get mired down in this bucket.

Table 4.2 Brandon and Teresa—Phase 3, Freedom

Goal/Bucket	Formula	A Balanced Path	Where You Are	Gap
No oppressive debt (No debt at a rate over 10 percent)	0	$ 0	$ 0	$ 0
Cash reserve, checking + savings	Base unit × 1	$ 24,000	$ 30,000	$ 6,000
Other (jewelry, cars, furniture)	Base unit × 1	$ 24,000	New category	
Long-term investments (after-tax)	Base unit × 3	$ 72,000	New category	
Retirement savings	Base unit × 5	$120,000	$ 30,000	–$ 90,000
Total debt (mortgage)	Base unit × 8	($195,000)	($195,000)	$ 0
Net worth	Base unit × 13	$317,000	$105,000	–$212,000
Total assets	Base unit × 21	$512,000	$300,000	–$212,000

But if you find you are significantly above the recommended value for this category, I would strongly encourage you to shift your priorities to closing the other gaps.

The Long-term investments category is also new. Generally, people are quick to build up retirement accounts and quick to build up a checking or savings account, but they are missing an investment account comprised of after-tax assets. Starting this account early unleashes a tremendous amount of flexibility with your long-term financial goals, including liquidity and the ability to harness the power of compounding.

In the Independence phase we called this a "big life changes" bucket. We discussed the importance of this bucket being lower risk and that it is a savings bucket for weddings, homes, grad school, and other big life changes. In the Freedom phase, this becomes an Investment bucket—one that you could access if you need to but one that can also afford short-term volatility for the potential of long-term higher returns.

Looking at Brandon and Teresa, you'll notice a massive gap in their retirement and long-term savings buckets. They need to work to fill up these two buckets. Which should they fill up first? A nice split to consider would be 60 percent to retirement savings and 40 percent to long-term investments but they could customize this to anywhere between 30 and

Table 4.3   Brandon and Teresa Balance Sheet—End of Freedom Phase

Assets	Amount	Liabilities	Amount
Cash	$ 24,000	Oppressive debt	$ 0
Personal/other	$ 24,000		
Long-term investments	$ 72,000		
Retirement investments	$ 120,000		
Home	$ 272,000	Mortgage	$ 195,000
Total assets	**$512,000**	**Total liabilities**	**$195,000**
Net worth	**$317,000**		

50 percent to long-term investments and the balance to their retirement savings. They should not be focused on paying down their mortgage at this time.

If they follow this road map, their balance sheet could look like Table 4.3.

Here the debt ratio is $195,000/$512,000 = 38.1 percent. *Notice that the debt ratio is falling considerably, even though they have not paid down any debt.* This happened because the assets around them have grown more significantly.

To keep this simple, I assume they are on an interest-only mortgage and only made the required interest payment. All other money went to building up assets. To be crystal clear, I am showing their debt ratio falling without paying down anything toward their debt.

With respect to their house, I valued it at $272,000. Their house may or may not have appreciated and, of course, it could have depreciated. It is likely that this phase will take more than 15 years to complete and most people like to assume that houses appreciate over a 10- to 15-year period so I have assumed a modest level of appreciation. If their house appreciates as indicated, their home equity would grow from $45,000 to $77,000, even though they didn't pay down any of their mortgage.

Significant events have now transpired in their financial life:

1. They have significant assets working for the long term.
2. They could easily move, change jobs, or survive an emergency.
3. They have almost $200,000 working for them, plus the home value, which could, over a long period of time, go up in value as well.
4. If they have a 15-, 20-, or 30-year time horizon, they have increased the chances of a solid retirement.

They have freedom to enjoy life, freedom to change jobs, freedom to do what they want. Money, debt, and finances do not oppress Brandon and Teresa—these things empower them. They liberate them. Brandon and Teresa are making informed, strategic choices. Behind the scenes, they are thinking and acting like a company, implementing some of the most powerful theories in finance, and exhibiting a balanced approach that is found throughout the natural world.[3]

Application

Use Table 4.4 by doing the following:

1. Write down your total liabilities (your total outstanding debt) = _____

2. Divide this number by 8 = _____

This figure is the base unit to use in completing the table.

As we move forward, it will become increasingly important to be flexible and consider these tables as broad guides. Keep in mind, you can't control the value of your home or the value of your portfolio. These figures will change regularly, so look for the big holes or, if your life is in fairly close balance, look at maintaining the ratios.

Table 4.4   A Blank Freedom Worksheet—Debt Based

Goal/Bucket	Formula	A Balanced Path	Where You Are	Gap
No oppressive debt (No debt at a rate over 10 percent)	0	$0		
Cash reserve, checking + savings	Base unit × 1			
Other (jewelry, cars, furniture)	Base unit × 1			
Long-term investments (after-tax)	Base unit × 3			
Retirement savings	Base unit × 5			
Total debt (mortgage)	Base unit × 8			
Net worth	Base unit × 13			
Total assets	Base unit × 21			

Frequently Asked Questions

Continuing to build on our foundation and trying to make the advice as specific as possible, let's address some of the most common questions that come up during this phase:

- What about student debt?
- What about income as a base unit? In other words, what if instead of basing the ratios off of debt, how could it be done with income as we did before?
- What if you don't own a home?
- How long will this phase take?
- What about children and children's saving accounts?

What about Student Debt?
Let's say Brandon and Teresa have $30,000 in student debt. If we apply the same framework, it would suggest their base unit is $28,125 ($195,000 mortgage + $30,000 student debt)/8 = $28,125. Our beacons would flash the same signals: de-prioritize paying down debt. Cash is OK. Build up retirement and build up long-term investments.

I would apply the same framework as before. If the after-tax rate is over 8 percent, I would aggressively pay down student debt. If the after-tax rate is between 4 and 8 percent, I would take a balanced approach. I would consider directing 50 percent of your after-tax savings to paying down student debt. For example, if 50 percent of savings goes toward retirement, you could choose to direct 25 percent to building up long-term investments and 25 percent to paying down student debt. If the after-tax rate is under 4 percent, I would not pay any more than you need to for the minimum required payment.

What about Using Income as a Base Unit?
I prefer you use debt as the base unit for this phase. However, if income is your preferred approach, then the table can be created with income as the base by doing the following:

1. Write down your gross annual pretax household income = _____

2. Divide the number by 12 = _____

Use this number as the base when completing Table 4.5.

Table 4.5 A Blank Balanced Path Worksheet—Phase 3: Freedom, Income Based

Goal/Bucket	Formula	A Balanced Path	Where You Are	Gap
No oppressive debt (No debt at a rate over 10 percent)	0	$0		
Cash reserve, checking + savings	Monthly income × 5			
Other (jewelry, cars, furniture)	Monthly income × 5			
Long-term savings (after tax)	Monthly income × 15			
Retirement savings	Monthly income × 25			
Total debt (mortgage)	Monthly income × 40			
Net worth	Monthly income × 65			
Total assets	Monthly income × 105			

You can use both ways as a framework for balance and see which areas need to be built up and which need to be reduced. In many cases, these two charts will look similar. In a balanced world, they should be close to equal. If liabilities are out of whack, your debt ratio will fall when you either build up assets or pay down debt. Until you get your net worth built up to more than five times your annual income, paying down debt should be off the table—with the exception of oppressive debt, which you should never have.

What If You Don't Own a Home?
Renting can be great. Depending on the market, you can find considerable value in renting for more of your life, and perhaps all of your life. I'm 41, live in downtown Chicago, and have three kids. There is at least a 50 percent chance I will rent for the next 10 to 20 years, if not the rest of my life. If you are a renter, use Table 4.6 to see how this works when you are in Phase 3.

Table 4.6 A Blank Balanced Path Worksheet—Phase 3: Freedom, No Home/Renting

Goal/Bucket	Formula	A Balanced Path	Where You Are	Gap
No oppressive debt (No debt at a rate over 10 percent)	0	$0		
Cash reserve, checking + savings	Monthly income × 5			
Other (jewelry, cars, furniture)	Monthly income × 5			
Big life changes (savings)	Monthly income × 10			
Long-term investments (after tax)	Monthly income × 15			
Retirement investments	Monthly income × 25			
Net worth	Monthly income × 65			

1. Write down your gross pretax annual income = _____
2. Divide this number by 12 = _____
3. Multiply this number by 5 = _____

Use five months of your gross, pretax earnings as the base unit to look at balance.

How Long Will This Phase Take?

Who knows? My guess is 8 to 15 years, but it depends on so many factors. That is why I focus on debt instead of income. To me, life is a lot like the games Sorry, Monopoly, and Chutes and Ladders—a few steps forward and a few steps backward. The best we can do is control the things we can control. You can control your savings rate. You can control where you direct your savings. You can control your debt ratio. You can't control your rate of return and you can't control the world around you.

Focus on what you can control and be prepared. From my experience, I think it is likely that you may move forward from one phase to another faster than you expected only to step back again, and then forward again, and then back again.

I encourage you to go with it. I think you will be disappointed—and maybe bored—if you approach life as a linear experience. When you are in the Freedom phase and moving toward Equilibrium, you are fully prepared to embrace the journey of life.

What about Children and Children's Savings Accounts?

For many households, children come into the picture during this phase. While children are a great gift, they add more complexity to our prioritization. In addition to wanting to enjoy life, save for the future, and pay down debt, we now also have the added challenge of providing for and possibly sending our children to college. This is another unfunded future obligation. It is another debt to your future self. Here again, the problem is that many people start saving too little, too late, missing out on the benefit and power of the compounding of interest.

The path I'm outlining and the 15 percent savings rate is designed to fulfill the debt to your future self. The good news is, we will see this path has a high probability of success. The bad news is, it doesn't include children. To include children, I would suggest you need to save an additional 2 percent of your income per child from the time they are 6 months old through 22. So if you are saving 15 percent and you have one child, you will need to save 17 percent. If you have two children, you will need to save 19 percent, and so forth. I recognize this is a lot of savings, but if you are willing to make the sacrifice, I will prove it works. If you save less, the trade-off is a few more years of work, which isn't necessarily bad, either. We will do some math later in the book to test and refine this process.

The bottom line theme is the same: Do not pay down your debt during the Freedom phase; build up your savings. For those with children, we are just adding an additional savings bucket, college. While you can do this in a number of different accounts, I recommend that you visit with your advisor about a 529 college savings program.

Phase 4: Equilibrium

Wouldn't it be awesome to have no debt? I think so. What is even more awesome is if you have the *ability* to pay off all of your debt but *choose* not to. Instead, you *choose* to be strategic, thoughtful, and balanced. You take a conservative twist on the strategies used by the largest and most successful companies in the world. You borrow from the greatest theories in finance. You are an empowered, flexible force. Thoughtful. Balanced. On track, and able to change course anytime you want to. You are in control.

In the Freedom phase, we saw your debt ratio can fall by paying down debt or by building up assets. In the Equilibrium phase, your assets are greater than five times your gross annual pretax income. At this point, your biggest debt is still the debt to your future self. You need to build up assets. We continue building up assets more than focusing on paying down debt.

For our base units, we can return to an income-based formula. This is because in the Equilibrium phase you are getting closer to retirement. Retirement is essentially an income-based goal: You want to have an income stream from your portfolio that replaces the income you used to get from working. Even if you choose not to retire, I assume that you would like the option to be able to do so. As with the other chapters, we begin with a case study and then provide a blank guide so you can apply it to your life.

Use Table 4.7 to see where you are in Phase 4.

1. Write down your gross pretax annual income = _____
2. Divide this number by 12 = _____

Always think about this like a ship in a channel of water. The bigger the ship, the wider the channel it navigates. The bigger the balance sheet, the more you want to look at this as a representation of balance but not strict rules to which you are expected to conform. Consider these beacons for which you can aim, not hard rules, which is why I use the word *approximate* throughout the table.

Recall Brandon and Teresa make $60,000, or $5,000 each month. Let's look at Table 4.7, where they finish the Freedom phase and enter the Equilibrium phase.

Table 4.7 Brandon and Teresa Entering Equilibrium

Goal/Bucket	Formula	A Balanced Path	Where You Are	Gap
No oppressive debt (No debt at a rate over 10 percent)	0	$ 0	$ 0	$ 0
Approximate cash reserve (checking + savings)	Monthly income × 7	$ 35,000	$ 24,000	–$ 11,000
Approximate other (jewelry, cars, furniture)	Monthly income × 7	$ 35,000	$ 24,000	–$ 11,000
Approximate mortgage	Monthly income × 35	($175,000)	($195,000)	($ 20,000)
Approximate long-term investments (after tax)	Monthly income × 56	$280,000	$ 72,000	–$208,000
Approximate retirement savings	Monthly income × 91	$455,000	$120,000	–$335,000
Approximate total investment assets	Monthly income × 147	$735,000	$192,000	–$543,000

Here our beacons are flashing many signals: Brandon and Teresa need to build up a little cash and perhaps reduce their debt, but they also need to build up long-term investments and retirement savings—a lot. The gaps in cash and debt are small. The gaps in investments and retirement savings are large.

Notice the beautiful balance the beacons show us:

• The debt ratio is $175,000/$735,000, or 23.8 percent.
• Retirement savings/Total investment assets = $455,000/$735,000, or 62 percent.
• This is approximately the same ratio of after-tax assets as a percentage of retirement assets ($280,000/$455,000), or 62 percent.

Here again, these ratios represent balance found throughout the natural world, art, and architecture.[4] See Appendix A—Phi Phound Me for details on the math, but, big picture, the beacons highlight a clear plan: a declining debt ratio and balance between our assets and our debts.

Table 4.8   Brandon and Teresa—Near Equilibrium

Goal/Bucket	Formula	A Balanced Path	Where They Are	Gap
No oppressive debt (No debt at a rate over 10 percent)	0	$ 0	$ 0	$ 0
Cash reserve, checking + savings	Monthly income × 7	$ 35,000	$ 30,000	–$ 5,000
Other (jewelry, cars, furniture)	Monthly income × 7	$ 35,000	$ 40,000	$ 5,000
Approximate mortgage	Monthly income × 35	($175,000)	($195,000)	($20,000)
After-tax savings	Monthly income × 56	$280,000	$300,000	$20,000
Retirement savings	Monthly income × 91	$455,000	$460,000	$ 5,000
Total investment assets	Monthly income × 147	$735,000	$760,000	$25,000

Let's fast forward several years, and their balance sheet looks like Table 4.8. This shows what their life might look like and compares it to the balanced path.

They are not just on track for retirement, they could potentially retire now. Even better, they can pay off their house if they want; their after-tax savings is greater than their mortgage balance.

HOW COULD THEY RETIRE NOW?

Let's assume their Social Security is $36,000 per year.[5] They also have a sizable portfolio. $38,000 is 5 percent of $760,000. If they take a 5 percent distribution, they would have $36,000 + $38,000, or $74,000 per year of income.[6]

In this example, they earn $60,000, or $5,000 per month, and are saving more than 12 percent of their income. Of course, they are also paying Social Security and Medicare, and in retirement are receiving benefits instead. The income can cover the mortgage, and they may never pay down the mortgage.[7]

Am I suggesting you never pay down debt and grow your assets instead? Yep. And do you know who else does this? Almost every single company in the world. In fact, companies strive to keep their debt ratios constant. As their assets grow, many companies actually take on more debt.[8]

Application

Use Table 4.9 to see where you are relative to a balanced path.

1. Write down your gross pretax annual income = _____
2. Divide this number by 12 = _____

Table 4.9   A Blank Equilibrium Worksheet

Goal/Bucket	Formula	A Balanced Path	Where You Are	Gap
No oppressive debt (No debt at a rate over 10 percent)	0	$0		
Approximate cash reserve (checking + savings)	Monthly income × 7			
Approximate other (jewelry, cars, furniture)	Monthly income × 7			
Approximate mortgage	Monthly income × 35			
Approximate long-term investments (after-tax)	Monthly income × 56			
Approximate retirement savings	Monthly income × 91			
Approximate total investment assets	Monthly income × 147			

Bonus Phase: No Debt!

As your net worth grows beyond 30 times your annual income, our debt journey may be able to come to an end. For example, Brandon and Teresa make $60,000 per year. Once their net worth crosses $1.8 million, they may have a limited need for debt in their life. In fact, depending on your age and time to retirement, when your investment assets cross 15 times your net income, you can carefully evaluate if the risk of debt is a needed risk. For example, when Brandon and Teresa's investment portfolio crosses $900,000, it would be very reasonable for them to just let the portfolio continue to grow and to direct any additional savings to paying down debt.

As we get older and closer to retirement, it is important that we begin to look at our net worth relative to how much money we need on an after-tax basis to cover our expenses in retirement. If you need a rate of return of less than 3 percent from your portfolio, you may not need debt in retirement. For example, you have $1 million and need less than $30,000 per year, or you have $2 million and need less than $60,000 per year. In these cases, debt may not add value. The juice may not be worth the squeeze.

If you need a rate of return between 3 and 6 percent, then a conservative and thoughtful amount of enriching debt will actually reduce taxes, reduce risk, and increase the odds you don't run out of money.[9] If you have $1 million and need between $30,000 and $60,000 per year, debt adds value. This was the theme of my book *The Value of Debt in Retirement*.[10]

If you need a rate of return of more than 6 percent, *then the unfortunate truth is that you need to take risk*. For example, if you have $1 million and need more than $60,000 per year from your portfolio, you can either take this risk through asset allocation or you can take it with debt. Faced with risk, I would rather take the least risky risk. Table 4.10 illustrates different distribution rates and the impact of debt on the degree of confidence that you will both run out of money. Here, the goal is to be as high as possible. For example, 100 means that historically there is a 100 percent chance on every tested rolling 30-year period that the strategy did not run out of money. Clearly, past performance does not predict future

Table 4.10 Trinity Study Summary Table: Probability of Success of Different Distribution Rates over a 30-Year Period—With and Without Debt

Payout Period	Annualized Withdrawal Rate as a % of Initial Portfolio Value									
	3%	4%	5%	6%	7%	8%	9%	10%	11%	12%
75% Stocks/25% Bonds										
Without debt	100	95	69	54	46	41	28	18	3	0
With debt	100	100	87	72	59	54	51	44	41	38
50% Stocks/50% Bonds										
Without debt	100	87	56	46	33	15	13	3	3	0
With debt	100	95	77	59	51	46	38	28	23	18
25% Stocks/75% Bonds										
Without debt	100	72	31	18	15	13	8	3	0	0
With debt	100	79	54	36	21	15	13	13	10	10

results, but the message is clear: Depending on your needs, debt can be a very powerful arrow in your quiver to increase the odds that you will not run out of money.

Pay yourself first. The biggest debt you have is to your future self. Don't pay off your low-cost debt until you know you are on track to be able to retire. If you are on track, or ahead of schedule, then you can 100 percent look at paying off your debt.

REDEFINE RETIREMENT: YOU MAY LIVE A LONG TIME

Advances in technology and life expectancy are changing your ability to do what you want, when you want. One of the single best things you can do is redefine your vision of retirement toward starting at 70 or 75. If you're on track and want to retire earlier, great! But if you retire 20 years from now at 65 and live to be 105, you'll play an awful lot of golf and bridge.

Many Americans are significantly behind with their retirement savings.[11] Given the L.I.F.E. glide path and even a relatively small starting base and a mid-level range of savings, you could easily be on track for retirement in 20 to 25 years. This triggers key observations with respect to paying down debt:

1. It is never too late to start!
2. If you have less than 25 years and are undersaved, deprioritize paying off your house.
3. If your mortgage is at a rate less than the required rate you need from your portfolio in retirement, paying it down will (1) reduce the amount of assets you have working; (2) mathematically increase the amount of time you have to work; and/or (3) reduce the odds you will not run out of money. If your mortgage is at a rate less than what you need from your portfolio, paying it down will likely increase the odds you will run out of money.

Congratulations! If you have made it this far, you now know what it takes to be on a glide path that creates balance, peace, stability, and flexibility. But is it better? We have one more step to look at before we determine that. Then we will look at tools to customize your path.[12]

Endnotes

1. Stephen R. Covey, *The 7 Habits of Highly Effective People: Restoring the Character Ethic* (New York: Free Press, 2004).
2. I love exploring the ways the Golden Ratio can apply to your life, especially your finances. This is a fun site where you can learn more about phi and the Golden Ratio: http://www.goldennumber.net/golden-section/.
3. The case studies presented are for educational and illustrative purposes only and cannot guarantee that the reader will achieve similar results. Your results may vary significantly and factors such as the market, personal effort, and many others will cause results to vary. All of the case studies throughout the book are hypothetical and not intended to demonstrate the performance of any specific security, product, or investment strategy. Opinions formulated by the author are intended to stimulate discussion.
4. http://www.goldennumber.net/golden-section/.

5. www.bankrate.com/calculators/retirement/social-security-beneifts-calculator
   .aspx. 70 years old / 70 years old, $60,000 of income, non-working spouse =
   $36,495

6. For probabilities of a 5-percent distribution, I encourage you to check out
   Chapter 4 of *The Value of Debt in Retirement,* by Thomas J. Anderson (Hoboken,
   NJ: John Wiley & Sons, 2015).

7. When they are working, Brandon and Teresa have $60,000 of annual income.
   This is $5,000 per month. From this, they would have approximately $565.83
   taken out for federal taxes, $310.00 for FICA (Social Security), and $72.50 for
   Medicare. This would leave them with a balance of $4,051.68. http://www
   .adp.com/tools-and-resources/calculators-and-tools/payroll-calculators/
   salary-paycheck-calculator.aspx. Note that we assume they also have savings
   of 12 percent of their income, which comes out to $7,200 per year. If $4,000
   of this savings is in their retirement account and $3,200 is taxable, then their
   withholding would adjust as follows: Gross pay $5,000, federal tax $515.88,
   FICA $310.00, Medicare $72.50, and 401(k) $333.00, for a take-home pay
   of $3,768.62 per month. Independent of the rate, if they are able to make
   their mortgage payment off of this income, then they are able to make it off
   of a $5,000-per-month income. For example, if they were on a 30-year fixed
   rate mortgage at 4 percent in 2016, their mortgage payment on $198,000 is
   $930.96 a month (leaving about $2,800 per month for their other expenses).
   http://www.adp.com/tools-and-resources/calculators-and-tools/payroll-
   calculators/salary-paycheck-calculator.aspx. At "retirement" as illustrated,
   they no longer need to save and they no longer have FICA and Medicare
   expenses. They would have $5,000 per month of income less their $930.96
   mortgage payment for a take home income of over $4,000 − $1,200 higher
   than what they had when they were working.

8. The notion of constant debt ratios over time for corporations, and therefore an
   increase of their outstanding debt over time (and my subsequent investigation of
   this phenomena), was triggered by a lecture that Joel Stern gave at the University
   of Chicago in the fall of 2012. For readers who want more information on this
   subject, see Chapter 1 of *The Value of Debt,* by Thomas J. Anderson (Hoboken,
   NJ: John Wiley & Sons, 2013), and specifically, endnotes 1–15.

9. Tax laws are complex and subject to change. Tax information contained in
   this presentation is general and not exhaustive by nature. It is not intended
   or written to be used, and cannot be used, by any taxpayer for the purpose
   of avoiding U.S. federal tax laws. This material was not intended or written
   to be used for the purpose of avoiding tax penalties that may be imposed on
   the taxpayer. Individuals are encouraged to consult their tax and legal advisors
   (a) before establishing a retirement plan or account, and (b) regarding any potential tax, ERISA, and related consequences of any investments made under such
   plan or account. These materials and any statements contained herein should

not be construed as tax or legal advice. Tax advice must come from your tax advisor.

10. Anderson, *The Value of Debt in Retirement*.

11. http://time.com/money/4258451/retirement-savings-survey/.

12. Author's note: The information in this chapter is to be considered in a holistic way as a part of the book and not to be considered on a stand-alone basis. This includes, but is not limited to, the discussion of the risks of each of these ideas as well as all of the disclaimers throughout the book. The material is presented with a goal of encouraging thoughtful conversation and rigorous debate on the risks and potential benefits of the concepts between you and your advisors based on your unique situation, risk tolerance, and goals.

Chapter 5

The Other Side of the Balance Sheet

"Debt is part of the human condition."

—Margaret Atwood

D ebt is neither good nor bad. It is simply a magnifier.
If you choose investments that deliver higher returns than the after-tax cost of your debt, then debt adds value. If you choose investments that return less than the after-tax cost of your debt, then debt destroys value. For example, if you borrow money at 3 percent and invest in assets that return 6 percent, debt added value. If you borrow money at 6 percent and buy assets that pay 3 percent, then debt destroyed value.

The goal is to capture the spread over time. By that I mean we want to earn a rate of return higher than your after-tax cost of debt. What follows are the ideas that influence me in trying to capture the spread. These ideas are unique because I know I do not know the future whereas, from what I see on TV, a lot of people seem to think they do. You can listen to your fortune teller, get a crystal ball, turn on the TV, and follow the lemmings or you can use the following facts—grounded in math and Nobel Prize–winning theories—to fundamentally shift your strategies and develop a comprehensive, holistic philosophy that transcends both sides of the balance sheet.

In order for me to prove *The Value of Debt in Building Wealth,* I have to spend time talking about the other side of the balance sheet—assets. When people hear my Value of Debt platform, they think it is a bull market strategy. Make no mistake about it: markets will crash. In fact, I predict 2008 will not be the worst crash you will see in your life. I predict most investors will be greatly disappointed with returns from U.S. stocks and bonds over the next five years. Perhaps counterintuitively, these beliefs are actually what anchor debt even more as a part of my integrated, comprehensive and holistic strategy.

The Probability of an 8 Percent Rate of Return Is Zero

Here is a fun math trick you can use the next time your friends start talking about investing. Many individuals like to say "If I average an 8 percent rate of return for the next 30 years I will have X dollars." Or they say things like, "I assume I will average 7 percent for the next few years on my portfolio." But, the probability of achieving those returns is zero. I know for a fact you will not average a return of 8.00 percent—or any other specific number—over the next 10, 20, 50 years.

If you flip a quarter one time, the odds of heads are 50 percent. If you flip it again the odds of landing on heads twice in a row falls to 25 percent. The odds of heads appearing three times in a row is 12.5 percent. The odds of heads 20 times in a row quickly approaches zero. In this simple example, you have two outcomes: heads or tails. In a portfolio you have a range of outcomes. Therefore, the odds of an exact 8.00 percent return, or any other specific number, quickly approaches zero over any given time period. What really matters is the range. For example, there is a big difference between having a 95 percent chance of being up between 6 and 12 percent and an 80 percent chance you will be up between −5 and +15 percent. *The tighter the range and the higher the degree of confidence, the more useful it is for predicting future outcomes.* The wider the range and the lower the degree of confidence, the greater the chance the data really is just a function of luck.

I don't count on luck. Therefore, I try to look at things that have a high probability of being within a certain range. A high probability in no way assures future results, it simply starts the conversation. Always remember that the probability of any given return over the rest of your lifetime is approximately equal to zero, including the returns in the data we are about to examine.

Risk, Return, and Diversification

We don't have a crystal ball, but we may have something better: it might be possible that with the right asset allocation, we don't even need a crystal ball. Figure 5.1 plots seven different asset classes over the past 46 years.

Many people are familiar with statements like "stocks average about 10 percent per year." This happened to be the case during the 46-year period of 1970–2015 where U.S. stocks in fact did average about 10.2 percent each year.

We also want to consider risk. Risk is like golf because, all things being equal, we want to have a low score or low risk. Risk is reflected on the bottom, or X, axis. And, all things being equal, the lower the number the better.

When we look at data like this, people tend to think U.S. stocks did well, having high returns and lower risk than many other assets. Bonds had less risk but a lower return. Commodities and gold had both more risk and a lower return.

Many people use charts like this to conclude they only want to own U.S. stocks and bonds. I think there is something else worth considering.

Figure 5.2 shows an equally weighted, globally diversified portfolio of all assets gave the magical combination of high returns and low risk.

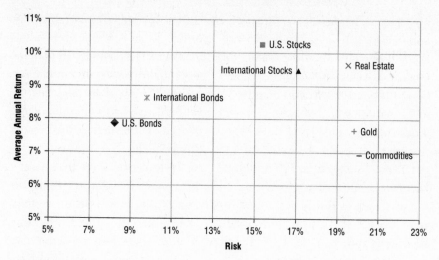

Figure 5.1   Risk/Return Trade-Off of Different Investments from 1970 through 2015

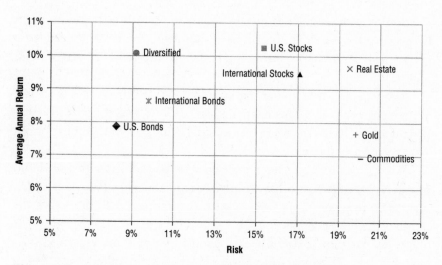

Figure 5.2   Risk/Return with an Equally Weighted Portfolio

During this time period, the diversified portfolio had a return similar to U.S. stocks and a risk similar to U.S. bonds.

I have friends who invest only in real estate, energy stocks, or gold. I don't understand this. In modern capital markets, investors have exposure to virtually every asset class at lower costs than ever before. Why would anybody pick just one asset when they can choose all of them?

Every individual asset has terrible years. Table 5.1 shows the six worst years of each of the assets individually. Diversified portfolios certainly have down years, but they're relatively bearable and not nearly as volatile. Risk is the standard deviation of the asset class returns over the time period. Steady, consistent returns are the key to long-term wealth accumulation.

Focusing on the worst years leads us to another important area to examine. Although these data represent one 46-year period, it is just that—a single 46-year period. It is a single data set, and a single data set that is unlikely, if not impossible, to repeat itself.

Therefore, while factually accurate, I think that long-term charts can be incredibly misleading. Figure 5.3 illustrates rolling 10-year periods. This gives us many data sets and sheds a better light on what type of returns we could expect on an asset class looking forward. By chopping the 46-year period into 37 different 10-year periods, we can get a better sense of historical reliability. We now have 37 data sets instead of one data set. This gives us a better sense of what historic returns were actually like and might give us a better sense toward the future.

Table 5.1 The Six Worst Years for Individual Assets (1970–2015)

U.S. Stocks	U.S. Bonds	International Stocks	International Bonds	Real Estate	Gold	Commodities	Diversified
−37.00%	−9.50%	−43.06%	−7.56%	−42.23%	−32.81%	−46.49%	−19.07%
−26.54%	−8.56%	−23.20%	−7.14%	−39.09%	−28.03%	−35.75%	−7.57%
−22.10%	−7.51%	−22.15%	−6.89%	−27.22%	−22.75%	−33.06%	−7.15%
−14.79%	−7.32%	−21.21%	−5.36%	−26.72%	−21.48%	−32.86%	−6.77%
−11.89%	−2.22%	−16.30%	−3.63%	−17.33%	−20.17%	−31.93%	−0.44%
−9.10%	−1.07%	−14.17%	−3.47%	−17.16%	−15.66%	−23.01%	0.76%

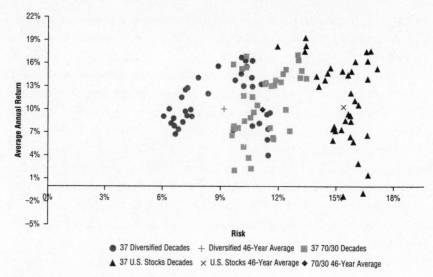

Figure 5.3   Rolling 10-Year Data Points

Why can long-term averages with respect to individual assets be very misleading? Consider U.S. stocks. While the 46-year average was 10 percent per year with a risk of 17 percent, during some 10-year periods investors may have had returns of 15 percent or more per year with less risk than the 46-year average, but during other 10-year periods they could have had returns below 2 percent per year with much more risk.

This highlights the concept of risk. *Any 10-year period was unlikely to look like the 46-year long-term average,* with investors likely either getting much better results, or much worse results, than the average led them to expect. Average tells us something about the past, but nothing about the future and nothing about what type of returns we could expect over any 10-year period, including the next 10 years.

I believe you will not get returns close to the long-term average returns from U.S. stocks over virtually any 10-year period. Your returns will likely be much better or much worse.

This phenomenon is true with diversified portfolios as well. For example, as demonstrated by Figure 5.3, a 70/30 U.S. stock-and-bond portfolio has been fairly consistent with respect to risk, but not with return. You can draw two vertical lines shooting up from the risk line of 10 and the risk line of 14. You will see there is a channel of risk—the risk is fairly consistent—but the return ranges from 2 to 16 percent.

I believe a 70/30 stock-and-bond portfolio has a high level of predictability with risk and a very low level of predictability with respect to return.

What is interesting to me is that during this time period, the diversified portfolio had a much tighter cluster. This cluster generally occurs with returns between 7 percent and 14 percent and with risk generally ranging from about 6 to about 12.

Importantly, in the periods when the portfolio was riskier, the returns frequently skewed higher, meaning that investors were at least often compensated for the risk. This is in stark contrast to U.S. stocks, where periods of higher risk often yielded lower returns. High-risk strategies are hard to stick with over the long term because of the extreme ups and downs. There can be no assurances that this will be what the future holds but this process influences my asset allocation tremendously.

LESSONS FROM MATH AND HISTORY SUGGEST CAUTION

While I know that I do not know the future, people request my opinions on what the future may bring. My outlook is based on a passion for economic history and theory combined with simple lessons from math. I simply look at big-picture beacons, and right now they are flashing bright with all signs warning of risks and dangers on the horizon.

Interest rates are at or near generational lows in many countries, including the United States, and the global economic and geopolitical situation could change enormously in coming years.[1] In the United States, Japan, and Europe we've watched interest rates and inflation go from high to low and government debt go from relatively low to high.[2] The macro trends of the past 30 years are unlikely to repeat—and in fact, things may go the other way.[3]

We could see rising interest rates (and therefore falling bond prices), rising taxes, and rising unemployment alongside falling stock prices, falling real estate values, and falling values of many major currencies, including the U.S. dollar—all at the same time. Virtually all of the traditional asset classes could fall at the same time, and perhaps for a prolonged period of time. This could create a sustained environment in which *past performance has virtually nothing to do with future results*. When you see that disclaimer, I suggest you heed it. I see little to no value in any past performance data from the past 30 years. That period is over and cannot repeat itself. It is not mathematically possible.

As an investor, you need to be familiar with how basic math and valuation impact expected returns. A Federal Reserve study found that significant busts have followed significant booms throughout the past 100 years in 10 countries.[4]

Corrections as high as 50 percent and even 65 percent occur more frequently than you might think. *I predict we will see at least one if not two equity corrections of at least 50 percent over the next 25 years.* This isn't that bold of a prediction. In fact, the U.S. stock market has seen two corrections of more than 49 percent since the year 2000.[5] Although it is true that when you are accumulating assets you may be in a stronger position to ride out volatility, buying overpriced assets is never a good idea.

If you don't know about The Shiller price/earnings ratio, you should learn about it or hire somebody who understands it. Professor Robert Shiller won a Nobel Prize on the concept so it is worth exploring. This barometer is flashing warning signs in late 2016 on many markets, such as the U.S. stock market. Assets that have recently gone up significantly may not deliver returns that are at all consistent with their long-term averages.[6]

In early 2016, as in every year I have studied, there were many assets that are trading at very attractive valuations and there were many assets that were trading at very expensive prices. The goal, of course, is to buy low and to sell high. Too often, people do the opposite, buying whatever has gone up and telling stories to justify why.

I am not simply asserting that one should buy things that have been risky and have gone down over the past five years.

However, I do feel investors should have a bias toward over-weighting asset classes that are trading at a discount to historic levels and underweighting assets that are trading significantly above historic levels.

If you are overweight in U.S. assets (and most U.S.-based investors are), consider making a change.[7] My research says any combination of U.S. stocks and U.S. bonds (70/30, 30/70, 50/50) has a high possibility of real returns of less than 3 percent for the next five years. This is a bold prediction because I know of no other prediction like it. My beacons actually warn of a high probability of negative real returns for most any combination of U.S. stocks and bonds for the next five years—and potentially as long as 10 years.

The bottom line is that if these indicators are correct this implies that even though interest rates are at generational lows, investors in these asset classes are unlikely to capture the spread relative to their cost of debt for a five-year period of time.

While I said what makes me different is that I know I don't have a crystal ball and I know that I don't know, I think economic history, theory, and math are reasonable barometers to use in making investment decisions. In this case, and to demonstrate the power of the guide posts, I will donate $100,000 to the Washington University in St. Louis Center for Finance and Accounting Research if between December 1, 2016, and November 30, 2021, any combination of U.S. stocks and bonds delivers an annualized real return greater than 3 percent. (For clarity to those in finance, I will stipulate any long, unhedged position combination, static percentage that could be set between the Russell 3000 and Barclays Aggregate U.S. bond indices on December 1, 2016, and held constant through November 30, 2021, measured in U.S. dollars—no other rules.)

What does this bet mean to you? Be careful. Many investors around the world in 2017 could be in for a big kick in the teeth. My research also suggests that history has been cruel to investors who are overweight in home country assets at times of high levels of government debt and record prices in their stock and bond markets.

Table 5.2 illustrates things to consider in the current environment. Global diversification and a world-neutral asset allocation model may help you be better prepared for a range of global outcomes.

Table 5.2   One Opinion on an Asset Allocation Framework to Consider

Asset Class	Weighting	Valuation in Mid-2016 Might Suggest
U.S. stocks	5–20%	Underweight
Developed international stocks	5–20%	Equal weight
Emerging market stocks	5–20%	Overweight
U.S. bonds	5–20%	Underweight
Developed international bonds	5–20%	Underweight
Emerging market bonds	5–20%	Overweight
Gold	10–20%	Overweight
Commodities	5–15%	Overweight
Real estate	5–15%	Equal weight

The problem for many people in the accumulation phase is that they opt for simple solutions such as target date funds or other asset allocation models that typically exhibit extreme home bias. Although you might think you are diversified, you may find that more than 70 percent of your assets are effectively in two positions: U.S. stocks and U.S. bonds. This does not represent diversification to me and may deliver disappointing results.

While I do not know what will happen, I believe that a diversified portfolio is the starting place for conversations relative to any other individual investment or asset class. I personally don't believe that portfolios should be equally weighted between each of these asset classes, but I do believe this should serve as the foundation.

That said, and since I'm in the betting mood, I will bet another $100,000 donation that an equally weighted portfolio between the nine asset classes in Table 5.2 will not only beat the S&P 500 over the 10-year period July 1, 2016, through June 30, 2026, but also will beat it with less risk.

I place these bets not because I'm a betting man. I place them to emphasize my confidence that what many investors are doing will lead to disappointment. I recognize I could be wrong, and I could be $200,000 poorer. If I'm right, hopefully I nudged some people into better decision making before it is too late. If I'm wrong, I supported a good cause. I'm more comfortable being wrong with my strategies than I am being lucky in a U.S. stock and bond portfolio mix.

What about Interest Rates and Cost of Debt?

While the previous tables are somewhat helpful in determining future returns, they do not address future interest rates or returns relative to those interest rates. They also do not address inflation.

Long term, what matters is capturing the spread. An investor captures the spread when they earn a higher rate of return, after tax, than their after-tax cost of debt. Ideally, an investor is looking to capture two spreads: one that gives returns higher than inflation, the other that gives returns higher than their after-tax cost of debt. If an investor earns, on average, a higher rate of return on their assets than they are paying on their debt then the strategy of having debt is a good one.

The time between 1970 to 2015 comprises periods of both rising and falling interest rates. Similarly, it comprises periods of both high and low inflation.

Diving into the numbers, we discover that over any individual calendar year, a diversified portfolio has outperformed U.S. inflation plus 4 percent only 63 percent of the time. This means that in 37 percent of the years it underperformed inflation + 4 percent.

While these figures may sound disappointing, they begin to change over 10-year periods. A diversified approach outperformed inflation plus 4 percent in 34 of 37 rolling 10-year periods, or 92 percent of the time. In the periods that it outperformed, it did so by an average of 2.78 percent per year. Of the three times that it underperformed, it did so by an average of 0.81 percent per year. Historically, a diversified approach did very well in terms of providing a solid return over and above inflation.

Let's examine two different inflation-adjusted goals:

- With respect to an inflation plus 2 percent goal:
  - The S&P 500 outperformed inflation + 2 percent in 78 percent of every rolling 10-year period of time.
  - A 70/30 U.S. stock-and-bond portfolio outperformed inflation + 2 percent in 78 percent of every rolling 10-year period of time.
  - The diversified approach outperformed inflation + 2 percent in 97 percent of every rolling 10-year period of time.
- With respect to an inflation plus 6 percent goal:
  - The S&P 500 outperformed inflation + 6 percent in 59 percent of every rolling 10-year period of time.
  - A 70/30 U.S. stock-and-bond portfolio outperformed inflation + 6 percent in 54 percent of every rolling 10-year period of time.
  - The diversified process outperformed inflation + 6 percent in 54 percent of every rolling 10-year period of time.

History provides us with a framework to guide our actions for the future. But we must understand that we do not know future interest rates (and therefore future borrowing costs), future inflation rates, and future rates of return. These are impossible to know. We must recognize that past performance does not guarantee future results and that it is virtually impossible for the historical data series to repeat.

Based on rolling 10-year periods since 1970, if your cost of debt is higher than inflation + 6 percent, then we can conclude there is an approximate 50 percent chance that debt will destroy value and you will not capture a spread. Debt that is at a rate that is closer to inflation + 2 percent is likely to have a higher probability enabling an investor to capture the spread. Historically, and during this one data set with one diversified asset allocation model, the odds of accomplishing the objective were 97 percent.

The purpose of the data is to form the basis for testing the glide path I proposed. It will help shape our conversation and we will look at what could happen in upside or downside scenarios. While none of us knows the future, we now have a framework to look at some of the probabilities.

Historically, the lower our cost of debt relative to inflation, the higher the chance that we can capture a spread. Also, we have seen that the higher our cost of debt relative to inflation, the lower our chance that we can capture a spread.

While it is possible that rates could stay lower longer than most people anticipate, it is also possible that crazy things could happen to interest rates and to inflation. This could come from a series of unprecedented monetary policy actions, a lack of fiscal policy discipline, or simply because rates are starting from generationally low levels. Depending on how debt and investments are structured, a prolonged period of rising interest rates may make it easier or harder to capture the spread, depending on how you are positioned. For example, if you lock in on generationally low interest rates, it could be easier to capture a spread in the future.

What about One of Your Biggest Assets? Your House

Your house might go up in value. Your house might go down in value. The simple truth is, we don't know the future returns on housing any more than we know the future returns on anything else.

Many people want to own their homes outright rather than waste money on mortgage interest, but it's important to look at something called *opportunity cost* before paying off a mortgage. The opportunity cost reflects the fact that you could pay down your mortgage or you could put that same amount of money into an investment.

If you believe that, on average and over time, you can earn returns at a *higher* rate than the after-tax cost of your mortgage, then you should consider investing the money instead of paying down on the house. If you believe that on average and over time your returns will be *lower* than your after-tax cost of debt, then you may want to consider paying down the debt. For example, if you have a mortgage at 4 percent and you are in the 33 percent tax bracket, your after-tax cost of that mortgage is 2.68 percent. If you invest that money, then 2.68 is what you need to beat to capture a spread.[8]

Keep in mind that when you pay down debt, you also generally lose a lot of the liquidity you had, so you also have to be comfortable with that risk. Liquidity is something to spend time thinking about, as it becomes very valuable at precisely the time when you need it the most.

Also, always keep in mind that the value of your house is 100 percent independent of the financing in place around it. If you own your house outright, it isn't worth any more. If you have a big mortgage, it isn't worth any less. You can't change your net worth or the value of an asset with financing.

When you list your house, you will not advertise the value of your mortgage as one of the attractive features. Your mortgage is completely independent of the buyer's perception of value. Your house may go up or down in value, but this movement is independent of the financing decisions you make.

What if you plan to hang onto the home for a while? Isn't real estate one of the best investments you can make in the long run? Residential real estate certainly may keep pace with inflation over long periods of time; just think about how much the home that your parents or grandparents lived in during the 1950s or 1960s is worth today. But it also may not. There are many examples around the world, such as in Japan, where the prices of real estate have fallen over extended periods of time.[9]

With housing, people often do bad math because determining a property's actual appreciation is tricky. This happens in part because we love to deceive ourselves into thinking we've done better than we actually have. If you buy a home for $500,000 and sell it for $1 million 10 years later, it *does* look like you doubled your money or had an approximate annual return of 7.2 percent. If during those 10 years, however, you paid $60,000 in property taxes and invested $150,000 in maintenance, upkeep, and remodeling, your actual basis is $710,000, which gives you just a 3.5 percent rate of return.

The total cost of ownership includes carrying costs plus financing (or opportunity) costs. In the current environment, and depending on the market, over a five-year period the total cost of ownership is likely to be between 6 percent and 8 percent per year. From these expenses, you can subtract any appreciation and add any depreciation. If the house goes down in value, that adds to the costs. And while appreciation is great, depreciation can be devastating. A leveraged asset's drop in value can be crushing to your finances.

MORTGAGES: THE ONE-WAY LIQUIDITY TRAP

I don't understand why Americans seem to hate cash. They rush to pay down debt at the expense of building up cash reserves, putting themselves at real risk. And what do they get for paying down a big chunk of principal on an amortized loan? A back rub? A free Starbucks latte? They get another bill the next month.

This is particularly notable in the housing market. People get a windfall—a hefty bonus or an inheritance—and decide to put all of it into paying down some of the principal on a 30-year amortized mortgage. The next week they lose their job. Can they get that money back? No, they can't. It's almost impossible to refinance anything without a job, and payments are still due every month. That's why I believe mortgages are one-way liquidity traps.

I recommend not paying down a mortgage unless you can pay off the entire thing—and even then, I'd think long and hard about whether that makes sense in your overall financial plan. Remember, the rate of return on paying down debt is exactly equal to the after-tax cost of that debt. If you have a fully tax-deductible 3 percent mortgage and are in the 35 percent tax bracket, that money is costing you 2 percent (3%/35% = 1%; 3% − 1% = 2%). The after-tax cost of paying off your mortgage is the equivalent of investing in assets that generate a 2-percent rate of return. Trading in your liquidity and flexibility to save 2 to 3 percent a year might not make sense.

Three Buckets of Money

"Let every man divide his money into three parts and invest a third in land, a third in business, and a third let him keep in reserve."

– The Talmud

Whether you have $100,000 or $1 million to invest, you must have a clear, precise investment philosophy. In 1986, economist Gary Brinson released a watershed study called "Determinants of Portfolio Performance."[10] He concluded that 90 percent of an investor's returns are attributable to their investment policy, or asset allocation, and less than 10 percent of the return was due to market timing and stock selection. Asset allocation refers to how much of your portfolio is in a particular asset, such as U.S. stocks or emerging market bonds. A take-away would be to center your investment philosophy around maximizing diversification in your portfolios, making the decision to always own a globally diversified, multi-asset class mix of investments.

In addition to diversified asset allocation, I believe accumulators should focus on having different buckets of money. To build wealth and mitigate risk, divide your investment assets into three buckets: Conservative, Core, and Aggressive.

Conservative

There is a difference between saving and investing. Your conservative money is not an investment; it needs to be safe. In this case, the Conservative bucket protects purchasing power and is easily accessible. I suggest you create one bucket designed to keep your money safe and keep pace with inflation.

When thinking about Conservative, you want to think about two factors. First, consider inflation. You want to be prepared for both low-inflation and high-inflation periods. This can be accomplished by having some of your Conservative bucket invested in inflation-protected bonds and some of this bucket invested in cash and regular bonds. Second, consider the strength of the U.S. dollar (or your home currency). Your Conservative bucket should be prepared for both strong-dollar periods and weak-dollar periods. If you were born in 1980, the purchasing power of the U.S. dollar has declined by 65 percent in your lifetime.[11] You can be prepared for strong-dollar periods by investing in U.S. bonds and cash, and you can be prepared for weak-dollar periods by investing in international bonds and international currencies.

SAFE, NOT SORRY

I'm willing to keep cash on hand that pays me zero interest while paying interest on a mortgage. It may appear that I'm "wasting money" on interest, but I value the liquidity and flexibility that having cash gives me. I look at it as a form of insurance.

In the current economic environment, investors should be very cautious with high-yield, long-term, and municipal bonds, which some investors turn to for safety and income. I believe many are trading at near record-high prices and may not provide as much safety as investors had hoped in either a rising-rate environment or a recession.[12] I'm not sure the juice is worth the squeeze. There are better ways to add value to a portfolio.

This bucket needs to be walled off and protected. Don't pledge it to a line of credit. Don't include it in a personal guarantee. Don't dip into it for a fun trip. Don't make a dumb investment decision with your safe money. Keep it safe and separate. Don't risk your conservative money—ever.

In the glide path, this would be the balances in your checking and savings accounts as well as the initial savings in your big life changes bucket. This is also where you park any money you need to withdraw from your investments within the next five years. For example, when you retire, you will want about five years of income in this bucket. This is liquid money you need, and the return on your Conservative bucket will have almost nothing to do with your long-term wealth accumulation.[13]

Once you have accumulated more than three months of money in cash, you could be a little riskier—a teeny bit riskier—with additional short-term money, but these funds should be designed to keep pace with inflation rather than increase principal. For example, Cash Reserve 2 or the home equity savings (if the purchase is a long way off) could be allocated to something that targets inflation plus 2 percent. If you choose to do this, be comfortable with the fact that it could go down.

SIX MONTHS PLUS IN CONSERVATIVE

I keep a six-month spending reserve plus any funds I will need to withdraw over the next five years in my Conservative bucket. As you get closer to retirement, you will want to build up your Conservative bucket so the year you retire, you have all the money you will need over the next five years. For example, if you need $100,000 per year, you will strive to build up $500,000 in your Conservative bucket.

Core

This bucket aims to keep your money prudently invested and working for you over time. Ideally, it would protect your principal and grow it by inflation plus 4 percent on average. I use the data from the diversified portfolio as the base of this bucket. Think of it as your personal foundation and endowment. If it is doing its job, the Core bucket will probably be boring in the short term but rewarding over time. When stock markets are up, it will generally be up but not as much as you would like. When stock markets are down, it will likely go down but not as extremely. Over time, you should see consistent results that build a foundation of wealth. You might fine tune it a little, but there should be no major shifts or changes in this portfolio.

There are many interpretations about the best way to build a Core portfolio. Too many people oversimplify this concept by assuming the S&P 500 or the U.S. stock market represents such a portfolio. The S&P 500 represents an asset class; it is not a diversified portfolio. A diversified portfolio should have assets with varying risk, return, and correlation. It should include stocks and bonds, U.S. and international markets, emerging and developed markets, real estate, and commodities.

More important than the number of asset classes is the correlation between those asset classes. Correlation is the way that assets move relative to each other. Positive correlation means that everything is moving in the same direction at the same time. That's great if all of your assets are going up and devastating if they tank. You should focus on balance and there should be no expectation that all assets will be positive in all markets. That's not how investing works.

If some assets in your Core portfolio aren't losing money, then:

1. You're not trying hard enough.
2. Your portfolio has too much positive correlation.

A Core portfolio should be diversified so that some assets are rising while others are falling. Some part of your investments should be losing money at any given point. Consider having no less than seven different low-correlated asset classes with a minimum weighting of 5 percent in each for a well-diversified portfolio. Ideally, rebalancing would lead you to buy more of the assets which had done poorly recently and to sell some of the assets which had recently done well.

Aggressive

The Aggressive bucket is composed of investments that take a measured but higher level of risk while striving for increased returns. These investments should not be taken lightly. Swinging for the fences without a backstop can bring glory or disaster.

I have seen more people retire with substantial portfolios because they tried to hit singles and doubles consistently over time than I have seen people accumulate large portfolios by trying to hit homeruns over long periods of time.

In general, the higher the risk of your investment philosophy, the lower the odds are that you will realize the long-term returns of that investment philosophy. This is because high-risk strategies inevitably have large drops in value at some point. Not only are those drops devastating, but from a behavior economics perspective most people can't stomach the downturn and are likely to exit the strategy at the wrong time. And to be clear, believing you have a strong stomach for investing is different than actually having one. I understand no one likes to lose money but losing money is part of an aggressive investment strategy.

Within Aggressive investments, one of the most important things is the size of your investment. Often called *position size,* it refers to how much of your money you invest in the idea. This is one of the most important things to monitor. Aggressive investments should account for

0 to 30 percent of your total portfolio. A 4 percent position is ideal because if you hit a winner and it goes up by 100 percent, the portfolio goes up by 4 percent. If you pick a dud and it drops by 50 percent, the portfolio goes down by only 2 percent. If the choice is a complete disaster and goes to zero, you lose only 4 percent of your net worth.

The problem with small positions, such as a 1 percent position, is that if you're right and the asset goes up 100 percent the portfolio only goes up by 1 percent. There's no point in taking that risk for a 1 percent increase. At the same time, if you make an Aggressive investment worth more than 10 percent of your holdings, you could lose 10 percent of your net worth if it tanks.

Stay concentrated within a position if you really like it but never bet more than 10 percent of your net worth—and you should stay closer to 4 percent. I've seen a few investors who had success with large concentrated positions, but I've seen a lot more people who were on track only to have their dreams wiped out by an unfortunate turn of events. I believe it's just a question of time until people who hold concentrated positions wake up disappointed. Among institutional investors (pension funds, endowments, insurance companies), you will find very few examples of professionals taking large, concentrated risks.

As a general rule, I prefer to restrict Aggressive investments to two types of investors. The first type is an investor who does not have enough assets to meet his or her long-term goals. This investor has to take higher risks in an effort to achieve their goals. The second type of investor is one who has more assets than they will ever need and merely wants some exciting, Aggressive investments in their portfolio. Absent being in one of these two groups, I would avoid Aggressive investing.

I would suggest that until you enter the Freedom phase, when your net worth is greater than two times your annual income, you should refrain from Aggressive investments.

AGGRESSIVE INVESTING: NOT WORTH THE DRAMA

Before I turned 40, I made more than $1.5 million on Aggressive trades. And before I turned 40, I lost between $1.3 million and $1.8 million on Aggressive trades. The wins were great. The losses were awful—and not worth the wins. I would take a boring $300,000 return any day. And I'd probably be about $300,000 richer.

I see many people start with Aggressive ideas early in life and do very little with them later in life. I believe this is because they eventually have an experience much like mine. I don't make a lot of Aggressive investments in the market anymore.

Risk Matters—The Risk of Time

Return is not the only consideration in investment portfolios. Risk is just as important.

From my experience, many people in the accumulation phase hesitate to minimize risk in portfolios because they believe they'll have to sacrifice return. Most investors—both individual and professional—believe risk and return have a lockstep relationship. If I tell an investor with a goal of averaging a 10-percent return that she could decrease risk by half she thinks her rate of return will also drop by half. It would be great if the world worked so predictably.

Risk and return operate independently of each other. It's possible to drastically decrease your portfolio's risk and give up only a fraction of the return, or possibly give up none of the return. This happens because of correlation, the yin and yang of your portfolio.

Why does all of this matter? Rarely, if ever, will your expected returns be your actual returns. What matters is how far your returns are off the mark. In *The Value of Debt in Retirement,* we saw that when you retire, risk is equally important, if not more important, than return. This is because of the sequence of returns. Although it is true that in the accumulation phase you might be able to afford more risk and more volatility—more risk—it simply may not be worth it.

Any way you multiply numbers, you get to the same result. If you take $3 \times 4 \times 2$ you get to 24. Similarly, if you take $2 \times 4 \times 3$ you also get 24. As a result, some people argue that it is OK to have higher risk while you are accumulating because it evens out in the end. This might be true and it might not be true. You see, when you are accumulating you have the benefit of time—but you also have the risk of time.

The way risk and accumulation work may be different than you expect. As you get closer to retirement, you cannot afford to have a bad decade. If you have a bad decade the decade before you plan to retire, it is punitive to your overall returns.

> Risk does matter. This suggests that if you are young, high-risk investments may not be worth it. High-risk investments usually have a wide range of future returns. They are a bet that may turn out well or may turn out poorly. Lower-risk, more consistent returns may be a better strategy.

Let's say Oliver starts with $100,000 and saves $10,000 per year every year for 30 years. He is an aggressive investor and averages a 9 percent rate of return. However, his returns are lumpy. He has one great decade, one OK decade, and one bad decade. Specifically, he has one 10-year period where his returns are a disappointing 3 percent per year, another decade that is exceptional at 16 percent per year, and a third that is in the middle at 8 percent per year.

It turns out that Oliver could end up with $2.2 million or $3.2 million depending on how lucky he was with the timing of the returns. Let me explain: If his first decade was the 3 percent decade and his second decade was the 8 percent decade, that would give him 20 years of saving and investing, and his portfolio would have grown to a considerable size making the final 16 percent per year decade really powerful. If he experienced the 16 percent decade first, the high returns would have a lesser impact because they are on a smaller portfolio. On average, you want your highest return years to be when your portfolio is largest. At the same time, this is the time that you can least afford a significant downturn. Therefore, I believe that in early years the risk isn't worth it and in the later years you can't afford it. Let me explain.

If instead Oliver simply averaged 9 percent the whole time, he would end up with $2.7 million. Granted, it is lower than the best-case scenario, but if the odds are equally distributed on the sequence, there is only a 33-percent chance that he would get better returns with the risky strategy. In this simple example, there is a 67-percent chance the consistent process is better than the risky process. More often than not, math will show not only that consistent returns are better, but also that slightly lower consistent returns are better than slightly higher but much riskier returns.[14]

Factoring Leverage into Returns

Used correctly, low-cost and tax-efficient debt may enhance your returns over time. Let's take a look at a few scenarios to understand how this works.

Erika and Raj rent a house, have no material assets, and just inherited $1 million. They are debt averse and decide to buy a home worth $500,000 outright, with no mortgage. This leaves them with a $500,000 investment portfolio. At this point, Erika and Raj have a net worth of $1 million, as shown in Table 5.3.

What about income? If their investment portfolio returns an average of about 6 percent, Erika and Raj would be making roughly $30,000 in income per year, as shown in Table 5.4. (To simplify things, we're ignoring other income sources.)

Table 5.3 Balance Sheet—Scenario A

Original Scenario A Balance Sheet

Assets		Liabilities
Real estate	$ 500,000	–
Investments	$ 500,000	–
Total	$1,000,000	–
Net worth	$1,000,000	**0 %** **debt ratio**

Table 5.4 Income Statement—Scenario A

Scenario A Portfolio Income

Portfolio		$500,000
Portfolio return	6%	$ 30,000
After-tax cost of debt	0%	–
Net income from portfolio		**$ 30,000**

Now let's consider Scenario B. Erika and Raj purchase the same house by putting down 20 percent and taking on a $400,0000 mortgage. This allows them to keep their money invested without changing their net worth. Erika and Raj now have $1.4 million of assets and a 29-percent debt-to-asset ratio ($400,000 / $1.4 million = about 29 percent). This is illustrated in Table 5.5.

What happens from an income perspective in Scenario B? Let's assume Erika and Raj have the same portfolio return of 6 percent, their mortgage is at a 3 percent rate, and they're in the 33-percent tax bracket (so that the cost of that additional $400,000 in their portfolio is effectively 2 percent, resulting in an $8,000 cost). What happens to their net income?

As the income statement in Table 5.6 shows, Erika and Raj now receive a net income from their portfolio of $46,000, or $16,000 more than they received in Scenario A. By taking on the mortgage at 3 percent, they've increased their portfolio income by $16,000 a year (assuming

Table 5.5   Balance Sheet—Scenario B

Scenario B Balance Sheet

Assets		Liabilities
Real estate	$ 500,000	$400,000
Investments	$ 900,000	–
Total	$1,400,000	$400,000
Net worth	$1,000,000	**29% debt ratio**

Table 5.6   Income Statement—Scenario B

Scenario B Portfolio Income		
Portfolio		$900,000
Portfolio return	6%	$ 54,000
After-tax cost of debt on $400,000	2%	–$ 8,000
Net income from portfolio		$ 46,000
Additional income compared to A		**$ 16,000**

a hypothetical 6-percent portfolio return). They have also substantially increased their overall liquidity.

In Scenario A, you would need a return of more than 9 percent on your investments to generate a $46,000 return ($500,000 × 9% = $45,000). In Scenario B, you can get to the same place with just a 6 percent average return.

There are two ways to get a 9 percent rate of return: Find assets that deliver a 9 percent rate of return or leverage assets that have a 6 percent rate of return.

> Everything else being equal, a lower-volatility portfolio with debt is better than a high-volatility portfolio with no debt. Similarly, a portfolio with no debt may actually be taking on more risk than a portfolio with debt while achieving the same result.

Debt as an Integrated Part of Your Investment Philosophy

Debt can be an integrated part of your overall investment philosophy. As your balance sheet grows, you may choose to reduce your debt ratios during market environments where you think there is a low probability of capturing a spread for the next five years and you may choose to slightly expand your debt ratios in times where you think there is a high probability of capturing a spread.

I point out this strategy because it is interesting to consider, but it comes with a big caveat. There is risk to intentionally moving your debt ratio up and down—the risk that you are likely to be wrong. So many people increased their debt in 2007 and paid it off in 2009.[15] In hindsight, they should have been doing the opposite. While you are in the L.I.F.E. glide path, I prefer a constant, systematic building up of assets rather than trying to change debt ratios based on market environments.

Equally important is that debt ideas are a way to express a view with respect to currencies. For example, Argentina has gone through a series of crises.[16] At certain points in time, if you borrowed in Argentinian pesos and invested in an Argentinian stock and bond portfolio, your portfolio and your balance sheet could have been destroyed. At the same time, if you borrowed in Argentinian pesos and bought virtually any asset anywhere else in the world, you could have made a tremendous amount of money as the currency fell apart and you were able to pay back the devalued debt at pennies on the dollar.

In January 2016, the U.S. dollar appreciated by about 20 percent versus a basket of global currencies between January 1, 2014, and January 1, 2016.[17] If you purchase a foreign bond at 4 or 5 percent and the dollar falls to its previous levels over the next 10 years, then you could average approximately a 7-percent annual rate of return, and have done so in bonds. Now, of course, there is considerable risk to the strategy as well. If the dollar continues to strengthen and the assets are denominated in other currencies, then you would receive the income but lose in the devaluation of the currency.

Similarly, borrowing is a great way to express views with respect to interest rates and inflation. While these strategies are best utilized with your advisors, here is the important point: *It isn't the borrowing that is good or bad, it is the investment decisions that you make with respect to the borrowing. Debt is a magnifier of your investment decisions.*[18]

Endnotes

1. https://data.oecd.org/interest/long-term-interest-rates.htm.
2. https://data.oecd.org/gga/general-government-debt.htm.
3. Thomas J. Anderson, *The Value of Debt* (John Wiley & Sons, 2013). For more details, I encourage you to see the citations and references on pages 204 to 207 of *The Value of Debt*. The notion that the past 30 years cannot be like the next 30 years is inspired by a presentation given by Jeffrey Rosenberg, Chief Investment Strategist for Fixed Income, Blackrock at the Barron's Top 100 Conference, fall 2012. Lectures from David Wessel, Luigi Zingales, Ed Lazear, Martin Feldstein, Paul Krugman, Gary Becker, and Naill Ferguson in 2012 and 2013 all inspired some of the views expressed in this section. Readers looking for additional detail should familiarize themselves with their work.
4. Federal Reserve Bank of St. Louis—Working Paper 2006-051A. See https://research.stlouisfed.org/wp/2006/2006-051.pdf.
5. http://www.nbcnews.com/id/37740147/ns/business-stocks_and_economy/t/historic-bear-markets/#.V8bsoZMrLUI.

6. John Y. Campbell and Robert J. Shiller, "Stock Prices, Earnings, and Expected Dividends," *The Journal of Finance* 43, no. 3 (July 1988): 661–676, Papers and Proceedings of the Forty-Seventh Annual Meeting of the American Finance Association, Chicago, Illinois, December 28–30, 1987. Paper available here: http://www.jstor.org/stable/2328190.

7. Rick Hakler, "US Investors' Home Bias," Nasdaq (July 23, 2015), http://www.nasdaq.com/article/us-investors-home-bias-cm499769.

8. Tax laws are complex and subject to change. Tax information contained in this presentation is general and not exhaustive by nature. It is not intended or written to be used, and cannot be used, by any taxpayer for the purpose of avoiding U.S. federal tax laws. This material was not intended or written to be used for the purpose of avoiding tax penalties that may be imposed on the taxpayer. Individuals are encouraged to consult their tax and legal advisors (a) before establishing a retirement plan or account, and (b) regarding any potential tax, ERISA, and related consequences of any investments made under such plan or account. These materials and any statements contained herein should not be construed as tax or legal advice. Tax advice must come from your tax advisor.

9. Jun Hungo and Kosaku Narioka, "Japanese Land Prices Rise for First Time Since Global Financial Crisis," *Wall Street Journal* (March 22, 2016), http://www.wsj.com/articles/japanese-land-prices-rise-for-first-time-since-global-financial-crisis-1458645819.

10. Gary P. Brinson, L. Randolph Hood, and Gilbert L. Beebower, "Determinants of Portfolio Performance," *Financial Analysts Journal* 42, no. 4 (1986): 39–44.

11. http://www.usinflationcalculator.com/.

12. https://www.ft.com/content/5ea2d076-4733-11e6-8d68-72e9211e86ab.

13. As of August, 2016, the return on your Conservative bucket will have almost nothing to do with your long-term wealth accumulation. For example, you can only earn 1.6% on the 10-year U.S. Treasury bond, and around 0.25 percent on a 30-day T-bill. Cash has a very low return in this environment.

14. The case studies presented are for educational and illustrative purposes only and cannot guarantee that the reader will achieve similar results. Your results may vary significantly and factors such as the market, personal effort, and many others will cause results to vary. All of the case studies throughout the book are hypothetical and not intended to demonstrate the performance of any specific security, product, or investment strategy. Opinions formulated by the author are intended to stimulate discussion.

15. "Quarterly Report on Household Debt and Credit," Federal Reserve Bank of New York (February 2016), https://www.newyorkfed.org/medialibrary/interactives/householdcredit/data/pdf/HHDC_2015Q4.pdf.

16. "Chronology: Turbulent History of Economic Crises," Reuters (July 30, 2014), http://www.reuters.com/article/us-argentina-debt-chronology-idUSKBN0FZ 23N20140730.

17. http://www.bloomberg.com/quote/DXY:CUR.

18. Author's note: The information in this chapter is to be considered in a holistic way as a part of the book and not to be considered on a stand-alone basis. This includes, but is not limited to, the discussion of the risks of each of these ideas as well as all of the disclaimers throughout the book. The material is presented with a goal of encouraging thoughtful conversation and rigorous debate on the risks and potential benefits of the concepts between you and your advisors based on your unique situation, risk tolerance, and goals.

Chapter 6

Proof of the Value of Debt

"In a gentle way, you can shake the world."

—Mahatma Gandhi

I've laid out a glide path for the different phases in your L.I.F.E. and I have talked about the other side of the balance sheet, assets. Key questions remain: Is the glide path better, and if it is better, how much better?

Let's do a quick recap. I created a four-phased glide path based on your net worth relative to your income. I suggested that in the Launch phase people should not have debt and should focus on savings. In the Independence phase, I outlined a prudent starting level for debt as a percentage of your net worth, leveraging the power of debt to get the things we otherwise cannot afford, such as a house. Then, in the

113

Freedom phase, I showed how this percentage can fall by building up assets instead of by paying down debt and encouraged you to build up assets. The benefits of an early base of assets are liquidity for emergencies and the ability to harness the power of compounding. In the Equilibrium phase, I showed how debt ratios can fall even further, toward an optimal range, by continuing to build up assets instead of paying down debt.

It is essential to remember that I started by saying that not everybody needs debt. If your net worth is more than 15 to 20 times your income, and/or if you have more than 20 years until retirement and your savings rate is higher than 20 percent, you can carefully consider if you need debt and the Value of Debt®. For the fortunate few of you that have a net worth of more than 30 times your annual income, then the risk of debt may not be worth the potential reward. However, for those who have a net worth less than 20 times their annual income, the vast majority of the population, I'm going to prove that debt can add value.[1] Table 6.1 summarized suggestions for determining how much debt to hold.

We then established ground rules, including:

1. All debt is not equal: There are different types of debt.
2. Your rate of return for paying down debt is exactly equal to your after-tax cost of debt.
3. Sh★t happens—Value liquidity.
4. Yes, you can—save.
5. Compounding matters to the upside and downside.
6. The past is the past. Focus on the future.
7. Behavioral economics matters.

Table 6.1 The Debt Glide Path

Net Worth Relative to Income	The Alternative Glide Path Suggestion
<50% 1-year income	Debt may add considerable risk and should be minimized.
50% to 2x	Keep a debt-to-asset ratio under 65%.
2x to 5x	Move your debt ratio toward 40%.
5x to 30x	Move your debt ratio toward 25%.
>30x	Debt may not be needed and may not be worth the risk.

After we examined the ground rules and outlined a glide path, we looked at historic returns as a reference point for discussion. As I said from the start, I cannot predict the future, but I can demonstrate what you need to believe in order to believe that a comprehensive balanced strategy that includes debt is better than a no-debt strategy.

We agreed these are the things we don't know:

1. Your future income
2. Your future savings rate
3. Your future rate of return, on investment assets or on your home
4. Future interest rates
5. Future inflation rates

What we do know:

1. By paying down debt, you get a rate of return equal to the after-tax cost of debt.
2. Liquidity is valuable.
3. But unfortunately, we don't really know how valuable it is until we need it. By this, I mean that while we can easily recognize it is valuable, we can't quantify exactly how valuable.
4. The value of an asset is independent of the financing in place around that asset.
   a. An asset is worth what an asset is worth.
   b. Your house is worth whatever your house is worth. The same is true with a car, a boat, or anything else. You have to separate the financing of an asset from the value of the asset.

With this foundation in place, let's dive in and test the ideas we have covered so far against conventional wisdom.

The Big Picture—Debt Can Be Valuable

If you anticipate that on average and over time, your investments will return a rate that is higher than your after-tax cost of debt, the L.I.F.E. glide path will always add value relative to the no-debt approach.

If you return an average return less than your average cost of debt you will have "destroyed value" from an investing perspective but you will have gained liquidity—liquidity that is valuable, especially early in life.

Critically, our debt journey doesn't begin until later in life. The glide path suggests renting, and building up liquidity and eliminating oppressive debt. Too often, people are so worried they are wasting money on interest and are lured into the illusion that home ownership is a "risk-free path," and they purchase homes too early in life.

Not rushing to buy a home is a valuable first step in the process from a liquidity and flexibility perspective. Make no mistake, if you buy a house early in life and it appreciates a lot then you were lucky and you could be ahead of where you would have been as a renter. However, if you buy a house with a small down payment and it falls in value by 20 percent, something that should be in your base case, then you may find yourself underwater, trapped, and, in the worst case, homeless or bankrupt. This risk isn't worth the reward.

Zero Oppressive Debt Is Valuable

The average U.S. household carries $15,310 in credit card debt, which totals $712 billion. According to NerdWallet, "Consumers and lenders are reporting vastly different credit card balances—to the tune of more than $415 billion as of 2013—likely because consumers are underreporting their debt. This means that Americans claim to have less than half of the debt they actually have."[2]

What is amazing to me is how many people have debt on a credit card and debt on their house, yet are paying down on their house. If your mortgage is at 4 percent and your credit card is at 14 percent, then by deemphasizing paying down your mortgage and by paying down credit card debt, you can save 10 percent per year. If you have $15,000 of debt, this simple step is worth $1,500 per year. Over a 40-year time period, this can be worth over $60,000.

Is Debt Valuable if It Costs Nothing?

If conventional wisdom says that all debt is bad, is debt that costs zero bad? Let's test it compared to the option to save over 35 years at 4 percent.

If it passes the test at 0 percent, then we can ask tougher questions, like how much we are willing to pay for debt.

Thirty-five years may seem like a long time, but life expectancy is changing. If you are 35 today, you can easily reframe retirement toward age 70. Of course it would be great to be able to retire earlier, but I will look at the glide path as a 35-year horizon from when you start the Independence phase. If you clear the Launch phase by 30 and have your heart set on retiring at 65, then you still have a 35-year time horizon.

Let's start with Brandon and Teresa. Remember, they are 30 years old making $60,000, the approximate average household income. They buy a $240,000 house, with a $195,000 mortgage. Their savings rate is 15 percent.

The no-debt camp would recommend Brandon and Teresa direct all savings to pay off the mortgage. To be extreme, let's say that even debt with no cost is evil in this view. Brandon and Teresa get a mortgage at 0 percent and decide to rush to pay it down.

In the current example, the savings rate of 15 percent is $9,000, which means that the mortgage would be eliminated in $195,000 / $9,000 = 21.6 years.

When they are 51.6 years old they have a party and celebrate by burning their mortgage documents. Unfortunately, they also have zero savings and are 51.6 years old.

Let's assume they start saving and their savings grows at 4 percent until they are 65 years old. They will accumulate $159,000 in total savings. It turns out that the average 60-year-old has about $172,000 in retirement savings.[3] So, you could embrace the no-debt mantra, save, and perhaps be in line with to slightly ahead of above average.

The problem with this outcome is that they "did everything right" yet they fell short of the goal line. They found the cheapest mortgage, one that cost zero in our extreme example, they paid it off, and they had a rate of return of 4 percent during their investing life. There is virtually no way this family can retire with the same lifestyle. Keep in mind, 4 percent of $159,000 is less than $10,000 per year. They are 70, undersaved and dependent on Social Security.

What if their rate of return was higher, say 8 percent? They would have $215,000. What if their rate of return was 12 percent? They would have $296,000. In the best of cases they are likely to have between

$135,000 and $300,000. Think about this for a minute. If Brandon and Teresa had a 0-percent mortgage and follow conventional wisdom and average an improbable 12-percent return per year, they would accumulate less than $300,000. While this is impressive, they are well short of having a comfortable retirement.

What if they followed the L.I.F.E. path I have outlined? By embracing the ideas of the book, they would have built up assets early rather than focused on paying down debt. What if instead of following conventional wisdom they directed the $9,000 of savings into an investment that paid 4 percent? At the end of 35 years, they would have built up about $685,000!

If they have a 4-percent rate of return on the $685,000, they would have about $27,000 of income, plus Social Security, which would be estimated to be approximately $26,000. Their total income is $53,000!

Importantly, they no longer have the expense of their savings, which was $9,000 per year. $60,000 − $9,000 = $51,000. *They actually have more income than they had when they were working.*

What if they don't trust Social Security? Incredibly, if they worked until 70, their assets would grow to almost $900,000 and their Social Security would be $36,000 per year.[4] Even if benefits were significantly reduced, they could retire with significantly more income than the no-debt family.

Granted, the no-debt family no longer has a mortgage, and the other family still has a $195,000 mortgage, but they have more assets.

We just took the average American family—that had no chance of being on track for retirement—and gave them a comfortable retirement using conservative returns, by embracing the Value of Debt in Building Wealth.

To be clear, by embracing a balanced approach to building wealth, Brandon and Teresa with a 4-percent return and a 35-year time horizon, have double the money of somebody who averaged a 12-percent return for a shorter period of time. *You cannot—and should not—underestimate the long-term power of compounding.* We all know it; the tortoise wins the race. In fact, consider that if Brandon and Teresa averaged an 8-percent rate of return, they would have $1.7 million. At 12 percent, they would have an astonishing $4.8 million. For Brandon and Teresa, the single biggest determining factor in their ability to retire is the decisions they make with respect to debt. Return is perhaps the least important factor in determining how much money they will have at retirement.[5]

There is considerable value to saving early. In the average American family, we just showed there could be well over $400,000 of value. If you make $60,000 and are saving $9,000, that is a big difference. And if your income is higher, the difference is even more impactful in terms of dollars.

Most people pay off their good and bad debt early and save later. They should do the opposite: Keep the good debt, build up assets early, and harness the power of compounding. You can always pay down good debt later.

However, we assumed things like a 0 percent cost of the mortgage and no inflation and we looked at a constant-rate-of-return environment. These are all unreasonable assumptions so we need to drill down further. We are right back at Chapter 1 and the examples of the Nadas, the Steadys, and the Radicals. With simple assumptions, it is easy to see the hypothetical value of debt, but what about the real world? From here, let's pull from the foundation we have built to answer many commonly asked questions:

- What happens if borrowing costs are higher?
- What if investment returns are higher or lower?
- What about the impact of the savings rate?
- What are the tax implications of the strategy?
- What if the mortgage interest tax deduction goes away?
- What about children/college savings and debt?
- What about debt service coverage ratios?

It is, of course, impossible for me to 100 percent prove without a doubt that debt can add value to you and your family. Obviously, it is possible that debt could destroy value. So the key question is, what do we need to believe to know that the glide path illustrated is better than conventional wisdom?

What about Borrowing Costs?

From a big-picture perspective, your borrowing costs are what they are and will change throughout time. On an absolute basis, you want to consider if you think your returns are likely to be higher than your borrowing costs over a long period of time. In the book, I have referred to borrowing at a rate close to inflation. If your borrowing costs are inflation, and your rate of return is inflation + 4 percent then over a long period of time, debt will add considerable value. So, can we borrow at a rate close to inflation?

Interest rates in most developed markets and in the United States are at or near generational lows.[6] In July 2016, 30-year fixed mortgages in the United States were approximately 3.5 percent and five- and seven-year adjustable rate mortgages were generally around 3 percent.[7] In the current tax environment, many borrowers receive tax benefits that range from 20 percent to 40 percent, depending on their income. Borrowing costs after taxes generally hover in the 2 to 3 percent range.

Although these rates are very low compared to historic standards, there is another side of the coin. Money market rates are generally under 1 percent and many are closer to zero.[8] While inflation was around 1.6 percent in 2014, it was about 0.5 percent for 2015. Cash, relative to mortgage rates, is at a negative spread. Importantly, borrowing costs, even after tax, are about 2 percent higher than inflation. This means that currently, even though rates are low, borrowing costs are higher than inflation and cash is paying less than inflation. In this environment, it may be hard to capture as much of a spread. But what about historically?

Table 6.2 lets us take a step back in time and look at mortgage rates compared to money market rates and inflation.

If interest rates are high and money market rates fall, you could find yourself in a position where you have a high borrowing cost and

Table 6.2 Interest Rates and Mortgage Rates from 1980 to 2015

	1980	1985	1990	1995	2000	2005	2010	2015
Money market rate	12.68%	7.71%	7.82%	5.48%	5.89%	2.66%	0.34%	0.08%
Inflation rate	13.51%	3.56%	5.40%	2.81%	3.38%	3.39%	1.64%	0.12%
30-year fixed mortgage	12.85%	13.10%	9.83%	9.22%	8.15%	5.77%	5.09%	3.73%
Tax adjusted (less 30%)	9.00%	9.17%	6.88%	6.45%	5.71%	4.04%	3.56%	2.61%

a lower return on investment.[9] For example, if you were in a mortgage in 1980 and didn't refinance by 1995, you could be paying 12.7 percent (8.9 percent after tax) on your mortgage and receiving 5.5 percent on your cash. A negative spread! A declining rate environment could make it hard to capture a spread if your interest cost is fixed.[10] The solution to this is to refinance the debt to a lower rate, which is what millions of Americans have done over the past few years.[11]

What about the opposite scenario? What if you borrow when rates are low and then over a long period of time they move higher? What is interesting is that borrowing money can be one of the best ways to express a view with respect to interest rates. For example, if you borrow money for 30 years at 3.5 percent and money markets move to 6 percent, which is below average from the past 45 years, then it would be possible to capture a significant spread and just be in cash![12]

I am in no way suggesting this will happen. It is my opinion, rates could stay lower longer than most people think and do more unusual things than most people think. But that is just my opinion, and I have no idea what will happen with interest rates—and it is my opinion that nobody else knows, either.

We can identify two things:

1. Interest rates are just a function of the economic environment we are in at any given time. High rates are not bad, low rates are not good. While mortgage rates looked awful in 1980, cash paid the same and long-term bonds paid even more.

   a. It would have been easier to capture a spread in 1980 with interest rates at high levels and stock market valuations near generational low levels.

   b. Today, low rates may make an illusion that it is easy to capture a spread. It is possible that future returns in both stocks and bonds have been pulled forward and that for investors in developed markets, it may be hard to capture a spread, even though rates are low.

2. On the other hand, if you were to lock in rates for a long period of time and try to capture a spread, you might try to do so with interest rates near generational lows, like they are in the United States and in many markets around the world in mid-2016.

Let's revisit the question: Can we borrow at a rate equal to inflation? Over the past 30 years, it appears that if we were borrowing long term (on a 30-year fixed mortgage) and comparing to short-term inflation, then no, we cannot. This includes today where even factoring in tax adjustments, borrowing costs for 30-year mortgages, even though they are at generational lows, are averaging higher than inflation.

However, this is misleading because it is comparing long-term fixed mortgages to short-term inflation. There are floating-rate mortgages that have a cost of approximately LIBOR + 2 percent. These rates change on a monthly basis. LIBOR is the London Inter Bank Offering Rate and is the rate at which banks can borrow and lend from each other. Since 2008, LIBOR has generally been between zero and 0.5 percent.[13] This means that there is a product through which an individual can borrow at a rate closer to 2.5 percent in the current environment, which can be close to 1.4 percent for borrowers in a high tax bracket. This is stunningly close to inflation. The risk with this product is that if central banks, like the Federal Reserve, raise interest rates, and if LIBOR rises alongside, which is what is generally anticipated, then borrowing costs will rise as well.

As was highlighted in Chapter 5, simply looking at the past 30 years may be misleading. It is a single economic environment in which interest rates went from generational highs to generational lows. While inflation may stay lower, longer than many people anticipate—and while the world continues to battle deflation—there is no question that we are at a different beginning place. The spreads that one needs to capture looking forward are starting from near all-time lows in the United States, Europe, and Japan. From these levels, on an absolute and relative basis investors need to capture a spread lower than ever before.

Therefore, we can conclude that borrowers following the L.I.F.E. glide path have an interesting choice between borrowing at a floating rate that is near inflation and borrowing at fixed rates that while higher than current inflation, are lower than historic inflation and starting at generational and in some cases—all-time lows.

It is important to note, in the examples above, we are comparing borrowing costs to inflation and to returns in cash. Remember our risk/return charts from before? Cash is not the only investment in which one can invest. An investor may choose from the universe of investment options on planet earth: U.S. stocks, U.S. bonds, developed market stocks, developed market bonds, emerging market stocks, emerging market bonds, commodities, gold, and real estate. Further, there are a myriad of alternative investments in which one can invest. This leads us to question investment returns relative to borrowing costs.

What about Investment Returns?

Starting again with the big picture, if your returns are higher than your after-tax cost of debt, the L.I.F.E. path will always be better. If you capture a larger spread, the power of the L.I.F.E. path is mind-blowing. Here is the ironic twist: If you think that investment returns will be low relative to your cost of debt over the next 30 to 70 years, then you need a bigger base of assets working for you as early as possible in life, not a smaller base of assets, in order to hit your long-term retirement goals. In a lower spread environment, the L.I.F.E. path is still better!

Let's say that you think returns will average 1 percent over your after-tax cost of debt. You still capture a spread and have more liquidity and flexibility as a result of the strategy. The L.I.F.E. glide path added value in higher returns and more flexibility.

If it is true that you think that no investments or diversified portfolios return a higher rate of return than your after-tax cost of debt, what should you do? Let's do the math on this. Let's assume that Brandon and Teresa think that their borrowing costs for the next 40 years will be 2.5 percent and their investment returns will be 2.5 percent. To try to keep things apples to apples, I will assume that they cover the interest expense from cash flow and that principal payments come from "savings." This will let them pay off their mortgage in the same 21.6 years. If they keep saving $9,000 for the next 18.4 years and have a return of 2.5 percent, Brandon and Teresa will retire with $207,000. Without Social Security, they are out of money in about five years. Paying down debt or investing, they are in bad shape for their retirement goals.

The bottom line is that if you think your returns from all assets on planet Earth will average less than your after-tax cost of debt, you are stuck. You will either need a very short retirement (working longer) or to save at a very high rate, or both.

If this is the case, it is difficult to solve the gap through savings. For an extreme example, consider if Brandon and Teresa are scared and hate debt, hate risk, and hate investing. They feel their investment returns will be less than 2.5 percent. Their mortgage is at 2.5 percent. Therefore, they decide to increase their savings, pay down debt, and then build up assets. If they increase their savings to 30 percent of their income, $18,000 per year, they would pay off their house in 17.3 years. Their portfolio at 2.5 percent would grow to about $540,000—double the savings rate of the L.I.F.E. glide path, five more years of working, and fewer assets! And while this is impressive, it likely is not enough for them to sustain for the next 30 years.

To be more extreme, if an individual has a return of zero and works for 30 years and then wants to retire for 30 years with the same income, she would need to save 100 percent of her income during her working years, which, of course, is not possible.

In fact, while it is true that she might have Social Security and be able to live on less, it is also true that due to inflation, her money might not go as far. If her return is truly zero, then even saving one year of income won't make it. For example, my mom was a teacher. In her first year of working, she made about $7,500 in the 1970s. If she saved all of that income for the whole year and had a return of zero, then it would potentially cover less than a month of her living expenses today.

Remember the diversified portfolio from Chapter 5? Over a 10-year period of time, a diversified approach outperformed inflation plus 4 percent in 92 percent of every rolling 10-year period of time. The diversified process also outperformed inflation + 2 percent in 97 percent of every rolling 10-year period of time. The diversified process outperformed inflation + 6 percent in 54 percent of every rolling 10-year period of time.

This is not a recommendation to follow the diversified process or any statement on what it will deliver in the future. What we can see is that if your borrowing costs are close to inflation, and your portfolio is diversified across many asset classes, there may be a chance that on average, and over a long period of time, you can capture a spread, and capturing even a modest spread can be valuable.

I do not know future returns, but there are two possibilities: Future returns will be lower than the after-tax cost of debt or they will be higher.

All of the strategies we are looking at have risks. Our job is to assess all of the possible strategies and choose the course which maximizes the odds of your success while minimizing the excess risk taken.

The combined implications of this are vast. If you truly believe that returns will be lower than your after-tax cost of debt, then you believe in a short retirement and/or a high savings rate. For this group, I would suggest that you consider a middle ground. Move your savings rate to 30 percent and embrace the L.I.F.E. path with 15 percent of your savings and the pay-down-debt path with the other 15 percent. If you are in this camp, then you are already signed up, knowing that your likely case is that you work for a long, long time, which is a clear possibility under your current assumptions. I think the alternative path is better, as you have little to lose relative to your alternatives and you have an added possibility that you could be on track for retirement.

What about the Impact of Savings Rate?

If Brandon and Teresa saved at a rate of 20 percent, $12,000 per year, then holding the rate of return constant and inflation plus 4 percent would result in a portfolio of $914,000!

The L.I.F.E. path works exceptionally well with a 20-percent savings rate. It's about right at 15 percent. If you save less than 15 percent, then the unfortunate news is that there is little mathematical chance of you being on track, unless you believe in large returns or have an exceptionally long time horizon (or never intend to retire). If you are saving less than 15 percent and have a time horizon less than 35 years, then I would strongly encourage you to consider the potential benefits and risks of embracing an optimal debt strategy. If you believe in large returns, then embracing debt will complement your strategy. If you believe in low returns and have a low savings rate, you have to have debt to make it, or you are doubly stuck.

If you save more than 20 percent, you have flexibility. The greater your savings rate, the more you can afford to consider paying down debt early in life. The lower your savings rate, the less of an ability you have to consider paying down debt early in life. At the same time, it is my position that until you build up enough assets to be able to pay off your house, you should not pay off your house. The risk is too great and you lose liquidity.

There are three interconnected levers: your savings rate, your existing assets, and time until you retire. If you have a long time, a high savings rate, and a good base of assets, then you should be on track for retirement and can choose to pay down debt. If you have a short time, a low base of assets, and a low savings rate, then you need as many assets working for you as you can and will want to direct savings toward investing rather than paying down debt, assuming that you can get your cost of borrowing close to inflation or inflation + 2 percent.

What about the Tax Factor?

This concept gets a sliver complicated, but a neat byproduct of this strategy is that you are consistently adding funds to your taxable and tax-deferred accounts, throughout your lifetime. Therefore, there should be little need to sell from your portfolio.

Let's say that I have a diversified portfolio of 10 exchange-traded funds (ETFs) and I start out with a weighting of 10 percent in each one. Half of them go up 5 percent and half of them go down 5 percent. Half would now have a weighting of 10.05 and the other half at 9.95. When you add funds, you will be buying up the areas that are underweighted and not adding to the areas that are overweighted. As a result, you can actually rebalance your portfolio through contributions rather than by selling. At a minimum, any sales should take place as long-term capital gains because the investment should have been held for at least a year.

Also, by maintaining a mortgage throughout your life, you maintain the tax benefits associated with that mortgage. This can not only create a tax-free retirement but also significantly reduce taxes during working years.[14]

What if the Tax Deductibility of Mortgages Goes Away?

The tax deductibility of mortgages may go away. This is constantly a topic of conversation in Congress. Who knows what will happen with Congress, but here is a framework to address it:

An elimination or phase-out in the tax deductibility of mortgages increases the cost of the mortgage. You always want to look at your after-tax cost of debt and compare it to your investment options. If you think you can capture a spread, over a long period of time, then there is value to the debt. If the deduction is eliminated, your spread may fall, but even a small spread is powerful over time, and you have the added benefit of liquidity, which gives more flexibility.

Children and College Savings

Brandon and Teresa had a child at 30, the exact time that they entered the Independence phase. They started saving 2 percent per year, or $1,200, for college. If they earn a rate of return of inflation plus 4 percent, this would grow to $30,744 by the time their child is 18 in today's dollars. Here comes the cool trick: for the four years the child is in school, they could also direct their $9,000 of annual savings to college instead of to savings. Plus, they could direct the money they were saving for college. This means that they would have $10,200 of annual cash flow that they could put toward college. $10,200 × 4 years = $40,800 + the $30,744 means a total ability to pay over $70,000 toward college. While it might not cover everything, this should go a long way and be supplemented with work, loans, or grants. Based on this income level, they might also be excellent candidates for grants.

What is great for Brandon and Teresa is that when their child enters school, they will have accumulated assets of over $230,000 ($260,000, including college savings). Granted, some of this is in their retirement program, but here is the really cool trick: If they stop saving for this 4-year period and their portfolio grows at inflation plus 4 percent, their portfolio will grow by about $9,200 per year. Their portfolio will do the savings for them.

What if they have more kids? To be extreme, consider if Brandon and Teresa never save again, and direct all of their future savings to paying for the kids' school. Their $230,000 will grow to $545,000 at age 70. Combined with Social Security, they would still be on track to retire. Granted, they will have a mortgage but they will still be richer than the no-debt camp, and will have saved 198,000 fewer dollars.

Magic. It is so powerful to build up a base of assets early in life.

I want to address the 2-percent figure with some more color. While the level of accumulation depends so much on income, so does financial aid. Make no mistake, more savings is always better. Due to the power of compounding, I recommend saving as much as you can as early as you can. Once your college savings crosses $25,000 per child ($50,000+ if you desire they attend a private school), you will want to work with your advisor to run some calculations to see if you are on track or under saved, but until then, just keep saving.

Interest Rates and Debt Service Coverage Ratios

In the L.I.F.E. glide path, I did not address interest rates. The mortgage started out at 39 times monthly income and stayed constant. In the current environment, it is possible to embrace the L.I.F.E. path and have payments that would be less than the average American household. But what if interest rates rise?

Typically, but not always, there is a relationship between inflation, interest rates, and your paycheck. If you are a young professional and anticipate that your income will be rising, you may have a different framework. For example, what if you buy a home when your income is at $60,000 and five years from now it is at $90,000? If you have not moved, you can cover a considerable spike in interest rates. Or, if your mortgage is fixed, you have very little of your income going to your mortgage. Either way, you should be ahead.

At some point in the future, when interest rates are considerably higher, you may want to adjust the glide path so that your payment is always less than 20 percent of your annual income.[15]

Endnotes

1. http://www.forbes.com/sites/nextavenue/2013/03/01/next-avenue-money-scorecard-how-do-you-rate/#6b613b3d7d12.
2. https://www.nerdwallet.com/blog/credit-card-data/average-credit-card-debt-household/.
3. TransAmerica Center for Retirement Studies, *Retirement Throughout the Ages: Expectations and Preparations of American Workers: 16th Annual Transamerica Survey of American Workers* (May 2015), http://www.transamericacenter.org/docs/default-source/resources/center-research/16th-annual/tcrs2015_sr_retirement_throughout_the_ages.pdf.
4. http://www.bankrate.com/calculators/retirement/social-security-benefits-calculator.aspx; 70/70 years old, includes nonworking spouse benefits.

5. The case studies presented are for educational and illustrative purposes only and cannot guarantee that the reader will achieve similar results. Your results may vary significantly and factors such as the market, personal effort, and many others will cause results to vary. All of the case studies throughout the book are hypothetical and not intended to demonstrate the performance of any specific security, product, or investment strategy. Opinions formulated by the author are intended to stimulate discussion.

6. https://data.oecd.org/interest/long-term-interest-rates.htm.

7. https://www.wellsfargo.com/mortgage/rates/.

8. Robert Schmansky, "Interest Rates May Rise but Your Money Market Yield May Not," *Forbes* (May 6, 2016), http://www.forbes.com/sites/feeonlyplanner/2016/05/06/interest-rates-may-rise-but-your-money-market-yield-may-not/#13c6942618af.

9. https://fred.stlouisfed.org.
https://www.fdic.gov/regulations/resources/rates/previous.html.
http://www.infoplease.com/ipa/A0908373.html.

10. For example, imagine if you borrow at 8 percent long term and invest all of your money in short-term bonds that also pay 8 percent. Imagine interest rates fall to 2 percent and all of your bonds have matured. You would now have to reinvest at 2 percent and would still be paying 8 percent interest, a negative spread of 6 percent!

11. If you had a mortgage at 8 percent in the early 2000s, you could refinance it to a lower rate near 3 percent in 2016. This refinancing makes it easier to capture a spread, but note in 2016 that interest rates are higher than bond yields and money market yields, which is still creating a negative spread, albeit a smaller negative spread.

12. http://www.allcountries.org/uscensus/822_money_market_interest_rates_and_mortgage.html.

13. http://www.macrotrends.net/1433/historical-libor-rates-chart.

14. For more detail on tax strategies, I encourage you to check out Chapter 5 of *The Value of Debt in Retirement,* by Thomas J. Anderson (Hoboken, NJ: John Wiley and Sons, 2015).

15. Author's Note: The information in this chapter is to be considered in a holistic way as a part of the book and not to be considered on a stand-alone basis. This includes, but is not limited to, the discussion of the risks of each of these ideas as well as all of the disclaimers throughout the book. The material is presented with a goal of encouraging thoughtful conversation and rigorous debate on the risks and potential benefits of the concepts between you and your advisors based on your unique situation, risk tolerance, and goals.

Chapter 7

Conclusion

"It is not easy to convey, unless one has experienced it, the dramatic feeling of sudden enlightenment that floods the mind when the right idea finally clicks into place. One immediately sees how many previously puzzling facts are neatly explained by the new hypothesis. One could kick oneself for not having the idea earlier, it now seems so obvious. Yet before, everything was in a fog."

—Francis Crick

I know we can embrace a sensible, balanced approach to debt, an approach that mimics the balance found in nature, art, architecture, music, even our own bodies. This balanced approach will increase your financial security and flexibility. It will increase the likelihood of a secure retirement, and reduce your stress along the way.

While it is impossible for me to know for sure that a balanced approach will be better, I know it increases the chances you will be on track. When compared to the no-debt path, I believe there is an approximate 95-percent chance the balanced path I have outlined will lead to greater wealth accumulation. I believe there is a 100-percent chance it will leave you better prepared for emergencies and the curve balls life sends all of us.

Taking a Stand Against Conventional Wisdom

Make no mistake, how you invest matters. But advice on investing is often based on conventional wisdom and using the past to try to predict the future, something that has virtually no chance of happening. Wall Street portfolios exhibit massive home bias. Most portfolios look nothing like the process that was outlined in Chapter 5. Most portfolios have over 80 percent of their assets in U.S. stocks and bonds—an allocation to two assets that are trading at or near absolute and relative all-time high prices. It is my opinion that this is a process that is virtually guaranteed to lead to massive amounts of wealth destruction.

If my two $100,000 charitable bets did not adequately make the point, let me try one more way. The average bear market is a 30-percent correction.[1] I do not need to know when the next bear market will take place. I simply need to know that if one happens anytime in the next five years there is a high probability of below average and potentially negative returns in U.S. stocks over that five-year period. Let's look at an extreme example and imagine stocks go up 50 percent between 2016 and 2020, making a bull market run that goes from 700 to 3,000. This would imply we are in the second-longest and second-biggest bull market ever, and then if what follows that run is an average bear market of a 30-percent correction, U.S. stocks would be flat for the next five years.

Keep in mind, the last two runs of similar size were the 1990s, which ended in the tech wreck, and one in the 1920s, that ended in the Great Depression.[2] The process the lemmings follow is virtually guaranteed to deliver returns that will disappoint and destroy value.

I am not saying investors should not own U.S. equities or that they shouldn't own cash or bonds. I am saying that I believe that if your portfolio is only composed of these assets you may have a difficult time capturing a spread for the next decade.

Conventional wisdom is not only wrong with respect to investing, it is really wrong with respect to debt.

You have been told debt is bad. You have been told paying off your mortgage is good. I believe it is a lie. I have found no mathematical basis to these claims.

The single biggest determining factor in your rate of return and in being on track for retirement is your debt, debt structure, and the choices you make with respect to debt. Do not underestimate the power of building up assets early and paying down debt later.

If you believe that you can capture a spread, at any level, over your after-tax cost of debt, on average and over a time period of more than five years, debt does not destroy value but, rather, adds considerable value to the accumulation of wealth. The greater the spread and the longer the time period, the greater the value of debt.

> *We can embrace a sensible, balanced approach to debt throughout our lives. This balanced approach will reduce stress, increase financial security and flexibility, and increase the probability of a secure retirement. Strategic debt is not a waste of money, but rather, an opportunity to increase the likelihood you will be able to accomplish your goals in the short, medium, and long term.*

Let's look one last time at Brandon and Teresa. Without drastically changing their savings rate, they cannot hit their retirement goals through the conventional approach. It isn't possible without unreasonable assumptions.

If they had a return of 7 percent, their retirement portfolio would only grow to about $318,000.

If their returns were 10 percent, it would only grow to $429,000.

In fact, they would need a return of 14 percent to equal the net worth of $850,000.

In the L.I.F.E. path, they achieved $850,000 with a return of 4 percent.[3]

What is more likely, your ability to consistently get a 4-percent rate of return or a 14-percent rate of return?

It is virtually impossible for me to express how little returns matter relative to the decisions you make with respect to debt.

And if you believe you can accomplish higher returns, then you believe you can capture a spread—and you should believe in debt.

If you believe returns will be low, *then you need to capture a spread* to have any chance of hitting your objective.

If you believe that no asset class on this planet can capture a spread over a 30-year period relative to generational low interest rates, then you need a high savings rate, perhaps upwards of 50 percent and potentially pushing toward 100 percent. Unless you like that idea, you have to take risk. And faced with risk you should take the least risky, highest probability path to accomplishing your goals. To me, this is accomplished by embracing strategic debt—throughout your life—accompanied with perhaps slightly lower but slightly more consistent returns.

You—and your advisors—should not manage one half of your balance sheet. It is not possible to do a good job if you do not use all of the tools that are at your disposal. Debt is a tool that is to be managed carefully. You would not have a doctor operate without a scalpel. You would not build a house without a hammer. Failure to look at your financial picture in a connected, holistic way is gross negligence.

You have the right to be mad at conventional wisdom. In fact, you should be outraged. Partial advice is bad advice. The future of wealth management is interconnected holistic advice. Comprehensive plans that look at how your assets and liabilities work together. Advisors that manage only half of the balance sheet, assets, are by definition managing one half of the picture. As my friend Duncan MacPherson says, "Without debt, there is no balance to a balance sheet."

Shoot for more conservative, more consistent returns with some debt rather than volatile, inconsistent returns with no debt. I can't say it enough: The single biggest determining factor in your overall rate of return is your debt ratio and your debt structure. But you have to be thoughtful, balanced, strategic, and comprehensive, or everything can go wrong.

So what does a balanced approach look like? In my opinion: If your net worth is less than 20 times your gross income and you want to retire, you have to carefully consider the potential risks and benefits associated with the value of debt in building wealth. To me, the benefits are compelling relative to the risks.

Here are some key takeaway thoughts:

Oppressive Debt:

- Get rid of it.
- Your number one goal is to eliminate oppressive debt and break the paycheck-to-paycheck cycle as quickly as possible.
- Be sure you aren't saving yourself into oppressive debt by putting money into your retirement plan while racking up charges on your credit card.
- Build up liquidity. Have money in your checking account so you have reserves and can ride out the storms.

Home Ownership:

- Too many people buy houses too early in their life.
- The risk and lack of liquidity is not worth it.
- Renting is not wasting money. It is about risk management, flexibility, and using other people's money so you can build up yours.
- There is considerable value to renting until: You have no oppressive debt and a net worth of at least 50 percent of your annual income and closer to two times your annual income, or you know you will be in that home for at least five years.

Borrowing:

- Try to keep your borrowing costs as close to inflation or inflation + 2 percent. If they get above inflation + 4 percent, it will be hard to capture a spread.
- Avoid 15-year mortgages unless you have the cash flow to be on a 15-year mortgage and save at a rate of at least 15 percent. A low savings rate combined with a 15-year mortgage virtually guarantees you will not be on track for retirement.
- Interest-only mortgages are not bad, if you stay within the guidelines outlined and save at a rate of 15 percent.
- 30-year mortgages might be good, but generally only if you plan to be in that specific property for more than seven years.

Capturing a Spread:

- A small spread of even 2 percent adds up to a lot of money over a lifetime.
- A spread of 4 percent could be the difference between being able to retire and not.
- A spread of 6 percent is a significant and material spread over a lifetime, but may not be worth the risk.
- I know I will not capture a spread every minute, hour, day, week, year or even every three-year period of time. I would like to capture a spread over most five-year periods of time. Properly positioned, I think there is a high possibility of capturing a spread over a 10-, 20-, 30-, and 50-year period of time.

Risk:

- The larger the spread you are targeting, the more risk you are taking on with your investment strategy.
- I would rather capture a smaller spread more consistently on a larger base of assets. It's a marathon, not a sprint.
- Over time, risk is equally important to return.
- A lot of risk isn't worth it early in life, and you can't afford it later in life.

Although conventional wisdom will tell you debt is bad, my advice is that debt is a powerful tool that can materially add value to your financial picture. It is one of the best ways to express a view with respect to currencies and interest rates. It is one of the best low-correlated assets in a portfolio.

The right debt, with the right balance, has a place in virtually everybody's life. Slow and steady wins the race. Consider taking your risk through a balanced amount of debt rather than through asset allocation. Tune out the news and market forecasts: Nobody knows what will happen in the future.

The 2015 Nobel Prize in Economics went to Angus Deaton. In discussing his award, the *Economist* magazine said: "*As well as his specific contributions to our understanding of the world, Mr. Deaton offers three lessons to aspiring economists. First, the theory should tally with the data—but if not, then do not despair. Puzzles and inconsistencies help to prompt innovation.*

Second, the average is rarely good enough. It is only by understanding differences between people that we can understand the whole. Finally, measurement matters. In the words of Mr. Deaton, "Progress cannot be coherently discussed without definitions and supporting evidence."[4]

I would suggest we apply the same framework to *The Value of Debt in Building Wealth.*

- The theory must tie with the data. But if not, then do not despair. Puzzles and inconsistencies help to prompt innovation.
- Average is rarely good enough. It is by understanding differences that we can understand the whole.
- Measurement matters. Progress cannot be coherently discussed without definitions and supporting evidence.

While Mr. Deaton's work has been called "a triumph for evidence-based economics," it is my hope that this book is a small step forward for an evidence-based approach to the value of debt in building wealth.[5]

Lastly, never forget the importance of behavioral economics. This growing field is perhaps the most important. Simply ask yourself, "Will I honestly have the discipline to implement the plan?" If the answer is no, then make no mistake, debt will most likely destroy value throughout your life. This plan requires discipline and requires you to be rational and thoughtful. I believe in your ability to implement the glide path through L.I.F.E. we've outlined and examined together. I believe in you.[6]

Endnotes

1. Julie Verhage, "Morgan Stanley Analyzed 43 Bear Markets and Here's What It Found," *Bloomberg* (January 26, 2016), http://www.bloomberg.com/news/articles/2016-01-26/morgan-stanley-analyzed-43-bear-markets-and-here-s-what-it-found.
2. http://us-history.com/1920s-the-great-depression/; Ironman, Political Calculations, "Here's Why the Dot-Com Bubble Began and Why It Popped, *Business Insider* (December 15, 2010), http://www.businessinsider.com/heres-why-the-dot-com-bubble-began-and-why-it-popped-2010-12.
3. The case studies presented are for educational and illustrative purposes only and cannot guarantee that the reader will achieve similar results. Your results may vary significantly and factors such as the market, personal effort, and many others will

cause results to vary. All of the case studies throughout the book are hypothetical and not intended to demonstrate the performance of any specific security, product, or investment strategy. Opinions formulated by the author are intended to stimulate discussion.

4. "Reality Cheque; Free Exchange." *Economist (US),* October 17, 2015.

5. Ibid.

6. Author's Note: The information in this chapter is to be considered in a holistic way as a part of the book and not to be considered on a stand-alone basis. This includes, but is not limited to, the discussion of the risks of each of these ideas as well as all of the disclaimers throughout the book. The material is presented with a goal of encouraging thoughtful conversation and rigorous debate on the risks and potential benefits of the concepts between you and your advisors based on your unique situation, risk tolerance, and goals.

Appendix A

Phi Phound Me

I n my other books, I proved debt can be beneficial, but my earlier books' inflexibility for people in the accumulation phase presented a series of new challenges:

- How can you create a flexible, dynamic debt ratio range that moves throughout your life in a responsible way?
- How can the range be customized for different levels of assets and different levels of income?
- How can a dynamic, flexible range be overlaid with some of the greatest theories in finance?
- How can we test results without knowing the future? Most people test using historic data, but the results can be incredibly misleading.
- Could we reverse the test by considering what assumptions you would need to believe to find value in debt?
- Could this process help create an informed discussion composed of a world of unknowns?

- In addition to giving debt mathematical value, can we test the value of debt in reducing stress?
- If it turns out that the theories test well, how could they overlap with behavioral economics and our tendencies as human beings?

As it turns out, all of this was too difficult. Every strategy I derived was too complex or too rigid. I couldn't form a flexible, simple strategy to accommodate people of virtually any level of net worth and income that are still accumulating assets. I was stuck.

Inspiration Arrived

I visited the Museum of Science and Industry in Chicago and saw a fascinating exhibit about math in nature and life. I learned about the sequences and proportions that can be found across objects young and old, big and small, created by nature or created by man.

Nature, art, architecture, and music all exhibit a natural balance. They have patterns that can be repeated and scaled. They aren't the same. There are a lot of differences between Saturn, the human body, and the Parthenon, but when looking at the balance of the proportions, you may be surprised how much they have in common.

What is even more amazing is how the proportions can be consistent throughout change. For example, your body exhibits similar proportions throughout your life, even as it grows and changes. Importantly, the proportions in your body are similar but rarely would be the exact same and they rarely, if ever, would conform exactly to a mathematical series.

Could we apply these ideas to your financial picture? Could we use this framework as inspiration to create a balanced glide path? Could this balanced approach be flexible and more dynamic than the simple example of the Nadas, the Steadys, and the Radicals? Could the result be a more beautiful and better representation of balance throughout our lives?

You likely remember the number pi from geometry class. Pi is an irrational number that cannot be represented by a fraction. It is an infinite series (3.14159…) that never ends nor moves to a permanent repeating pattern. This transcendental number represents the ratio of a circle's circumference to its diameter.

There is another irrational number that you may or may not be familiar with: phi. Like it's friend pi, phi is an infinite series starting at 1.618. This is a super cool number that is often called the golden ratio. The golden ratio is often called God's ratio because phi can be found literally everywhere, including in the proportions in:

- The human body
- Other animals
- Plants
- The solar system
- Mother Nature
- DNA
- Architecture
- Music
- The Bible

The Italian Renaissance artist Leonardo Da Vinci used the golden ratio in many of his paintings—and in fact, the golden ratio had a central role in the book and movie *The Da Vinci Code*. Phi is 1.618. Let's say that a line has a length of 1. Imagine that you break this line into two sections—one that is 0.618 in length and other 0.382. This break represents phi, or the golden ratio, which is sometimes rounded to "one third/two thirds."

I have been familiar with phi for a long time and considered that perhaps the golden ratio of personal debt is 38.2 percent—which is really close to (though a bit higher than) the optimal ranges I recommend. In fact, the one third/two thirds ratio is the basis of the tests I conducted with some wonderful assistance from the Olin School of Business at Washington University in St. Louis in *The Value of Debt in Retirement*.

Still, phi represents a single number. It represents balance, but it is rigid. This is unsatisfactory, because as we have discussed, people's lives and incomes change over time. One number, one ratio, cannot give the flexibility people want and need. I had the seed of an idea, but I still lacked a flexible, dynamic framework.

The golden ratio can be derived many ways, including the Fibonacci sequence, which is named after an Italian mathematician. In *The Da Vinci Code*, the Fibonacci sequence plays a central role as the protagonist attempts to break an ancient code. The neat thing about the sequence is that it provides a series of ratios that can be used to look at proportions across objects young and old, big and small, created by nature or created by man. A series is more flexible so it can more easily evolve throughout life. For example, your body exhibits similar proportional ratios through-out your life, even as it grows and changes. Importantly, the proportions in your body are similar as you grow but they rarely, if ever, would be the exact same, and they rarely, if ever, would conform exactly to a mathematical series.

Not Perfect Makes Perfect

Leonardo Da Vinci, Beethoven, the ancient Greeks, Mother Nature, and your body all exhibit balanced traits from the Fibonacci sequence, but none are an exactly perfect fit to the series. I look to the Fibonacci sequence as an inspiration, but have no intention to force a fit nor to be precise. Some of the greatest works of art, architecture, music, and even our own bodies are not perfectly conforming! Perfection is boring. Perfect is not beautiful. Therefore, I am not looking for perfection, I am looking for a balanced path of inspiration that can accommodate a wide variety of shapes and sizes.

Applying the Fibonacci Sequence

The following is intended only for readers who find the inspiration for the math behind the book interesting. This book went through a dramatic evolution. The first version laid out concepts, but it wasn't specific or actionable and offered no proof to the underlying thoughts. I wasn't satisfied. Once phi found me, I rewrote the whole book emphasizing the math. In the second iteration of this book, the first chapter was called "The Debt Hypothesis." In it, I formed a "null" hypothesis which, to me, represented the conventional wisdom held by most members of society:

Debt adds zero value. While most consumers use debt at some point, they desire to eliminate it as fast as possible because they believe that being debt free is financially responsible and will increase their financial security, reduce stress, and put them on a better path to financial freedom.

It is my belief that in the anti-debt hysteria world most people are (1) taking on too much debt too early in life; and then (2) paying down that debt too aggressively; and as a result they are (3) not beginning saving until later in life. It is my hypothesis that this strategy might be coming at a considerable cost to society and that there could be a better, more balanced path. This formed the basis for an alternative hypothesis:

We can embrace a sensible, balanced approach to debt throughout our lives; an approach that rhymes with the balance exhibited in nature, art, architecture, music, and even our own bodies. This balanced approach will reduce stress, increase financial security and flexibility, and increase the probability of a secure retirement. Used appropriately, strategic debt is not a waste of money, but rather, an opportunity to increase the likelihood you will be able to accomplish your goals in the short, medium, and long term.

From here, the book was a contest: a mathematical proof of *The Value of Debt in Building Wealth.* I laid out the alternative hypothesis and then tested the null hypothesis against it. Because I do not know your rate of return or your cost of debt, the book concluded with what you would need to believe in order to conclude that debt adds or destroys value in building wealth. While the second version was very math forward, the version you just read was more "concept forward." For those who desire more specifics on the math, here are highlights behind the phases.

The Fibonacci sequence is written as follows:

0, 1, 1, 2, 3, 5, 8, 13, 21, 34, 55, 89, 144 …

You can see that each number is the sum of the two numbers before it. For example, $5 = 2 + 3$; $21 = 13 + 8$. This sequence can be graphed as shown in Figure A.1. As the series grows, the numbers become closer and closer to the golden ratio. For example, $144/89 = 1.61797…$

Notice that the first square has the dimensions 1×1, as does the second. Two is a 2×2 square. Its sides equal three and three is a square that is 3×3. As we know, the golden ratio itself is a static infinite series $1.618033…$. The Fibonacci sequence not only gives us a single number but also a series of numbers and therefore a series of ratios.

The following are examples of Fibonacci ratios:

$$13/21 = 61.9\%$$

$$8/21 = 38.1\%$$

$$5/21 = 23.8\%$$

$$2/21 = 9.5\%$$

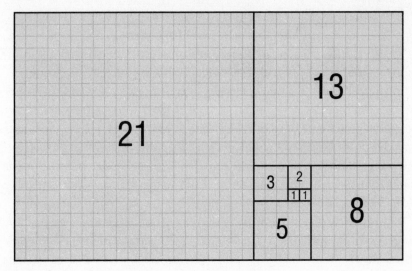

Figure A.1   A Representation of the Fibonacci Sequence

$$1/21 = 4.8\%$$

$$0/21 = 0\%$$

These ratios actually form the basis for the glide path presented in the book. We began with Phase 1: Launch! Table A.1 is a reprint of Table 3.3, which outlined the Launch Phase path in Chapter 3.

Recall the Fibonacci sequence begins: 0, 1, 1, 2. Our Launch phase series began with zero oppressive debt, 1 month cash reserve, 1 month of income in a retirement plan, and 2 additional months of savings. This could be written as follows:

0 = Zero oppressive debt

1 = 1-month cash reserve

1 = 1 month of income in a retirement plan

2 = 2 additional months of savings

The Launch phase starts out with a perfect tracking of the Fibonacci sequence. From here, we entered Phase 2: Independence. Table A.2 is a reprint of Table 3.8 from Chapter 3.

In math, we often use different units to measure. For example, something could be 30 yards away, 90 feet away, or 1,080 inches away.

Table A.1 Blank Phase 1: Launch!

Step/Goal/Bucket	Formula	A Balanced Path	Where You Are	Gap
No oppressive debt (No debt at a rate over 10 percent)	0	$0		
Cash reserve, build to a one-month reserve (checking account)	Monthly income × 1			
Start a retirement plan. Build to a balance of one month's income	Monthly income × 1			
Continue building cash savings until you have an additional two months' reserve (savings account)	Monthly income × 2			

Table A.2 A Blank Balanced Path Worksheet—Phase 2: Independence, No House

Goal/Bucket	Formula	A Balanced Path	Where You Are	Gap
No oppressive debt. No debt at a rate over 10 percent.	0	$0		
Cash reserve, checking account	Monthly income × 3			
Cash reserve, savings account	Monthly income × 3			
Retirement investing	Monthly income × 6			
Big life changes	Monthly income × 9			

Each is the same distance, it is simply presented with different units of measurement. As the size grows, we typically use a different basic unit of measurement. You would not, for example, typically state the distance of Washington, D.C., to New York City in inches.

In the Independence phase, our goals were to have zero oppressive debt, build a three-month cash reserve, build retirement savings to six months' income, and establish a big-life-changes fund equal to six months of income. The Fibonacci sequence is written: 0, 1, 1, 2, 3, 5, 8. At the surface the numbers 0, 3, 3, 6, 9 appear to have little in common with the sequence. However, if you restate each of the goals into a basic unit where a unit is equal to three months of income, you could write it as follows:

- 0 = Zero oppressive debt
- 1= Cash reserve checking (equal to 3 months income / 3 = a basic unit of 1)
- 1 = Cash reserve savings (equal to 3 months income / 3 = a basic unit of 1)
- 2 = Retirement savings (equal to 6 months income / 3 = a basic unit of 2)
- 3 = Big life changes (equal to 9 months income / 3 = a basic unit of 3)

Said another way, if you divide each number of the series 0, 3, 3, 6, 9 by 3, you get 0, 1, 1, 2, 3, which is the Fibonacci sequence.

Next we discussed buying a house. Table A.3 is a reprint from Chapter 3 of Table 3.13. In Table A.3, however, I replace the columns "A Balanced Path," "Where You Are" and "Gap" with "Fibonacci Numbers" and "Basic Unit," which is the "Formula" column divided by the basic unit, in this case 3.

Note that the last number in the basic unit column is 20, where the Fibonacci sequence would have been 21. And note that net worth is a 7 in the unit column where it would have been an 8 in the Fibonacci sequence. This is where it is essential to recall that I am not trying to force a fit, I'm turning to the natural world for inspiration to test the alternative hypothesis against the null hypothesis.

In Chapter 4, we covered Phase 3: Freedom. From Chapter 4, "*The goal of the Freedom phase is to reduce your debt ratio. Since reducing debt is the primary goal, then we need a different base unit, one that relates specifically to your debt. Therefore, do the following:*

1. Write down your total liabilities (your total outstanding debt) =

_____

2. Divide this number by 8 = _____

This is your base unit for this phase."

Table A.3 A Blank Balanced Path Worksheet—Phase 2: Independence, with a House

Goal/Bucket	Formula	Fibonacci Numbers	Basic Unit (3 months income)
No oppressive debt (No debt at a rate over 10 percent)	0	0	0
Cash reserve, checking account	Monthly income × 3	1	1
Cash reserve, savings account	Monthly income × 3	1	1
Retirement savings	Monthly income × 6	2	2
House equity	Monthly income × 9	3	3
Net worth	Monthly income × 21	8	**7**
Mortgage	Monthly income × 39	13	13
Total assets	Monthly income × 60	21	**20**

The number 8 is a Fibonacci number, but let's look at what is happening. Let's assume that you embrace the glide path outlined in the Independence phase.

0 = Oppressive debt

1 = Cash reserve 1

1 = Cash reserve 2

2 = 401(k)

3 = House equity

5 = Equity in long-term investments (house equity and 401(k))

8 = Approximate net worth

13 = Liabilities (mortgage)

21 = Total assets

The problem that you are facing is that your long-term assets are a 5 and liabilities are a 13. Assets, of course, could not support your debt, and therefore, you are dependent on income. There is no chance to retire at this time. This creates two goals: You want to have less debt and you want to have more assets.

There are two ways to lower your debt ratio:

- Pay down debt.
- Build up assets.

Path 1 is that you could pay down debt. If you do this, then (1) your rate of return will be equal to your after-tax cost of debt; (2) your investments will grow by the rate of return they earn; and (3) your liquidity will be reduced.

Path 2 is that you could choose to build up assets. I assert that the debt ratio should be reduced by building up assets and harnessing the long-term power of compound interest.

From 13 to 8

From the example in Chapters 3 and 4, Brandon and Teresa had a mortgage of $195,000, or 13. Their total assets were $300,000, or 20. In the Fibonacci sequence, 13/21 implies a debt ratio of 61.9 percent. At the end of the Independence phase, Brandon and Teresa's debt ratio is $195,000 / $300,000 (or 13/20), which is 65 percent. I think most people can comfortably agree that long term this is too high; they have too much debt. The question we are analyzing is if they should reduce debt by paying down debt or by building up assets.

To do this, I need their debt to be a lower number in the Fibonacci sequence. I need it to move from 13 to 8. This is why debt is the center of this phase and why 8 is the basic unit of measurement.

From Chapter 4, "*Therefore, Brandon and Teresa would divide 195,000 by 8, which would give them a base unit of 24,375. Now while you may choose to be that precise, I prefer to round it to 24,000. You could also round it to 25,000.*"

Table A.4 is a reprint of Table 4.4 from Chapter 4. Here you can see the series: 0, 1, 1, 3, 8, 13, 21: all Fibonacci numbers but with debt moving from 13 to 8.

Table A.4   A Blank Freedom Phase Worksheet—Debt Based

Goal/Bucket	Formula	A Balanced Path	Where You Are	Gap
No oppressive debt (No debt at a rate over 10 percent)	0	$0		
Cash reserve, checking + savings	Base unit × 1			
Other (jewelry, cars, furniture)	Base unit × 1			
Long-term investments (after-tax)	Base unit × 3			
Retirement savings	Base unit × 5			
Total debt (mortgage)	Base unit × 8			
Net worth	Base unit × 13			
Total assets	Base unit × 21			

For Brandon and Teresa, their debt ratio falls to 8/21, or 38.1 percent. Here is how their life looked in the chapter:

0 = Zero oppressive debt

1 = $24,000 = Cash savings

1 = $24,000 = Other (value of "things" cars, jewelry)

2 = $48,000 = (not listed in the chapter but is likely close to their house equity)

3 = $72,000 = Long-term savings

5 = $120,000 = 401(k)

8 = $195, 000 = Total liabilities (mortgage)

13 = $317,000 = Net worth

21 = $512,000 = Total assets

Their debt ratio is falling considerably, even though they have not paid down any debt! Importantly, they now have a significant level of assets that are working for them long term. They have just materially increased the chances that they will be on track for retirement.[1]

Later in the chapter, I show an income approach to the Freedom phase. The goals are laid out in monthly income goals of 0, 5, 5, 15, 25, 40, 65, 105. If you use a basic unit of five months' income, the series becomes 0, 1, 1, 3, 5, 8, 13, 21. In both approaches, the ending debt ratio is 8/21, which is 38.1 percent.

This phase will likely take a decade of time, and during that time many life events, good and bad, are likely to happen. Therefore, as the scale grows, it increasingly becomes important to look at this as a glide path more than to force a fit.

From 8 to 5

In Phase 4: Equilibrium, we continued the assumption of never paying down debt and building up assets, but with a desire to have a lower debt ratio and a desire to be able to pay off the home. Table A.5 is a reprint of Table 4.7 from Chapter 4.

As listed, the series appears to be 0, 7, 7, 35, 56, 91, 147. If you assign a basic unit of seven months' income, the series can be rewritten: 0, 1, 1,

Table A.5 A Blank Equilibrium Worksheet

Goal/Bucket	Formula	A Balanced Path	Where You Are	Gap
No oppressive debt (No debt at a rate over 10 percent)	0	$0		
Approximate cash reserve (checking + savings)	Monthly income × 7			
Approximate other (jewelry, cars, furniture)	Monthly income × 7			
Approximate mortgage	Monthly income × 35			
Approximate long-term investments (after-tax)	Monthly income × 56			
Approximate retirement savings	Monthly income × 91			
Approximate total investment assets	Monthly income × 147			

5, 8, 13, 21. There is balance not only in the assets and liabilities but also in how the assets are weighted relative to each other. From Chapter 4, *"Notice the beautiful balance the beacons show us:*

The debt ratio is \$175,000 / \$735,000, or 23.8 percent.

Retirement savings / Total investment assets = \$455,000 /\$735,000, or 62 percent.

This is approximately the same ratio of after-tax assets as a percentage of retirement assets (\$280,000 / \$455,000), or 62 percent."

A fun side note is that while I do not discuss it in Chapter 4, they are eligible for a line of credit against their long-term investments. This strategy is the theme of my first book, *The Value of Debt,* and is discussed in Appendix C. They could comfortably borrow up to a 2 on their securities-based line of credit (or 14 months' worth of income), which would be 2/8, or a 25-percent debt ratio against their portfolio.

Super Cool Math

As presented, when your investment assets equal 21, then you are nearing the strike zone for retirement. If you assume a 5-percent distribution in retirement then 21 × 5 percent equals 1.05, which means that savings will generate about 7.35 months of your income. This is calculated by taking the base unit of 7 months × 1.05 = 7.35 months of income. You would need pension, Social Security, and changes in lifestyle to cover the rest. (For a detailed discussion on distribution rates, see *The Value of Debt in Retirement.*)

If you do not want to depend on Social Security we can turn to another number in the Fibonacci series, 34. When your investment assets equal 34, then 34 × 5 percent equals 1.7. This is equal to about 12 months of income (7 months × 1.7 = 11.9).

How long does it take to get to 21 or to 34? It depends on your savings rate, time, and on your rate of return. Table A.6 illustrates what Fibonacci number you can mathematically achieve with different savings rates and different periods of time, holding constant a 6-percent rate of return.

This chart tells you what you intuitively know and what I said earlier in the book: If you save a little, for a short period of time, there is little chance you will be on track for retirement. If you save a lot for a long

Table A.6   Savings Rate and Years to Get to Various Fibonacci Numbers

		Number of Years				
		15	20	25	30	35
Savings Rate	**5%**	2	3	5	7	10
	10%	4	6	9	14	19
	15%	6	9	14	20	29
	20%	8	13	19	27	38
	25%	10	16	24	34	48

period of time, your chances increase significantly. Specifically, if you save less than 10 percent of your income, there is little chance you will have enough assets to retire, even counting Social Security and even with a 35-year time horizon of savings.

Of course you could challenge my return assumptions, but *return hardly matters!* I have held the rate of return at 6 percent. Although that might seem conservative, I am excluding inflation from these assumptions. Inflation plus 6 percent is difficult to achieve for any investor (see Chapter 5 discussion on returns relative to inflation). But let's play with it a little. Even if you have a rate of return of inflation plus 8 percent, there are no savings rates below 10 percent that will let you get to 21 in less than 30 years.

I can go on: Inflation plus 10 percent, a vastly unreasonable assumption, would still require a 10-percent savings rate and a time horizon of 25+ years to get to 21. *Bottom line: If you are saving less than 10 percent, you need to wake up now. You are not on track and you cannot make it up with return.*

However, if you save 15 percent to 20 percent, then even at an inflation plus a 4-percent rate of return, you should be in a good zone in 30 to 35 years. If your returns are higher, you could potentially retire earlier. If you think returns will be lower, say inflation plus 2 percent, then you need a savings rate greater than 20 percent and a time horizon longer than 35 years.

And herein lies the proof to the alternate hypothesis and to the strategy outlined in the book. If you embrace the glide path outlined in the book, the investment ideas highlighted in Chapter 5, combined with a 15 to 20 percent savings rate for 35 to 40 years, then I am approximately 95 percent confident that you will be able to retire comfortably.

The higher the savings rate and the longer the period of time, the greater my belief that the glide path as presented will lead to a comfortable retirement.

If you follow conventional wisdom, the null hypothesis, and first pay off your debt, then holding the other assumptions constant, I am less than 5 percent confident in your ability to replace your income in retirement in the same amount of time. In fact, my math simply shows it isn't possible for most people to adhere to conventional wisdom to pay off their debt, have a less than 20-percent savings rate, and retire in less than 35 years.

Therefore, I conclude that debt adds value in building wealth. More specifically, if you choose to use good debt, working debt like a low-cost mortgage—especially one at generational lows, like in the year 2016—then not directing your precious savings to pay down low-cost debt is when debt is most valuable. It is my opinion that yes, our anti-debt hysteria is massively contributing to the savings crisis in America and that a thoughtful, balanced approach is significantly better.

But here is perhaps my most powerful math: The above is assuming that you are starting from zero! It is true that about 50 percent of Americans have less than $400 in savings, but by virtue of the fact that you are reading this book, there is a good chance you have more than $400 saved up.[2] If you are in that category, then even if you are behind, you can 100 percent get on track.

Remember how at the end of the Launch phase there was a base of retirement savings? If you can clear this phase by the time you are 40 and save at a rate of 15 percent, then you should be on track to have more than 21 within 25 to 30 years; yes—if you start today you can still be on track!

Much of America is significantly behind in retirement savings. If this is you, then you need to:

1. Immediately focus on building up assets.
   a. Target at least a 15-percent savings rate.
   b. Understand that you need a 20+ year horizon of saving at that level.
2. Do not pay down debt that has a cost less than your estimated (or required) return.

Given even a relatively small starting base, a mid-level range of savings, and 20 to 25 years, then there is a high chance of being able to be on track for the retirement you have dreamed of.

If your net worth is less than 12 times your annual income, you have a debt to your future self and need to keep the focus on building assets. For the fortunate few, if your net worth grows beyond 30 times your income, or approximately equal to a Fibonacci score of 55 in the above tables, while you may choose to embrace the strategic benefits of debt, you generally do not need debt.

Please visit the website valueofdebt.com to learn more about how the L.I.F.E. phases are inspired by and tie to the Fibonacci sequence.[3]

Endnotes

1. The case studies presented are for educational and illustrative purposes only and cannot guarantee that the reader will achieve similar results. Your results may vary significantly and factors such as the market, personal effort, and many others will cause results to vary. All of the case studies throughout the book are hypothetical and not intended to demonstrate the performance of any specific security, product, or investment strategy. Opinions formulated by the author are intended to stimulate discussion.
2. https://www.federalreserve.gov/econresdata/2014-report-economic-well-being-us-households-201505.pdf and as cited by Darla Mercado's August 31, 2016, CNBC article, "Americans' Top Financial Priority Isn't Investing."
3. Author's note: The information in this chapter is to be considered in a holistic way as a part of the book and not to be considered on a stand-alone basis. This includes, but is not limited to, the discussion of the risks of each of these ideas as well as all of the disclaimers throughout the book. The material is presented with a goal of encouraging thoughtful conversation and rigorous debate on the risks and potential benefits of the concepts between you and your advisors based on your unique situation, risk tolerance, and goals.

Appendix B

Understanding the Power of Securities-Based Lending

S ecurities-based loan (SBL) facilities allow you to borrow against liquid investable assets to finance almost anything except the purchase of additional securities. They offer many advantages and better terms: rates under prime, no amortization, no required monthly payments, no cost to establish or maintain, and limited underwriting. If you have $300,000 of qualifying investable assets, you could put an SBL in place with a maximum loan of $150,000—though you should never draw more than 50 percent of your available line, or $75,000 in this example.

How does this work? Suppose you just got a bonus and need a new car. You have your eye on a $40,000 car. Your first impulse—like most people's—is to get a 4-percent loan with a four-year amortization schedule, resulting in a monthly payment of about $900 per month. Those terms stink.

Instead, you could put the $40,000 on your SBL at a cost of about 4 percent. You would pay about $1,600 a year, or $133 a month, in interest ($40,000 × 4% = $1,600/12 = $133 per month), as opposed to roughly $900 a month.

Is this an apples-to-apples comparison? Not exactly, because the amortized loan includes a principal payment. But you can never underestimate the financial flexibility that a lower monthly payment provides. You can pay down principal whenever you want. The key is that you—not the bank—are in control of the payment schedule. You're not tying up capital in a depreciating asset.

In fact, as long as your line is in good standing, you don't even have to make a payment. You can let the interest capitalize, which is where it is added to the loan. While this might not be a good long-term strategy, it can provide a tremendous amount of flexibility during a tumultuous time, such as a job loss or emergency.

Case Study

The power of a securities-based line of credit starts to come into your life during Phase 3: Equilibrium. Let's look at Brandon and Teresa at the end of this phase. When their after-tax investment portfolio is at $280,000, they would have access to a line of credit for about $140,000. I recommend that they never use more than $70,000 of that line. Often times, these lines have a minimum of $75,000 and therefore require that you have at least $150,000 in liquid, after-tax assets to set one up. So at some point as they follow the beacons and focus on building up assets more than paying down debt, they will gain access to this tool. People who don't ever build up liquid assets lose the potential power of these borrowing strategies and get stuck in inflexible debt.

Table B.1 shows Brandon and Teresa at a hypothetical midpoint of the Freedom phase. They have built up savings and are building up their taxable and tax-deferred retirement savings accounts.

Since they have accumulated $200,000, Brandon and Teresa could set up a line of credit for $100,000 (50% of $200,000). I recommend that they borrow less than $50,000. Let's assume that they

Table B.1 Brandon and Teresa Midpoint of Equilibrium

Goal/Bucket	Formula	A Balanced Path	Where You Are	Gap
No oppressive debt (No debt at a rate over 10 percent)	0	$ 0	$ 0	$ 0
Approximate cash reserve (checking + savings)	Monthly income × 7	$ 35,000	$ 35,000	$ 0
Approximate other (jewelry, cars, furniture)	Monthly income × 7	$ 35,000	$ 35,000	$ 0
Approximate mortgage	Monthly income × 35	$(175,000)	$(195,000)	$(20,000)
Approximate long-term investments (after tax)	Monthly income × 56	$ 280,000	$ 200,000	−$ 80,000
Approximate retirement savings	Monthly income × 91	$ 455,000	$ 300,000	−$155,000
Approximate total investment assets	Monthly income × 147	$ 735,000	$ 500,000	−$235,000

want to buy a $40,000 car and that their borrowing cost is 4 percent. Table B.2 compares Brandon and Teresa to Amy and Bill who decide that they want a traditional car loan, also at 4 percent, amortizing over four years. Let's assume the following:

- Portfolio return: inflation + 4 percent
- Inflation: 3 percent
- Time horizon: 7 years
- Value of car at end of 10 years: $10,000
- Savings rate: $9,000 ($6,000 to retirement accounts)
- Cash flow available for car payment: $300 per month

Individual specific assumptions:

- Cost of securities-based line of credit: 4 percent
- Amount of principal paid down on car loan: $0
- Cost of car loan: 4 percent
- Amortization period of car loan: 4 years

158

Table B.2   Brandon and Teresa vs. Amy and Bill—7 Years after Midpoint of Equilibrium

Goal/Bucket	Beginning Balance	Brandon & Teresa Ending Balance after 7 Years	Amy & Bill Ending Balance after 7 Years
No oppressive debt (No debt at a rate over 10 percent)	$ 0	$ 0	$ 0
Approximate cash reserve (checking + savings)	$ 35,000	$ 35,000	$ 35,000
Approximate other (jewelry, cars, furniture)	$ 35,000	$ 35,000	$ 35,000
Car loan	($ 40,000)	($ 40,000)	$ 0
Value of car	$ 40,000	$ 10,000	$ 10,000
Approximate mortgage	($195,000)	($195,000)	($195,000)
Approximate long-term investments (after tax)	$200,000	$364,426[1]	$323,562[2]
Approximate retirement savings	$300,000	$533,659[3]	$533,659[4]
Approximate total investment assets	$500,000	$898,085	$857,221
Investment assets + Car − Car loan		$868,085	$867,085

Notes:

[1]$200,000 at 7 percent (3 percent inflation + 4% return = 7%) for 7 years grows to $321,156.30. They have $3,000 of after tax savings. They have a "car budget" of $300 per month, or $3,600 per year. Their interest expense on the car is $40,000 × 4% = $1,600 so they have excess cash flow of $2,000. The Value of Debt is about better ways to pay for things you can afford, not ways to buy things you can't afford. Therefore, they choose to save the additional money, meaning that they save $5,000 per year. $5,000 per year at 7 percent for 7 years is $43,270.11. Therefore, their total portfolio is $321,156.30 + $43,270.11 = $364,426.41

[2]$200,000 at 7 percent (3 percent inflation + 4% return = 7%) for 7 years grows to $321,156.30. They have $3,000 of after-tax savings. They have a "car budget" of $300 per month, or $3,600 per year. Their car payment on $40,000 at 4% for 4 years is = $903.16. The car budget of $3,600 + the $3,000 of cash for excess savings = $6,600. Since $903.16 × 12 is $10,837.92, they have a negative savings of $4,237.92 per year for the first four years. This "negative savings" is going toward paying down the car so they likely feel that they are "doing the right thing" by paying down debt. The "negative savings" reduces the value of their portfolio by $18,812.53. At the end of four years, they again begin saving $3,000 per year, plus they freed up the cash from the car budget of $300 per month ($3,600 per year) so they save a total of $6,600 for the final three years. This grows to a total of $21,218.34. Therefore, their total portfolio is $321,156.30 − $18,812.53 + $21,218.34 = $323,562.11

[3]$6,000 per year at 7 percent for 7 years grows to $51,924.13. $300,000 existing assets at 7 percent for 7 years grows to 481,734.44. The total is $51,924.13 + 481,734.44 = $533,658.57.

[4]Same formula as footnote 3.

Notice, I held all of the assumptions the exact same in both scenarios. This is why you would expect the final answer to be very similar. And that is my point: You don't have to pay down your debt to increase your net worth. You can increase your net worth by building up assets. Brandon and Teresa enjoyed more flexibility, more liquidity, and more freedom—and have a little more money in their pocket. Due to their savings and some investment gains, their net worth was rising considerably during the seven-year period: an increase of $368,000—even though they didn't pay down a dime on their car or their house. This is the power of debt.[1]

The Power of Securities-Based Lending

If you live in the United States, you've been programmed to want to buy things since you could understand language (and possibly before). There's nothing wrong with that, as long as you're fully aware that "things" will never make you happy if you're not happy already. *As long as you're not living beyond your means*, you have a right to acquire some of the better things in life—and believe it or not, careful and responsible use of debt may help you do that. Once you understand how debt works—and how to work it—you can begin to make use of working and enriching debt to finance cars, homes, raw land, horses, boats, or whatever luxury items you desire. SBLs are not just about rate, they are about flexibility. A few quick examples:

- $300,000 boat × 4% = $12,000 per year in interest expense, $1,000 per month
- $200,000 lot to build a house × 4% = $8,000 per year in interest expense, $667 per month
- $50,000 advanced degree × 4% = $2,000 per year in interest expense, $167 per month
- $40,000 car × 4% = $1,600 per year in interest expense, $133 per month
- $20,000 new home furnishings and moving costs × 4% = $800 per year in interest expense, $67 per month
- $10,000 jewelry × 4% = $400 per year in interest expense, $33 per month

> It is essential to always remember: Using a securities-based line of credit never should be about buying things you can't afford. It is about better ways to pay for things you already can afford.

The prize on the other side of Equilibrium is tremendous. Brandon and Teresa will have tremendous financial flexibility. They could sell down $40,000 from their portfolio and pay off their car loan. They would still have an investment portfolio of $324,000, which would be eligible for a $160,000 line of credit. They could, for example, buy a $50,000 car (which, with the $10,000 trade-in would cost $40,000) and do a combination of new furnishings, jewelry, etc. They can now afford these luxuries. They have saved, and now they should enjoy—but of course, within guidelines and limits.

Before embracing securities-based lending, it is important to start with some important principles:

1. The value of an item is 100 percent independent of the financing for that item.

    The value of an item remains the same whether you pay cash, take out an amortized loan, or finance it through an SBL. The value you receive upon selling the asset has nothing to do with whether you have a loan against it. Your house—or a vacation home, a Renaissance painting, a rare coin collection—will either appreciate in value or depreciate in value, regardless of how it's financed. This important root principle allows you to think more holistically and creatively about financing opportunities.

2. Amortization stinks!

    Amortization requires the borrower to repay parts of the loan over time. What's wrong with this? An inflexible minimum monthly payment (including both interest and principal reduction) that you have to make no matter what else is going on in your life decreases liquidity just when you need it most. You're locked in until that loan is paid off. Your capital is tied up in fixed assets, and you can't put that money into savings and investments. Avoid these loans whenever possible.

WOULD APPLE AGREE TO AMORTIZATION?

When you buy a corporate bond from Apple, you will never receive monthly interest payments that include a locked-in portion of the principal. No CFO would agree to that. One hundred percent of corporate debt in America is issued on an interest-only basis, with the principal due at the bond's ultimate call date or maturity. If you purchase a bond from Apple, you receive an interest payment every six months. You receive principal repayment when the bond matures.

3. Mortgages trump SBLs all day long.

I refer to securities-based lending often because I believe it's a fantastic tool for people who have the assets and can use the facility responsibly. I talk about it a lot during trainings with financial advisors across the country, and I've become known as the "SBL Guy." That's funny because, all things being equal, I'd always rather see my clients take out debt against their homes than against their portfolios.

A mortgage is considered *permanent debt* because you're locked in as soon as the bank wires the money. You own the house, and you'll lose it only if you stop making payments. Even if the home's value falls below the amount of the loan—which is what happened to a lot of homeowners during the housing crisis of 2008—you will not lose your home unless you stop making payments.

When you borrow against a portfolio, banks typically require you to maintain a certain percentage of collateral above the amount you've pledged to the line of credit. If you draw a high amount and the market falls, the bank can require you to pay down the loan with outside assets or it can legally sell off your securities—in a down market—to make up the difference. No one wants that.

When I was a financial advisor, I would almost always recommend that clients finance their homes through mortgages—which also have tax advantages—and use SBLs for bridge financing; buying cars, boats, and other luxuries; or emergencies.

First Bank of Mom and Dad

While you may not currently have assets that qualify for a line of credit, if your parents have an investment portfolio and are willing to help you out, there is a way to lessen your debt burden with lower interest and more flexible terms, freeing you from required monthly amortized payments. Using an SBL, your parents can borrow against their portfolio to pay off your credit card debt or student loans while continuing to invest their own assets.

Though you and your parents may choose to work out a monthly payment plan, you have the option of paying small amounts or interest only on an SBL—or nothing at all—without racking up penalties and fees while you're getting on your feet. Instead of juggling several different lenders with differing terms and interest rates, you'll be able to track just one loan with flexible terms. And you can always increase the payments or even pay off the entire loan once you find your dream job.

How does this work? Let's say you had a tough time finding a job and racked up $25,000 on your credit card at 20 percent interest (unfortunately, this is all too easy to do). At this rate, you're looking at paying $5,000 a year in interest, or over $400 per month in interest alone, on the card if you don't pay it off. If your parents have a $250,000 investment portfolio eligible for a line of credit against it, they can use the SBL facility to pay off your credit card at closer to 4 percent interest. Instead of owing $5,000 in interest a year, you owe $1,000 per year, or $83.33 a month ($25,000 × .04 = $1,000/12 = $83.33). Right off the bat, you're saving about $4,000 a year. And because the loan is not amortized, you can skip a few payments while you get settled into your new career—without penalty.

WHY CHOOSE AN SBL?

1. Interest rates on SBLs are typically a combination of a standard index such as LIBOR plus a spread, which is generally lower than a Parent PLUS or private student loan.
2. The only fee associated with an SBL is simple interest, calculated as the interest rate times the dollar amount drawn.

3. SBLs generally have no prepayment penalties, credit, or application fees and no intensive underwriting process or costs.
4. The existence, status, and draw amount of an SBL is generally not reported to the credit bureaus.
5. SBLs don't require monthly payments. You can allow interest to accrue or pay down only interest, providing valuable flexibility.

You can use securities-based lending to finance virtually anything and everything except the purchase of more securities. Typically, there is no cost to set them up, no ongoing fee, and no downside to having one in place. But make no mistake, these lines are not for everyone. You must be adequately invested in a portfolio that's strategically balanced across asset classes and countries before you borrow against it. And you must thoroughly understand the potential risk. Have sufficient cash to cover the loan in an emergency and never borrow more than 25 percent of your portfolio's value.[2]

Endnotes

1. The case studies presented are for educational and illustrative purposes only and cannot guarantee that the reader will achieve similar results. Your results may vary significantly, and factors such as the market, personal effort, and many others will cause results to vary. All of the case studies throughout the book are hypothetical and not intended to demonstrate the performance of any specific security, product, or investment strategy. Opinions formulated by the author are intended to stimulate discussion.
2. Author's note: The information in this chapter is to be considered in a holistic way as a part of the book and not to be considered on a stand-alone basis. This includes, but is not limited to, the discussion of the risks of each of these ideas as well as all of the disclaimers throughout the book. The material is presented with a goal of encouraging thoughtful conversation and rigorous debate on the risks and potential benefits of the concepts between you and your advisors based on your unique situation, risk tolerance, and goals.

Appendix C

Home Purchase and Financing Considerations

Hopefully, I made it clear throughout the book that it is my opinion that too many people are too focused on home ownership too early in their life. Home ownership is a big topic during our 30s, 40s, and 50s—and it is an important topic. I am neither for or against renting, buying, fixed rates, floating rates, long amortization schedules, and short amortization schedules. Like many things in life, (1) the answer depends on your specific situation; and (2) so often I see people doing the opposite of what might be optimal. The following should be considered to be my personal opinions that are designed to help the debate around your kitchen table.

Before we dive in, if you are interested in this topic I would encourage you to turn to the Resource Guide, where I provide a list of videos with education and calculators on the following topics:

- Renting vs. Buying
- How Much Home You Can Afford

- Introduction to Mortgages
- Understanding Alternative Mortgage Options
- Adjustable Rate Mortgages
- Fixed vs. Adjustable Rate Mortgages

Being familiar with these resources will help your understanding of my perspective.

Don't Rush to Buy a House

Especially when you're young, think twice before you purchase a home. This advice isn't always popular because it goes against the American Dream. We've been taught that home ownership is the first step to financial security and stability. But owning a home comes with many hidden costs, and unless you stay in a home for at least three years—ideally, five to seven years or more—the math on this investment doesn't pencil out.

When you purchase a home, you need to be prepared to cover the following expenses:

- **Depreciation/maintenance:** A house will depreciate by approximately 2 percent to 3 percent of the building's value, excluding the land, per year. If the physical building of your home is worth $500,000, it's reasonable to assume that you will spend somewhere between $10,000 and $15,000 a year just to keep the building in the same condition.

  New construction is a bit tricky. You might perceive that there aren't as many maintenance issues—which is often true—yet many times there are a lot of finishing touches that need to be done: curtains/window treatments, landscaping, decorating, electronics, paint, and so on. After the tenth year, pretty much everything that plugs in is in danger of retiring. Carpets, potentially the roof, and certainly the paint will also need replacement (not to mention, the entire decorating scheme will be outdated). After 20 years, maintenance costs may normalize in the 2 percent to 3 percent range, but that could mean $5,000 in windows one year and a $20,000 driveway the next. If you are in a condominium or association, you may see some of this deprecation expense reflected in your dues.

These all need to factor in to your budget. Importantly, while the expenses of depreciation might not be immediate, you need to be setting aside the money early: setting aside $700 per year for the roof that needs to be replaced in 20 years instead of having a $14,000 surprise bill. From my experience, new house or old house, you should anticipate 2 percent to 3 percent of the building value in expenses.

- **Property taxes:** Although they range across markets, these will generally be between 1 percent and 2 percent of the property's value, depending on where you live.
- **Closing costs and upfront transaction costs:** These range by area but are generally between 1 percent and 2 percent of the property's value, and many markets now have mansion taxes and/or mortgage taxes on mortgages over a certain size.
- **Selling costs:** When you close on a property, unless you're very lucky, it's likely that you paid the highest price for that property at that point in time. If you turned around and resold the property immediately, you would have a 5-percent to 6-percent real estate commission, and you would probably have to sell it for 2 percent to 3 percent less than you paid for it. It is possible you would take a 7 percent to 9 percent hit.

Despite all this, many people still feel like they're wasting money on rent. Like most things, this can be quantified. Adding the above expenses together, I estimate that if you are in a property for five years, you need to offset the following expenses:

Depreciation: 2 percent × 5 years = 10 percent

+ Property taxes: 1 percent × 5 years = 5 percent

+ Selling and closing costs: 10 percent (to offset the commission and value)

= Approximately 25-percent appreciation required, within five years, *just to break even.*

Generally, the longer the time period, and the more you believe in appreciation, the more the formula shifts toward buying; the shorter the time period, the more it shifts toward renting.

When Home Ownership Can Go Wrong

Imagine a couple, Patrick and Emily, who just moved into their new $500,000 home with a $400,000 mortgage. Shortly after the move, 2008 repeats. Their house falls in value by 20 percent. Patrick and Emily's house is worth $400,000, but they would likely net $380,000 after sales commissions if they sold it. Not only is their home equity wiped out, but also they would have to bring money to the closing table to get out of their home. At the same time, the market is crashing so their portfolio falls by 30 percent. Adding insult to injury, Patrick loses his job. Then to top it off, the home needs a major repair. This will undoubtedly be a stressful situation.

Too often, people are surprised when things like this happen. It should not be a surprise: When the economy turns south, which will happen, it is easy to envision an environment where housing prices are going down in value, stock market prices are going down in value, and unemployment is going up. At the same time, homes do need repairs, and oftentimes you cannot control the timing of those repairs.

Renting protects your liquidity. You don't have to tie up assets! Renting is a form of insurance. It protects you from a wide range of outcomes. It is much easier to get out of a lease than it is to get out of a house in a down market. You should always quantify the cost of renting versus buying to determine how much this insurance costs. In markets where renting is less expensive than buying, this insurance is free! In other markets, renting is much more expensive than buying, but the cost of your insurance is dependent on the price of the property you buy.

Let's say that Patrick and Emily could have rented their house for $2,500 per month. They certainly would have felt like they were "wasting" $2,500 per month—but would they be? At 5-percent interest for the full purchase price of $500,000, Patrick and Emily's annual interest expense would be $25,000. In addition, the property taxes might be around $7,000 and the property likely has about $4,000 per year of maintenance expenses. The total expenses of owning the property are about $36,000 per year, or $3,000 per month. Granted, they could be missing out on some tax benefits and some potential appreciation, but they would have a lot more flexibility with a rental. In many cases, the tax benefits might not be as great as you think and while properties can go up in value, they also can go down in value.[1]

DO THE MATH

From my experience, many people tend to overestimate or under-estimate the tax benefits from home ownership. Stop Guessing With Your Money™! I recommend that you use an online estimator, like one from Turbo Tax, or work with your tax and financial advisors and see how much benefit you do or do not receive from deductions associated with home ownership.[2]

Save Yourself the Anguish

Home ownership brings many risks, from price variations to natural disasters, and requires upfront transaction costs as well as cash for major repairs and maintenance. During the critical early years of your financial life, you're better off building up cash reserves and your investment portfolio. With those in place, you'll have many more options and a lot more flexibility when the time is right to invest in a home.

GUIDELINES FOR RENTING VS. BUYING

Age: Most young professionals move frequently before they are 35 years old. If you are under 35, you should have a heavy bias toward renting. Use this time to build up assets, liquidity, and flexibility!

Time: If you think that you will be in a property for less than three years, consider renting. If you think you will be in a property for more than seven years, consider buying. If you're somewhere in the middle, it depends.

Resources: If you have enough liquid assets to withstand a 20-percent correction in the price, a 5-percent commission, and a 2-percent home repair project should you want or need to move, then you are in a good position to buy. If you do not have this level of resources, consider renting.

Markets: Real estate prices go up and down. They do not just go up. If prices are at significant discounts to where they have traded recently, buying might make more sense. If they are trading at or near all-time highs, tread cautiously!

Be Careful!

Most people don't buy a house for a price but instead buy a monthly payment. This has significant implications on the value of the underlying asset. If you can afford a $1.2 million house with a loan at 5 percent, what happens if interest rates rise to, say, 8 percent? All things equal you could afford to buy a home worth about $750,000. This is a stunning change in value.[3]

You likely believe that, given enough time, housing prices go up. Most people do because of our tendency to extrapolate recent trends into the future. I worry most people oversimplify. We need to look at what happened with growth in the 1960s, inflation in the 1970s, and declining interest rates from 1980 through 2015. Housing prices did well in each environment. People look at this data and conclude that houses must be a good investment, but I'm not certain this is the case.

While it is possible that housing prices could grow with inflation, it is, of course, possible that they could grow by less than inflation or even go down—potentially a lot—in value. This is especially risky if interest rates are starting at generational lows. In Japan, even with interest rates at generational lows, house prices today are *approximately where they were in 1985*.[4] This type of data should influence rent-versus-buy decisions.

All Mortgages Are Not Created Equal

Most Americans first encounter working debt through mortgages. And even though they'll live in their primary homes for a median duration of only 5.9 years, they'll pay to lock in interest rates on those mortgages for 30 years. This is silly.[5] Yes, they have the security of knowing they've locked in rates for decades, but they're paying to ensure that their interest rates don't change for a good 20 years longer than they're likely to keep the home. Why would anyone pay to lock in a 4 percent rate for 30 years when they're likely to sell the home and pay off the mortgage in less than 10?

Unless you know that you're going to hang onto a home forever, a five- or seven-year interest-only adjustable-rate mortgage could make a lot more sense. On a $1 million home, you could pay as much as $10,000 less per year in interest than you would with a 30-year fixed-rate product. That extra money can be invested so that it's working for you but available should you need liquidity. (Note that taking on interest-only payments because it's the only way to buy a house you can't afford is highly likely to land you in financial distress.)

Before you even begin talking to a real estate agent, make sure you understand all your options.

One-Month LIBOR Interest-Only Floating Rate ARM

Interest rates for this product are adjusted monthly based on a rate such as LIBOR, one of the most common benchmark interest rate indexes used to make adjustments to adjustable-rate mortgages. Most of these products are LIBOR plus 2 percent, which in today's environment is roughly 2.5 percent. So if you borrow $1,000,000, your fully tax-deductible interest payments would be a little more than $2,000 per month—and that payment is reduced every time you pay down principal.

Most floating-rate products are capped at 10 to 12 percent, so your rates can't skyrocket to 20 percent—which is good—but they *could* spike to, say, 6 percent in a couple of years, and they could go as high as the interest rate cap. It's important to self-insure when using this option. If you use one of these products, I recommend that you live your life as if you needed to make a payment equal to a 30-year fixed amortizing loan and put the additional money into your portfolio—where you might be able to capture the spread and make more money on it. That way you not only are used to making the higher payments, but also have a reserve to pay down the mortgage if you run into a high-rate situation.

5-, 7-, 10-Year Interest-Only ARM

The benefit to adjustable-rate mortgages is that you can lock in an interest rate for a set amount of time. When you take on a 5/1 interest-only loan, generally you lock in a rate somewhere between a one-month LIBOR and a 30-year fixed-rate mortgage (assuming a "normal" yield curve). The low interest rate is locked for five years, and then—depending on the details of your loan—it becomes an amortizing loan.

The beauty of this is that during the first 5, 7, or 10 years of the loan, you have the option to pay only the interest every month or also pay down principal, which puts you in the driver's seat. If you think you'll be in a home for 7 years or less, this is an excellent option—but you should self-insure by putting the amount you would pay on the principal into your portfolio, where it can be making money for you but is available if for any reason you choose to pay off the debt.

15- and 30-Year Fixed Rate

I rarely believe in 15-year fixed-rate mortgages. I think they're a trap. Many people are lured in by rates as low as 2.5 percent for this product, but guess what? They owe thousands of dollars in mandatory payments every month—no matter what happens. CFOs would never sign up for that. When you're young and accumulating wealth, it makes more sense to take on an interest-only or even a 30-year fixed-rate mortgage and invest the savings so that they can compound during your "go" years. If your savings rate is over 20 percent, then I do think that a 15-year mortgage can be a very powerful piece of your financial picture—assuming you can make the mortgage payments and keep saving at the 20-percent rate. If your savings rate is below 20 percent then I cannot get the math to come out in any way that shows that you can afford to be in a 15-year fixed mortgage.

A 30-year fixed-rate mortgage is a different animal. If you believe you will live in the house you're buying for a long, long time and are worried about rising interest rates, this is a good option. The risk, of course, is that you're paying a lot of money to "insure" an interest rate for 30 years. If you stay in the home for less than seven years, it might not be worth it. However, with interest rates at generational lows, the incremental cost of the insurance is relatively low, and this could turn out to be a great time to have locked in low-cost debt. See the Resource Guide for more information about interest rates and inflation.

First Bank of Mom and Dad—Part 2

I shared ideas about the First Bank of Mom and Dad in Appendix B. If your parents have a sizable investment portfolio and are willing to help you get into a house, they could consider using their securities-based line of credit to help you. Let's say you have a decent income, but you live in Chicago, where rent for a two-bedroom apartment with parking is $4,000 a month. That rent isn't tax deductible, and due to high income you could potentially benefit from deductions. How will you ever get ahead when you're paying $48,000 a year just in rent? If you're in the 25-percent tax bracket, you have to generate $64,000 a year in income just to pay the rent. That's ridiculous. How the heck can you save for a down payment while you're paying $4,000 a month in rent?

Assuming you need to come up with a down payment of 20 percent, or $100,000, you can ask your parents to pledge $300,000 in taxable securities from their portfolio and take out a securities-based loan using the securities as collateral. Your parents' money remains invested—though not accessible—and you can pay only the interest on the loan until you've saved up enough to pay it off. Your parents are on the hook for the pledge, but they're not taking on the full responsibility of cosigning a loan.

You could buy a $500,000 apartment, put down $100,000, and put $400,000 on a mortgage. Your monthly payment might be $3,000 (including taxes and homeowners association fees), but you might receive about $1,000 of tax benefits, for a net cost of about $2,000 a month.[6]

First-Time Home Buyers, Low- and No-Down-Payment Mortgage Options

There are numerous programs that enable low- and no-down-payment options. Some of these are offered by the United States Department of Veterans Affairs, the United States Department of Agriculture, and the FHA (Federal Housing Administration). Other programs are available through Private Mortgage Insurance, also known as PMI. Further, some online entrants into lending are offering lower down payment options without PMI for borrowers that fit certain criteria. It is outside of the scope of this book to discuss the eligibility, pros, and cons of each program. However, if you are set on purchasing a home these alternatives are well worth researching or visiting with a professional for their advice.

With respect to the L.I.F.E. path and how these solutions relate to the concepts in this book, if you follow the glide path outlined in the book, these can be wonderful solutions *if*:

1. You have cleared the Launch phase.
2. You have completed or have almost completed the Independence phase.
3. You expect the following to be true:
   a. You will be in the property for more than five years.
   b. Property values are low and are more likely to appreciate than depreciate over the next five years.

BUY LOW, SELL HIGH

My personal experience is that if I have paid a record-high price for a property (like I did in 2006), I have not had much, if any, appreciation. If I paid a relatively low price (like I did in 2009), I have had a better chance at appreciation.

Many real estate prices are back to near record highs, with generational low interest rates. All things equal, it is my belief that if you pay a record-high price for a property, there is a lower chance of significant appreciation over the next five years.

Look back at Brandon and Teresa. If they could buy their home with $25,000 down at the same mortgage interest rate, then it could be wonderful for them. They would have more money invested for a longer period of time and they would have more liquidity and more flexibility. If you are in this camp and can check off on the three points just listed, I strongly recommend that you learn more about the power of low-down-payment mortgage options.

Owning Can Be Great

All of this material can make it sound like I'm against home ownership, which is not at all the case. The examples of homeownership being a disaster in my personal life and during the crisis are vast—but I do think it is important to share three short examples of ownership success.

A dear friend bought a home in a Midwest town 15 years ago—when she was about 27 years old—for about $150,000. She is handy and has done some nice improvements. The home is likely worth about $240,000, and her mortgage is down to $75,000. She refinanced her mortgage onto a 15-year fixed at 2.5 percent. Her mortgage payment is $500 per month and she is on track to own her home by the time she is 57, but may pay it off earlier. She also has a great pension and is a wonderful saver. She has built up a very impressive retirement savings account. She has a nice balance in her checking and savings account. I could nitpick the fact that she has limited liquid investable assets (she can't have a securities-based line of credit), and she has a 15-year amortizing loan—but that would be absurd! She can afford the 15-year amortizing loan, and she is on track. Is she doing something wrong? Heck no! She is amazing!

A couple I know was in their mid-thirties in 2011 and bought a little more house than the L.I.F.E. guidelines would suggest. They did so taking advantage of a low-down-payment mortgage. This risky combination so far has turned out to be a good decision. Due to the growing family, the larger house likely prevented a move they might have otherwise made by now. Further, their timing was great and (at least to now) the house has appreciated considerably.

A third friend—a dual-income couple—moved across the country for a job. They had two young children and had been renting from college through age 35. In the market they moved to, the rent-versus-buy math was very much in favor of buying. Like professional surfers, they rode the waves perfectly. The math in their former market suggested rent, which they did, and avoided the housing crisis during a time where their affairs were more fragile. The math in their new market suggested buy, which they did in the years immediately following the crisis and when they were at a more stable time in their personal life.

At the end of the day, this is the custom suit business. Combine the thoughts in this chapter, with the glide paths in the book, the market environment in your community, and the tools in the Resource Guide, and hopefully you can feel a bit more empowered with the decisions you make![7]

Endnotes

1. The case studies presented are for educational and illustrative purposes only and cannot guarantee that the reader will achieve similar results. Your results may vary significantly and factors such as the market, personal effort, and many others will cause results to vary. All of the case studies throughout the book are hypothetical and not intended to demonstrate the performance of any specific security, product, or investment strategy. Opinions formulated by the author are intended to stimulate discussion.

2. Tax laws are complex and subject to change. Tax information contained in this presentation is general and not exhaustive by nature. It is not intended or written to be used, and cannot be used, by any taxpayer for the purpose of avoiding U.S. federal tax laws. This material was not intended or written to be used for the purpose of avoiding tax penalties that may be imposed on the taxpayer. Individuals are encouraged to consult their tax and legal advisors (a) before establishing a retirement plan or account, and (b) regarding any potential tax, ERISA, and related consequences of any investments made under such plan or account. These materials and any statements contained herein should not be construed as tax or legal advice. Tax advice must come from your tax advisor.

3. Focusing on the interest portion alone: $1.2 million × 5 percent = $60,000. $60,000 is 8% of 750,000.

4. Jun Hungo and Kosaku Narioka, "Japanese Land Prices Rise for First Time Since Global Financial Crisis," *Wall Street Journal* (March 22, 2016), http://www.wsj .com/articles/japanese-land-prices-rise-for-first-time-since-global-financial-crisis-1458645819.

5. "The Median Homeownership Duration Is Too Short to Build Real Wealth," Financial Samurai (August 13, 2012), http://www.financialsamurai.com/the-median-homeownership-duration-is-too-short-to-build-real-wealth/.

6. $400,000 mortgage at 4 percent 30-year fixed mortgage is $1,909.66. $700 per month in taxes and $400 per month in home owner's association = about $3,000 per month. Total amount of tax benefits will depend on the amount and composition of their income.
7. Author's note: The information in this chapter is to be considered in a holistic way as a part of the book and not to be considered on a stand-alone basis. This includes, but is not limited to, the discussion of the risks of each of these ideas as well as all of the disclaimers throughout the book. The material is presented with a goal of encouraging thoughtful conversation and rigorous debate on the risks and potential benefits of the concepts between you and your advisors based on your unique situation, risk tolerance, and goals.

Appendix D

The Millennial's Guide to Debt and Getting Started

Chances are you have some debt—and it might not be "good" debt. Two-thirds of all millennials have at least one outstanding source of long-term debt, generally student loans, home mortgages, and car payments, and 30 percent have more than one. Most millennials feel burdened by that debt and have trouble making payments, and more than half carried over a credit card balance in the last year.[1] With a median income of $57,000, millennials are struggling to keep up.[2]

Ongoing credit card debt is virtually always bad debt. Avoid it and pay it off as soon as possible. Already high-interest credit card debt can go even higher if you miss a payment. It has no tax advantages, limits your flexibility with monthly payments, and makes it very difficult to get a greater return on the money you borrow. You should have a few credit cards, however, because using and paying them off fully each month improves your credit score, which is important for getting mortgages,

179

business loans, and so on. For emergency and logistical purposes, you should have a large line of credit available on at least one card, but never draw more than 50 percent of your available credit because that could harm your credit score.

Many credit card companies offer low teaser rates, and they count on the fact that sooner or later you will be late or miss a payment so they can increase those rates. Some people try to play the roulette of taking on new credit card debt at very low rates and then shuffling it around with each new offer. Don't do this. Even if you don't miss a payment and you pay off the balance before the rates rise, this can wreak havoc on your credit score.

Saddled by Student Loans

Recent college graduates' struggles to pay back massive student loan debt has been in the headlines a lot lately. It's a real problem for our economy and our country, with very real consequences, including stalled lives as young borrowers struggle to pay back tens of thousands of dollars to multiple loan servicers. Seventy percent of today's college students have school debt, and the average they owe is $28,400. The total amount of U.S. student debt is $1.2 trillion.[3] Some believe this will trigger the next financial crisis, and it's certainly never good to have a big group of potential consumers enter the marketplace with unattractive debt-to-asset ratios that hold them back from buying and borrowing.

High student debt burdens affect your ability to buy a house or take on any other debt, according to the Federal Reserve Bank of New York.[4] These debts may cause you to put off settling down and buying a home. Only one-third of millennials head their own households, Pew Center for Research found, a nearly 40-year low.[5] Thirty-six percent of millennials—21.6 million young Americans—live in their parents' homes. The trend is so pervasive that GQ wrote "A Millennial's Guide to Having Sex While Living at Home."[6]

Young debtors have more depression, family dysfunction, higher suicide and divorce rates, and are less likely than nonborrowers to apply to graduate school (a move that would boost their lifetime earnings) than those without such debts. They contribute less to employer-sponsored retirement plans, losing early years of compounding and causing a lifetime wealth loss of more than four times the amount borrowed.[7]

We call student loans *working debt* because investing in a degree is well worth it—you will earn more and have an easier time finding a job than someone without a degree—but it can come with oppressive terms. Federal and private student loans are draconian to defaulters, who are handed over to private collection agencies that earn a percentage of recovered fees. After penalties and collection agency fees of up to 20 percent, a 10-year loan can nearly double in size.

The Federal Trade Commission received 181,000 complaints—more than any other industry—about abusive debt collection practices such as incessant phone calls, bullying, misrepresentation, and threats.[8] If you default, collection agencies can garnish up to 15 percent of your paycheck and seize Social Security, disability income, and federal and state income tax refunds. You could lose state-issued professional licenses or public employment. Even if you declare bankruptcy, you'll remain liable for the original principal balance, all accrued interest, court costs, and collection fees—with no statute of limitations.

If you grew up in a middle-income or upper-middle-income family, you got caught in a rough deal. A "moderate" annual college budget today is $44,000 for private colleges and $22,000 for public universities, and your family probably didn't qualify for federal aid or loans (most middle- and upper-income families don't).[9] You or your parents likely had to take out a higher-interest federal Parent PLUS loan or private amortized loans.

Loans are now the largest funding source for college education expenses and the second-largest liability on household balance sheets after mortgages—and families in higher income brackets are taking on student loans faster than any other demographic, according to a Federal Reserve report.[10] Most parents have great intentions of paying for their kids' education, but when it comes down to it, meeting skyrocketing tuition costs with stagnating wages hasn't been easy for anyone. The typical family can cover just 30 percent of college expenses, the Lawlor Group found.[11]

A lot of families turn to private student loans, with variable and fixed rates as high as 13 percent. These come from multiple vendors with a tangle of terms, conditions, and repayment schedules that many people find confusing. A Consumer Financial Protection Bureau survey about debtors' experiences with private student lenders found that borrowers had difficulty deciphering why payment amounts change, negotiating alternate payment plans, and dealing with lost payments. Unlike the federal government, most private lenders don't allow deferments or income-contingent repayment plans, and loans may go into default after one missed payment.[12] Oftentimes there's no way to strike that black mark from your record.

CAREFULLY CONSIDER DEBT CONSOLIDATION PROGRAMS

There are a variety of debt consolidation programs out there, some originating with the federal government or a state or municipal agency, and many for-profit ones that are privately owned and operated. Sometimes consolidating some or all of your existing debts can be incredibly helpful and end up saving you a lot of money. But be wary. Private agencies and programs exist to make a profit, and you can't necessarily trust that they have your best interests in mind.

Facing the possibility of student debt, credit card debt, a low savings rate, and the desire to do fun stuff, what are things that millennials can consider? The following suggestions are designed to help buck this trend.

The Best Budget: Spend Less Than You Make

Many, if not most, of the financially responsible people I know have the following in common:

1. They know how much they make. If they are on a commission or bonus system, they use a very low number for their planned monthly earnings, often directing all of their bonuses to savings.
2. They save first. Generally, they save at the higher end of my suggested ranges: between 15 and 25 percent of their income.

3. They save automatically. This happens in a few ways:

    a. Money automatically comes out of their paycheck and into their 401(k) or other employer-sponsored plan, before it even hits their checking account.

    b. That money automatically gets matched over time by their employer.

    c. They automatically move money each month out of checking and to their investment or savings accounts.

4. They do not carry balances on credit cards—ever. As a result, they wait to buy things until they have saved up for them.

5. They hold at least a three-month (and generally six-month) reserve in their checking account. They would never let it get anywhere near zero.

6. They generally do not want things and live life more simply than many of the people around them.

From here, I find two different personality traits to those that are financially on track: the bloodhound and the ostrich.

The Bloodhound Bloodhounds track every expenditure every month across every account. They bark loudly when anything is off track or they find an error. One of the greatest benefits of the bloodhound is that they are on top of things; they know what is happening in all of their accounts at all times.

One of the most formidable challenges is that while they can be great savers—and perhaps because they are great savers—often they are not great investors. You cannot, and should not, track your long-term investments the same way you track your checking account. Portfolios go up and down. Too often, bloodhounds react in the down cycle and change their philosophy. Because they track things so closely, the bloodhound can have a tendency to buy high and sell low.

The Ostrich It turns out that it isn't true that ostriches bury their head in the sand to avoid danger. The ostrich has amazing fight-or-flight capabilities. They are the fastest birds on land (and one of the faster animals overall) and they have the ability to fight—and even kill—lions.[13] The ostrich is a symbol of simplicity, to enjoy the little things and to uncomplicate our lives. While bloodhounds track everything, the ostrich wants for little, looks around at other birds flying and doesn't care. They prefer being grounded. Economically, they don't track their finances daily because they simply live within their means. Money is not the center of their life and they have little concern for it because they regularly save and regularly spend less than they make.

One of the greatest advantages is their ability to be excellent long-term investors and to shrug off short-term market movements. One of their greatest challenges is that they could tend to over-simplify complex issues that could require a little more attention.

The Millionaire Next Door

This concept of saving and spending less than you make is captured well in the book *The Millionaire Next Door: The Surprising Secrets of America's Wealthy* by Thomas Stanley. Most millionaires *do not*:

- Wear a $5,000 watch
- Drive a current model car
- Drive a foreign luxury car
- Lease their cars

They have an average income under $250,000, and only 13 percent make more than $500,000. They live in an average home of $320,000, and about half of them have occupied the same home for more than 20 years.[14]

Budgeting

Those who are financially on track spend less than they make, are not wanting for a lot, and are not wanting for more than they can afford. It is that simple. Budgeting can be powerful, but if you go through the effort to make a budget and don't adhere to it, what is the point? If you save the money off the top and don't use credit cards, then you are forced to live within what you have.

In my experience, I have not seen that budgets impact people of different income levels differently. In fact, from my experience many people with incomes between $50,000 and $150,000 save as great a percentage of their income, if not more, than people who make more than $150,000.

Aside from savings, most ways of accumulating wealth are dependent on markets and other things that are out of your control. Therefore, savings is the key driver that will put you on track for your long-term goals. If you are making above-average household earnings, it is 100 percent within your power to save 15 percent to 20 percent of your income.

"I Can't Afford It"

No one likes having to say they can't afford something. It was the hardest thing for me to say for years. The honest truth is that it's still hard for me to say. It has a stigma about it. Saying that I can't afford something must mean that I'm not successful enough to do things that I believe I should be able to do and am not good enough at providing for my family. "I can't afford it" gives me anxiety and challenges my manliness.

This is ridiculous, of course, and it's a slippery slope to financial disaster and unhappiness. If you reach for something that you can't afford and life throws you a curve ball (and trust me, life throws curve balls at all of us), you have the added stress of paying for something you truly can't afford. According to the *Huffington Post*, a *Money* magazine poll of married adults ages 25 and over with household incomes above $50,000 found that 70 percent of couples argued about money (frivolous purchases, credit card debt, insufficient emergency savings and insufficient retirement savings) more than household chores, togetherness, sex, snoring, and what's for dinner.[15]

Debt-to-Income Ratios

Throughout the book I recommend more conservative debt ratios than most banks use when determining how much you can borrow. Maxing out what banks are willing to give you is a very risky path. Throughout my life I have made probably 50 spreadsheets looking at expensive toys that I wanted to buy or investments that could "make me rich."

My results were always the same. If I had to make a spreadsheet, I couldn't afford these things. I wish I could have all that time I spent building spreadsheets back.

HOW TO GET A PERFECT CREDIT SCORE

Perfect can be a stretch, but at a minimum, *you should target a score above 800*. Some steps to accomplishing this goal:

1. Use credit, but use it responsibly.
2. Never draw more than 50 percent of your available credit.
3. Pay your bills on time and in full every month.
4. Don't have more than one or two primary cards and two or three store cards.
5. Use the same card for a long time; don't switch a lot.
6. Use a credit monitoring service.

Perhaps most importantly, drop your ego. At some point in your life you will have an annoying (doctor's, utility, cell phone, etc.) bill that you think is wrong. Pay it and then fight it. I saw somebody not pay a $50 bill "out of principle." All he did was show credit agencies that he was not willing to pay his bills rather than formally addressing them. The borrower's credit fell to below 620, and he ended up paying more than 1 percent more on a $300,000 loan, costing him well over $3,000 per year. Had he paid the $50 when it was due, he would have had 60 times the return on that investment per year!

Our culture focuses on debt-to-income ratios because they make it possible for people—especially young people—to buy things like houses and cars that they could otherwise not afford. Focusing on debt-to-asset ratios makes it very difficult to buy these things, especially when you're young. For example, if you wanted to buy a house, you would have to have saved more money than the value of the house you want to purchase. This is an unrealistic proposition for most people.

Points to consider about debt-to-income ratios:

1. The goal is not to borrow as much as the bank will let you borrow. How much the bank is willing to lend you should have nothing to do with how much you wish to borrow.
2. Do not count on raises or higher future income. When we make assumptions on future income that do not materialize, we become sad, frustrated, and mad. Those feelings manifest at work and at home.
3. If you're worried whether or not you can afford something, then you have your answer: you cannot. There are lots of things in life you can't afford. Get over it.
4. If you have to use a calculator, make a spreadsheet, or do any detailed math when looking at a purchase, you definitely can't afford it.
5. Pay cuts happen. When using income to buy things, assume a 10-percent pay cut and no raises.
6. Saving is mandatory—unless you like the idea of eating cat food when you're old or depending on the government or your kids to take care of you. Therefore, savings is not a part of income that can be used for the calculation. If you make more than $50,000, you should be able to save 20 percent of your income.

Always assume that you will be unemployed for at least three to six months at some point in your career.

If your income is commission-based, assume a 30-percent lower income. Commission is fabulous, but the most successful and happiest people I know who have had long careers in commission-based industries have lived well within their means. I think this is why they had such wonderful careers. Those who became dependent on high incomes blew themselves up.

To pull this all together, take your current income minus a 10-percent pay cut assumption, minus 20-percent savings, and that's the income you can use for debt-to-income ratios. This equals a 28-percent reduction in your income. Remember to be more conservative if you work on commission.

The Consumer Financial Protection Bureau states that debt-to-income ratio is "one way lenders measure your ability to manage the payments you make every month to repay the money you have borrowed." It is calculated by adding up monthly debt payments and dividing them by gross monthly income (before taxes and deductions). The Bureau found that mortgage loan studies suggest that borrowers with higher debt-to-income ratios run into more trouble making payments. A 43 percent debt-to-income ratio is the highest you can have to get a mortgage,[16] and Bankrate encourages people to keep it under 36 percent.[17] I recommend keeping it under 33 percent and ideally at 25 percent.

Pulling These Concepts Together

Here are ideas to pull it all together:

1. Spend less than you make.
2. Save off the top—and set a ramp to the 15 percent to 20 percent number.
3. If your net worth is less than 50 percent of your annual income, do not take on new debt, of any type.
4. Pay off your oppressive debt as quickly as possible.
5. Strive for a perfect credit score.
6. 36 percent of millennials are living at home: if you can't beat them, join them. If you save $750 a month in rent for 48 months, you just put yourself $36,000 ahead!

Combine these ideas with the material about the Launch phase in Chapter 3, and the rest of your life will be different because you will have broken the paycheck-to-paycheck cycle.[18]

Endnotes

1. Annamaria Lusardi, "The Alarming Facts About Millennials and Debt," *Wall Street Journal* (October 5, 2015), http://blogs.wsj.com/experts/2015/10/05/the-alarming-facts-about-millennials-and-debt/.
2. Megan Leonhardt, "Saving Comes Second for Many Millennials," Wealthmanagement.com (June 10, 2014), http://wealthmanagement.com/blog/saving-comes-second-many-millennials.
3. Sophia McClennen, "The Staggering Ways America Is Rigged to Traumatize and Impoverish Kids Coming Out of College," Alternet (October 8, 2015), http://www.alternet.org/news-amp-politics/staggering-ways-america-rigged-traumatize-and-impoverish-kids-coming-out-college?akid=13560.3367.PkuR0D&rd=1&src=newsletter1043763&t=2.

4. Ibid.

5. Richard Fry, "Millennials Still Lag in Forming Their Own Households," Pew Research Center (October 18, 2013), http://www.pewresearch.org/fact-tank/2013/10/18/millennials-still-lag-in-forming-their-own-households/.

6. Ramona Emerson, "A Millennial's Guide to Having Sex While Living at Home" *GQ* (September 2, 2016).

7. Robert Hiltonsmith, "At What Cost? How Student Debt Reduces Lifetime Wealth," Demos.org, http://www.demos.org/what-cost-how-student-debt-reduces-lifetime-wealth.

8. https://repository.library.northeastern.edu/files/neu:332683.

9. Jane C. Timm, "Students Seek Debt Forgiveness in Record Numbers," MSNBC (April 22, 2014), http://www.msnbc.com/morning-joe/students-seek-debt-forgiveness-costs-surge.

10. http://www.federalreserve.gov/econresdata/scf/scf_2010.htm.

11. http://www.cic.edu/Research-and-Data/Making-the-Case/Liberal-Arts/Documents/Lawlor2.pdf.

12. Deanne Loonin and Alys Cohen, *Paying the Price: The High Cost of Private Student Loans and the Dangers for Student Borrowers* (March 2008), http://www.studentloanborrowerassistance.org/wp-content/uploads/2013/05/Report_PrivateLoans.pdf.

13. "Ostrich," *National Geographic*, http://animals.nationalgeographic.com/animals/birds/ostrich/.

14. Thomas Stanley and William Danko, *The Millionaire Next Door: The Surprising Secrets of America's Wealthy (with a new preface for the 21st century)* (Lanham, MD: Taylor Trade Publishing, 1996). References from the 2010 edition.

15. Taryn Hillin, "New Survey Sheds Light on What Married Couples Fight about Most," *Huffington Post* (June 4, 2014), http://www.huffingtonpost.com/2014/06/03/marriage-finances_n_5441012.html.

16. http://www.consumerfinance.gov/askcfpb/1791/what-debt-income-ratio-why-43-debt-income-ratio-important.html.

17. http://www.bankrate.com/calculators/mortgages/ratio-debt-calculator.aspx.

18. Author's note: The information in this chapter is to be considered in a holistic way as a part of the book and not to be considered on a stand-alone basis. This includes, but is not limited to, the discussion of the risks of each of these ideas as well as all of the disclaimers throughout the book. The material is presented with a goal of encouraging thoughtful conversation and rigorous debate on the risks and potential benefits of the concepts between you and your advisors based on your unique situation, risk tolerance, and goals.

Appendix E

The Math Behind
the Examples

The L.I.F.E. glide path included case studies that helped demonstrate how you can get from one phase to the next. But does it work to guide you through the whole cycle? The math was intentionally limited in the core chapters to make the book approachable. This appendix contains more detailed math behind a number of the examples in the book and is the proof behind the process.

Let's revisit the hypothesis I outlined in Appendix A:

We can embrace a sensible, balanced approach to debt throughout our lives; an approach that is similar with the balance exhibited in nature, art, architecture, music, and even our own bodies. This balanced approach will reduce stress, increase financial security and flexibility, and increase the probability of a secure retirement. Used appropriately, strategic debt is not a waste of money, but rather, an opportunity to increase the likelihood you will be able to accomplish your goals in the short, medium, and long term.

In my experience working with clients of all ages, I discovered the zone where a strategic debt philosophy can have the greatest impact. I learned that people who save more than 25 percent of their income for more than 30 years before retirement likely don't need debt to make it. On the flip side, for people who save less than 10 percent for less than 10 years, they are likely not on track for retirement regardless of their debt strategy. If you are undersaved some strategic debt might help a little, but it isn't a magic bullet and it can't solve giant gaps in the overall plan. Chances are, you're somewhere in the middle. If that is indeed the case, it is my belief that if you are between 10 and 30 years away from retirement and target saving between 10 and 25 percent of your income, the decisions you make with respect to debt will have one of, if not *the*, biggest impact on your future net worth and your ability to comfortably retire.

So many people are dramatically undersaved, yet keep rushing to pay off their low-cost debt. These are areas where I see people focus when accumulating wealth:

1. Returns
2. Fees
3. The news
4. Asset allocation
5. Risk

Debt is nowhere to be found. If this is where you were before reading this book, you're not alone. But I hope you'll think more about a list that looks like this:

1. Asset allocation and debt

Everything flows from there. Your asset allocation and debt strategy will drive your net worth. As we discussed in Chapter 5, the effective use of asset allocation and debt can reduce your risk while maintaining your expected returns. Fees matter a little, but not as much in the big picture. And what you hear in the news should not matter at all.

I have been to hundreds of financial conferences and none of them discussed the long-term impact of the other side of the balance sheet. This makes no sense.

There is a belief that people do not like debt because, behaviorally, people cannot handle it. This is largely because debt that most people have had access to is oppressive. Behaviorally, people tend to buy high and sell low, when they should do the opposite, but we still encourage people to invest. Behaviorally, people typically don't want to eat vegetables or work out, but we encourage them to do so. I don't buy it that the issue is that Americans are so irresponsible that they can't handle debt. Even if that is sometimes the case, we owe it to ourselves to try and shift the behavior. I think you deserve the right to know what tools and resources are available to you over the course of your life: to enjoy the present, be prepared for emergencies, and be on track for a secure retirement.

Take a look at the math in this appendix and then you can decide if a debt strategy can help you better meet your financial goals.

Chapter 1: The Nadas, Steadys, and Radicals

Chapter 1 began with an example of the Nadas, the Steadys, and the Radicals. Recall that, "They live in a magical world with no taxes or inflation, interest rates never change, and investment returns are certain. This world is also magical in that banks will let people borrow however much they want for homes."

The purpose of this hypothetical world is to lay out a simple laboratory to test the hypothesis that debt adds value. The rest of the book is designed to create a more specific glide path that conforms to "the real world" of how we live and to introduce variables such as returns, interest rates, and taxes.

The following were the base assumptions for all three families:

- They each start at 35 years old.
- They start with zero assets.
- They both make $120,000 per year and never make a penny more or a penny less.
- If they invest money, they earn a rate of return of 6 percent.
- If they borrow money, they can borrow at 3 percent.
- Their house appreciates by a rate of 2 percent per year.
- They both save $15,000 per year ($1,250 per month).

- They never move.
- Home purchase: $300,000
- Initial mortgage: $300,000

A 30-year fixed mortgage at 3 percent results in a monthly payment of $1,264.81. While it isn't specifically discussed, the chapter effectively assumes that the families have the following breakdown of income:

$120,000 per year =

$10,000 per month

−$1,250 savings ($15,000 per year)

−$1,250 mortgage payment

= $7,500 for taxes, insurance, maintenance, and living expenses
    per month

It is further assumed in this that they could choose between being interest only on their mortgage and amortizing the mortgage.

The Nadas

Table E.1 illustrates the Nadas at month zero, immediately after home purchase.

The Nadas pay down their debt as quickly as they can, directing all cash and all savings toward reducing their debt.

- Present value: $300,000
- Interest / Year: 3%
- Payment: $2,500 per period = $30,000 year/12 = ($15,000 + ($1,250 x 12))

Table E.1   The Nadas, Month 0

Assets	Amount	Liabilities	Amount
Investments	$ 0		
Home	$ 300,000	Mortgage	$ 300,000
Total assets	**$300,000**	**Total liabilities**	**$300,000**
Net worth	**$ 0**		

Table E.2   The Nadas, Month 142

Assets	Amount	Liabilities	Amount
Investments	$ 0		
Home	$380,000	Mortgage	$0
Total assets	**$380,000**	**Total liabilities**	**$0**
Net worth	**$380,000**		

- Future value = $0
- Periods per year = 12
- Solving for number of months = 142.8 (rounded to 143)

The house appreciates at a rate of 2 percent per year, compounded monthly for 143 months, $380,664, which we round to $380,000. This results in the following balance sheet shown in Table E.2.[1]

After 142 months, the Nadas are debt free. From here, they direct all of their savings toward building up assets.

- Present value of savings: $0
- Interest / Year: 6%
- Payment: $2,500 per period = $30,000 year/12 = ($15,000 + ($1,250 × 12)) ($15,000 savings + former home payment)
- Periods per year: 12
- Periods: 360 − 143 = 217
- Solving for future value = $983,103

The house appreciates at a rate of 2 percent per year, compounded monthly for 217 months, which is $545,409. (I round the future value of the house to $550,000 in all of the examples.) Table E.3 illustrates their balance sheet at age 65.

Table E.3   The Nadas, Month 360 (age 65)

Assets	Amount	Liabilities	Amount
Investments	$ 980,000		
Home	$ 550,000	Mortgage	$0
Total assets	**$1,530,000**	**Total liabilities**	**$0**
Net worth	**$1,530,000**		

196   APPENDICES

Table E.4   The Steadys, Month 0

Assets	Amount	Liabilities	Amount
Investments	$ 0		
Home	$300,000	Mortgage	$300,000
Total assets	**$300,000**	**Total liabilities**	**$300,000**
Net worth	**$ 0**		

The Steadys

Table E.4 illustrates the Steadys at month zero, immediately after home purchase.

The Steadys pay down their 30-year mortgage as scheduled and save $15,000 per year every year for 30 years.

Value of investments:

- Present value: $0
- Interest / Year: 6%
- Payment: $1,250 per period ($15,000/12)
- Periods per year = 12
- Number of months = 360
- Solving for future value = $1,255,644

The house appreciates at a rate of 2 percent per year, compounded monthly for 360 months. Table E.5 shows the Steadys' balance sheet at age 65.

The Radicals

Table E.6 illustrates the Radicals at month zero, immediately after home purchase.

Table E.5   The Steadys, Month 360 (age 65)

Assets	Amount	Liabilities	Amount
Investments	$1,260,000		
Home	$ 550,000	Mortgage	$0
Total assets	**$1,810,000**	**Total liabilities**	**$0**
Net worth	**$1,810,000**		

Table E.6 The Radicals, Month 0

Assets	Amount	Liabilities	Amount
Investments	$ 0		
Home	$300,000	Mortgage	$300,000
Total assets	**$300,000**	**Total liabilities**	**$300,000**
Net worth	**$ 0**		

The Radicals pay down zero on their mortgage for 30 years. Value of investments:

- Present value: $0
- Interest / Year: 6%
- Payment: $1,750 per period = ($15,000/12 annual savings) + (House payment budget of $1,250/month × 12 = $15,000 less interest expense of $300,000 mortgage × 3% interest ($9,000) = $6,000 excess cash per year/12 = $500 per month).
- Periods per year = 12
- Number of months = 360
- Solving for future value = $1,757,901

The house appreciates at a rate of 2 percent per year, compounded monthly for 360 months. Table E.7 shows the Radicals' balance sheet at age 65.

Aside from having more money by the age of 65, the Radicals had more liquidity each month for 30 years. Rainy days will happen. The Radicals have flexibility and survivability. They have $7,750 each month, which they can use to handle a curve ball the moment it's thrown at them.

Table E.7 The Radicals, Month 360 (age 65)

Assets	Amount	Liabilities	Amount
Investments	$1,760,000		
Home	$ 550,000	Mortgage	$300,000
Total assets	**$2,310,000**	**Total liabilities**	**$300,000**
Net worth	**$2,010,000**		

The Nadas, Steadys, and Radicals in Retirement

The Chapter 1 conclusion stated, "If the Nadas don't change their spending habits, they are on track to run out of money in 18 years."

- Present value of savings: $983,103
- Interest / Year: 6%
- Payment: $7,500 per period
- Future value = $0
- Periods per year: 12
- Solving for periods: 213 months = 17.75 years, which the chapter rounds to 18 years.

Granted, the Nadas will have a considerable amount of home equity and could consider selling their home or a reverse mortgage.

The chapter also said, "If the Steadys don't change their spending habits, they are on track to run out of money in 30 years."

- Present value of savings: $1,255,644
- Interest / Year: 6%
- Payment: $7,500 per period
- Future value = $0
- Periods per year: 12
- Solving for periods: 363.8 months = 30.3 years, which the chapter rounds to 30 years.

Here again, the Steadys, like the Nadas, will have a considerable amount of home equity and could consider selling their home or a reverse mortgage.

Finally, the chapter said that the Radicals would have $8,750 per month in income in retirement. The actual answer is $8,789.

If the Radicals keep $1,757,901 invested at the same 6-percent return they would have monthly income of $8,789 ($1,757,901 × 6% = $105,474/12 = $8,789 per month).

They would still have to make the $750 interest payment on their mortgage ($300,000 × 3% = 9,000/12 = $750 per month). This would leave them with $8,039 per month in income, after mortgage expense.

Table E.8   The Radicals, Age 105

Assets	Amount	Liabilities	Amount
Investments	$4,330,000		
Home	$1,220,000	Mortgage	$300,000
Total assets	**$5,550,000**	**Total liabilities**	**$300,000**
Net worth	**$5,250,000**		

From the chapter, "This is more than the $7,500 they were spending when they were working." Remember from the assumptions, the Radicals' income was $120,000 / 12 = $10,000 per month. They were saving $15,000 per year ($1,250 per month) and making a mortgage payment of $1,250 per month. But remember that they had the option to be amortizing or interest only. All three families were living on $7,500 per month; their target living expense budget, net of mortgage, was $7,500. Therefore, *the Radicals' monthly income increases during retirement.*

Finally, the chapter states, "If the Radicals don't change their spending habits they are on track to have about $4.3 million when they are 105 years old." If we assume that "don't change their spending habits" means that they continue spending $7,500 per month, then we get:

- Present value of savings: $1,757,901
- Interest / Year: 6%
- Payment: $7,500 per period
- Periods per year: 12
- Periods: 480 months = 40 years
- Solving for future value = $4,325,938

The Radicals will never *need* to sell their home, though they could sell or do a reverse mortgage. But why would they? Table E.8 illustrates the Radicals at age 105.

Chapters 3 and 4: Brandon and Teresa

Remember that Brandon and Teresa are the average Americans. They have $60,000 of income, want to buy an average house, want to retire, and they want to make conservative assumptions all along the way.

The goal of this section is to show how the glide path works from beginning to end using the average household earnings, average rental rates, average home prices, the current tax code and current Social Security system, and current interest rate environment.

Assumptions:

- Income: $60,000, never changes
- The $60,000 earnings could be from two people earning $30,000 each, one earning $20,000 and one earning $40,000 or one person earning $60,000.
- Savings: 15%, which also never changes ($9,000 per year)
- Starting age: 25
- Employer match: 3% ($1,800 per year)
- No child savings expenses (that savings would be additional, as discussed in the book)
- No oppressive debt—If they have it then they would follow the guidelines to pay it off, which would simply extend the time period by the amount of time it takes them to repay the debt.
- No student debt—Here again, if they have it then they would follow the guidelines, and it would simply extend the time period by the amount of time it takes them to repay the debt.
- No inflation, but also no raises. If their raises are exactly equal to inflation, then we can remove the complexity of inflation from the equation.
- Investment rate of return of inflation plus 4 percent (Chapter 5)
  - I will simplify this to a 4-percent real return.

  - For the Nadas/Steadys/Radicals I assume a real return of 6 percent. In this example, I am assuming a real return of 4 percent, which is materially more conservative.

  - See Chapter 5 and the Resource Guide for more information on real returns and historic probabilities.
- Rental cost: $1,250[2]
- Home cost of $240,000 (from the book and approximately equal to average home cost)

Table E.9 Phase 1, Launch—Brandon and Teresa Starting at Zero, Age 25

Step/Goal/Bucket	Formula	A Balanced Path	Brandon & Teresa	Gap
No oppressive debt (No debt at a rate over 10 percent)	0	$ 0	$0	$ 0
Cash reserve, build to a one-month reserve (checking account)	Monthly income × 1	$ 5,000	$0	–$ 5,000
Start a retirement plan. Build to a balance of one month's income	Monthly income × 1	$ 5,000	$0	–$ 5,000
Continue building cash savings until you have an additional two months' reserve (savings account)	Monthly income × 2	$10,000	$0	–$10,000

Table E.9 illustrates the objectives of the Launch phase. Brandon and Teresa make $60,000 or $5,000 per month.

During this time their expenses look like this:

$5,000 per month of income

–$1,250 per month for rent

–$750 per month savings ($200 per month to retirement and $550 per month to checking/savings)

–$536 federal taxes

–$310 FICA

–$73 Medicare

= $2,081 after taxes to cover the rest of their expenses.[3]

Keep in mind that they are renting so they don't have any property taxes, homeowner's association expenses, or surprise maintenance expenses. The $2,081 is their budget for food, health care, clothing, travel, and transportation.

TurboTax shows that their taxes due are likely to be $4,631. If their withholding is $535.83 × 12 = $6,429.96, then they are likely on track for a $1,799 refund.[4] We won't factor this refund into our math and will assume they use it for some fun, furniture, travel, and so on.

Table E.10 illustrates where they are in three years.

Retirement is calculated: $200 per month for three years at 4 percent = $7,636 plus three employer matches for $1,800 ($1,800 × 3 years at 4% growth = $5,617) = $13,253. The total taxable savings is $550 per month for 36 months, which is $19,800. $5,000 of this is allocated to checking and the balance, $15,000 to building additional savings. From here they solidly enter the next phase: Independence. Table E.11 illustrates exiting Launch and entering Independence.

The total of the goals is 21 months' worth of income. Currently, they have saved a little over 6 months' worth of income so they have a savings gap of 15 months. Table E.12 let's us check in with where they are in 7 years on the same path.

Retirement after seven years is calculated: $200 per month for seven years at 4 percent = $16,244 plus seven employer matches for $1,800 (compounded at the same rate, annually) = $14,216. Plus, they have the

Table E.10   Phase 1, Launch—Brandon and Teresa, Three Years Later

Step/Goal/Bucket	Formula	A Balanced Path	Brandon & Teresa	Gap
No oppressive debt (No debt at a rate over 10 percent)	0	$ 0	$ 0	$ 0
Cash reserve, build to a one-month reserve (checking account)	Monthly income × 1	$ 5,000	$ 5,000	$ 0
Start a retirement plan. Build to a balance of one month's income	Monthly income × 1	$ 5,000	$13,000	$8,000
Continue building cash savings until you have an additional two months' reserve (savings account)	Monthly income × 2	$10,000	$15,000	$5,000

Table E.11 Year 4, Starting Phase 2, Independence

Goal/Bucket	Formula	A Balanced Path	Brandon & Teresa	Gap
No oppressive debt (No debt at a rate over 10 percent)	0	$0	$ 0	$ 0
Cash reserve, checking account	Monthly income × 3	$15,000	$ 5,000	–$10,000
Cash reserve, savings account	Monthly income × 3	$15,000	$15,000	$ 0
Retirement investing	Monthly income × 6	$30,000	$13,000	–$17,000
Big life changes	Monthly income × 9	$45,000	$ 0	–$45,000

growth of the existing $13,036 for seven years = $17,154. Total retirement savings = $16,244 + $14,216 + $17,154 = $47,614.

The total taxable savings is $550 per month for 72 months, which is $39,600. $10,000 of this is allocated to checking and the balance, about $30,000, to building additional savings.

They are close to completing the phase from a dollar perspective but they have a gap in the "big life changes." This could be problematic, as they are 35 years old and it is reasonable that they may be at a time in their life when they want to own a home. With their current savings, it would take them approximately 42 months to fill the "big life changes bucket," which would let them build up a traditional 20 percent down payment on the average home. This is one reasonable option for them. At the same time, they may have reached a point where they would like to own a home. They may be eligible for a variety of first-time home buyer programs, which might require much less than a 20-percent down payment. Tools to understand these options are outside of the scope of this book but resources to learn more are identified in the Resource Guide.

Since many first time home buyers take advantage of low down payment solutions, Table E.13 illustrates a bridge period of five years where their resources are directed to complete the phase regardless of the timing. By this, I mean that they do the following: direct $550 per month for 60 months to cash or paying down the mortgage, and continue directing

Table E.12   Phase 2, Independence after 7 years

Goal/Bucket	Formula	A Balanced Path	Brandon & Teresa	Gap
No oppressive debt (No debt at a rate over 10 percent)	0	$ 0	$ 0	$ 0
Cash reserve, checking account	Monthly income × 3	$15,000	$15,000	$ 0
Cash reserve, savings account	Monthly income × 3	$15,000	$15,000	$ 0
Retirement investing	Monthly income × 6	$30,000	$48,000	$18,000
Big life changes	Monthly income × 9	$45,000	$30,000	–$15,000

$200 per month to their retirement plan: 60 months × $550 per month = $33,000. Their gap from the glide path is $15,000, which means that they will have $18,000 excess cash ($33,000 – $15,000), which I will park in their savings account for now. To be clear, the purpose of this assumption simply lets them make a decision to buy a home at any point between 35 and 40 without overcomplicating the math.

Retirement savings is calculated: $200 per month for five years at 4 percent = $13,260 plus five employer matches for $1,800 (compounded at the same rate, annually) = $9,749. Plus, they have the growth of the existing $47,614 for five years = $57,930. Total retirement savings = $13,260 + $9,749 + $47,614 = $70,623. Table E.14 illustrates their balance sheet after they purchase their home.

During this time their expenses look like this:

$5,000 per month of income

–$930 per month for mortgage payment (30-year fixed at 4 percent)

–$250 per month for real estate taxes

–$70 per month to maintenance/depreciation

–$750 per month of savings ($200 per month to retirement and $550 per month to checking/savings)

–$536 federal taxes

Table E.13 Phase 2, Independence—Buying a House, Brandon and Teresa Age 40

Goal/Bucket	Formula	A Balanced Path	Brandon & Teresa	Gap
No oppressive debt (No debt at a rate over 10 percent)	0	$ 0	$ 0	$ 0
Cash reserve, checking account	Monthly income × 3	$ 15,000	$ 15,000	$ 0
Cash reserve, savings account	Monthly income × 3	$ 15,000	$ 33,000	$18,000
Retirement savings	Monthly income × 6	$ 30,000	$ 70,000	$40,000
House equity	Monthly income × 9	$ 45,000	$ 45,000	$ 0
Net worth	Monthly income × 21	$105,000	$163,000	$58,000
Mortgage	Monthly income × 39	($195,000)	($195,000)	$ 0
Total assets	Monthly income × 60	$300,000	$358,000	$58,000

Table E.14 Brandon & Teresa Approximate Balance Sheet after Home Purchase, Age 40

Assets	Amount	Liabilities	Amount
Checking account	$ 15,000	Oppressive Debt	$ 0
Savings account	$ 33,000		
Retirement investments	$ 70,000		
Home	$240,000	Mortgage	$195,000
Total assets	**$358,000**	**Total liabilities**	**$195,000**
Net worth	**$163,000**		

−$310 FICA

−$73 Medicare

= $2,081 after taxes to cover the rest of their expenses.[5]

Interestingly enough, when their taxes are input into TurboTax, they remain the same, $4,631.[6] There is a good chance that they perceived that there would be a tax benefit to owning a home, but in their case, it is not apparent that there is any tax benefit to them at all.[7] Proper tax assumptions should be an important consideration in your rent-versus-buy decision.

It is my view that $70 per month is well short of the actual cost of depreciation and maintenance (as discussed in Appendix C). This number is derived to show a common monthly living budget (it was $2,081 and remains $2,081 with the assumption). This makes the framework more neutral on the buy versus rent debate. Now that they are homeowners, they will likely have to spend their $1,800 tax refund on keeping up the house instead of doing fun things. The potential benefit of ownership is that they may get some home appreciation over time as well.

For better or worse, I am going to assume that they enter into a 30-year fixed mortgage. This is to test if this path works using readily available, common practices. Let's assume that they hold this path for 10 years, through age 50. The guide instructs them to do the following during the Freedom phase:

1. Write down your total liabilities (your total outstanding debt) = $195,000
2. Divide this number by 8 = $24,375 (rounded to $24,000)

Table E.15 shows us what their life would look like at age 50.

During the Freedom phase, Brandon and Teresa begin to build up their long-term investments. Their cash was at $48,000 and the glide path suggests $24,000 will be sufficient. They begin an investment account with $24,000 and add $550 per month at 4 percent for 120 months. This grows to $116,767. Retirement savings would be calculated as follows: $200 per month for 10 years at 4 percent = $29,450 plus 10 employer matches for $1,800 (compounded at the same rate, annually) = $21,611. Plus, they have the growth of the existing $70,263 for five years = $104,539. Total retirement savings = $29,450 + $21,611 + $104,539 = $155,600. The value of the home is unknown, but if we assume appreciation of inflation plus 1 percent, the home is worth $265,229. Table E.16 illustrates their balance sheet at age 50.

Now that they are 50, Brandon and Teresa solidly moved into Equilibrium and continue doing the same thing for the next 17 years. Table E.17 gives us a picture of where they end up at age 67.

Table E.15 Phase 3, Freedom Worksheet—Brandon and Teresa Debt Based at Age 50

Goal/Bucket	Formula	A Balanced Path	Brandon & Teresa	Gap
No oppressive debt (No debt at a rate over 10 percent)	0	$ 0	$ 0	$ 0
Cash reserve, checking + savings	Base unit × 1	$ 24,000	$ 24,000	$ 0
Other (jewelry, cars, furniture)	Base unit × 1	$ 24,000	$ 15,000	–$ 9,000
Long-term investments (after-tax)	Base unit × 3	$ 72,000	$116,000	$ 44,000
Retirement savings	Base unit × 5	$120,000	$156,000	$ 36,000
Total debt (mortgage)	Base unit × 8	($195,000)	($155,000)	$ 40,000
Net worth	Base unit × 13	$317,000	$421,000	$104,000
Total assets	Base unit × 21	$512,000	$576,000	$ 64,000

Table E.16 Brandon and Teresa Balance Sheet at 50 Years Old

Assets	Amount	Liabilities	Amount
Checking account	$ 24,000	Oppressive debt	$ 0
Other (personal items)	$ 15,000		
Long-term investments	$116,000		
Retirement investments	$156,000		
Home	$265,000	Mortgage	$155,000
Total assets	**$576,000**	**Total liabilities**	**$155,000**
Net worth	**$421,000**		

Brandon and Teresa continue building up their long-term investments; however, now they shift their savings $200 a month to long-term investments and $550 a month to their retirement savings. Their existing assets of $116,000 + $200 per month at 4 percent for 204 months grows to $287,009.

Retirement savings would be calculated as follows: $550 per month for 204 months at 4 percent plus the growth of the existing $156,000 = $467,899. Plus 17 employer matches for $1,800 (compounded at the same rate, annually) = $42,655. Total retirement savings = $467,899 + $42,655 = $510,554.

Table E.17 Phase 4, Equilibrium Worksheet for Brandon and Teresa at age 67

Goal/Bucket	Formula	A Balanced Path	Brandon & Teresa	Gap
No oppressive debt (No debt at a rate over 10 percent)	0	$ 0	$ 0	$ 0
Approximate cash reserve (checking + savings)	Monthly income × 7	$ 35,000	$ 24,000	–$ 11,000
Approximate other (jewelry, cars, furniture)	Monthly income × 7	$ 35,000	$ 15,000	–$ 20,000
Approximate mortgage	Monthly income × 35	($195,000)	($ 43,000)	$152,000
Approximate long-term investments (after-tax)	Monthly income × 56	$280,000	$287,000	$ 7,000
Approximate retirement savings	Monthly income × 91	$455,000	$510,000	$ 55,000
Approximate total investment assets	Monthly income × 147	$735,000	$797,000	$ 62,000

How do they look in retirement? If their investment assets of about $800,000 generate the same 4 percent return, then they will have $32,000 per year of income. Their Social Security is estimated to be $30,000 per year.[8] Total income is $62,000. They just got a significant raise in retirement. Importantly, they no longer need to save, so they can increase their monthly expenditures by what they were saving.

If their home is worth more than $250,000 (what they paid for it 30 years earlier), they are now millionaires! Look what else happens with their debt. Yes, they retired with a mortgage but they are able to cover the payment. In three years they will own their house outright, leading to yet another raise. Or better yet, they have the money in the bank to be able to pay it off now. I would be 100 percent comfortable with them selling down from their investments on the day they retire and paying off the mortgage. This would lead to a significant increase in their cash flow.

Testing the Assumptions

We took the average American, with an average income, average housing prices, and average rental rates, used conservative assumptions and turned them into millionaires using the power of debt.

One assumption that might strike you as conservative is that I assume that they will have a real return of inflation plus 4 percent. Often times, I refer to inflation plus 5 percent as a distribution rate. The difference between 4 and 5 percent is simply a level of confidence. Four percent is a more conservative assumption. This is based on my research and the reasons I identified in Chapter 5. For what it is worth, state and local government retirement systems hold assets of $3.56 trillion and they assume an average real return of 4.6 percent. So while the figure is conservative, the range of 4 to 5 percent is in line with the assumptions used by most state and local governments.[9] If your returns are higher, this will be much better, decreasing the age at which they can comfortably retire.

Also, I assume that you are going to live well past 100 years old. This may or may not be an assumption you want to make. If you want to assume a shorter life expectancy, you could retire earlier.

Another assumption that might not sit well is that the savings rate might seem high. Well, even with these assumptions, their after-tax, after-savings income is higher than 40 percent of American households' *gross* income.[10] So if you can't live within these assumptions, I think it is a good time to reflect on where you are in life.

What about children and other expenses? To keep the illustration simple, I excluded children. Obviously, many of the 40 percent of American households that have lower incomes do have children so it is possible to raise them within this budget. With this income there is a good chance of being eligible for grants and student aid. However, let's say that expenses from children totaled $150,000 over their lifetime. Depending on timing, mathematically this would be similar to not having paid down the mortgage, which pulls it back to the example in the chapter. Their income would still be sufficient to cover their mortgage in retirement and they would still have a raise in retirement. Further, they are still on track to retire early. They could easily work through age 70, which would increase their Social Security payment and the value of their portfolio.

Higher Income

If your household income is $60,000 the glide path outlined is powerful. Let's look at what happens if your income is higher, say dual income with $240,000 of income. Let's look at a couple, Ryan and Allison.

Income: $240,000
Savings: 15%
Starting age: 35
Employer match: 3%
Rate of return: Inflation + 4%
Cost of mortgage debt: Inflation + 2%
Cost of student debt: Inflation + 4%
Home appreciation: Inflation + 1%
Wage increases: Inflation
Payment structure: Interest only, they never make a principal payment
Property taxes: $15,000 (1.5% of $900,000)
Home price: $1,000,000

Further, I am going to introduce inflation into the equation to illustrate the power of capturing a spread over time. I am going to hold inflation at 2 percent. This implies that borrowing costs will be 4 percent and investment returns will be 6 percent and housing appreciation will be 3 percent. To simplify the number of moving pieces I will not apply inflation to wages or savings. We will start at age 35.

Let's intercept them in the Independence phase where their net worth is between 50 percent and two times their annual income. Table E.18 shows general assumptions based on the mid-30s, large urban professional crowd. They bought an expensive place (but they consider it to be reasonable based on their market) and took advantage of a low-down-payment solution. They have some cash, but not much relative to their income, and most of their money is tied up in their home. They are ahead on their retirement savings versus the guideline because they directed a lot of their early savings to that bucket.

The glide path does not include student debt, so Table E.19 reflects the above information plus $30,000 of student debt.

Table E.18 Phase 2, Independence—Dual Income Ryan and Allison, Age 35

Goal/Bucket	Formula	A Balanced Path	Ryan & Allison	Gap
No oppressive debt (No debt at a rate over 10 percent)	0	$ 0	$ 0	$ 0
Cash reserve, checking account	Monthly income × 3	$ 60,000	$ 25,000	–$ 35,000
Cash reserve, savings account	Monthly income × 3	$ 60,000	$ 15,000	–$ 45,000
Retirement savings	Monthly income × 6	$ 120,000	$ 160,000	$ 40,000
House equity	Monthly income × 9	$ 180,000	$ 100,000	–$ 80,000
Net worth	Monthly income × 21	$ 420,000	$ 270,000	–$150,000
Mortgage	Monthly income × 39	($ 780,000)	($ 900,000)	($120,000)
Total assets	Monthly income × 60	$1,200,000	$1,200,000	$ 0

Table E.19 Ryan and Allison Balance Sheet at Age 35

Assets	Amount	Liabilities	Amount
Checking account	$ 25,000	Oppressive debt	$ 0
Savings account	$ 15,000	Student debt	$ 30,000
Retirement investments	$ 160,000		
Home	$1,000,000	Mortgage	$900,000
Total assets	**$1,200,000**	**Total liabilities**	**$930,000**
Net worth	**$ 270,000**		

Let's test the glide path. During this time, their expenses look like this:

$20,000 per month of income

–$3,000 per month mortgage payment (assume inflation of 2% as starting figure for 4% cost: $900,000 × 4% = $36,000/12 = $3,000)

–$1,250 per month real estate taxes ($13,500/12)

–$1,000 per month to maintenance/depreciation/homeowners' association

–$3,000 per month savings (60% to taxable savings = $1,800 and 40% to retirement savings = $1,200/month to retirement)

–$4,000 federal taxes[11]

–$1,250 FICA

–$300 Medicare

= $6,200 after taxes, after savings, after mortgage to cover the rest of their expenses

When their taxes are input into TurboTax, they receive a $15,000 refund.[12] I will exclude this refund from the math for "wiggle room" (child-related expenses, state taxes, additional income, etc.). Here it is possible that the tax benefits to owning a home might in fact be bigger than they would estimate if they did not do the math. Due to their high income, in many markets this may impact the rent versus buy math considerably.

Let's assume that they pay down zero on their mortgage, they just make interest payments, and that they direct their $1,800 per month of savings to $600 per month to student debt and $1,200 per month to building up their checking and savings.

Let's assume that they hold this path for five years, through age 40. The guide instructs to take your debt and divide it by 8. Remember that Brandon and Teresa's debt was too high, therefore for Ryan and Allison, I am going to use what their debt should be, as suggested in the glide path, rather than what it is. The Independence phase suggested a balanced amount of $780,000 (which we will round to $800,000) and use that as the target.

1. Write down your total liabilities (your total outstanding debt) = $800,000
2. Divide this number by 8 = $100,000

The $1,200 per month of savings for 60 months at 2 percent (inflation) would grow to $75,000. (They are building up cash so there is little return.) The $600 per month for five years would pay off their student debt over the five years ($575 per month at 6 percent pays off $30,000 in 60 months).

Retirement savings would be calculated as follows: $1,200 per month for five years at 6 percent = $83,724 plus five employer matches of $7,200 (compounded at the same rate, annually) = $40,587. Plus, they have the growth of the existing $160,000 for five years = $214,116. Total retirement savings = $83,724 + $40,487 + $214,116 = $338,327, rounded to $340,000. Table E.20 shows us what their life would look like at age 40.

A few powerful changes have taken place in their life. First, they have $115,000 in the bank. They can ride out most any storm that life sends them. Keep in mind that while their income is $20,000 per month, they are living on $12,000 ($5,000 is going to taxes and $3,000 to savings). This means that the $115,000 reserve could get them through about 10 months of crisis, and that is with no changes to their lifestyle! They can move, change jobs, and should feel very little financial anxiety about the short term.

They built up some assets in cars and things (but it is a big part of the overall picture). They have eliminated their student debt but kept their mortgage. Their home appreciated a little so they now have $250,000 of home equity. Their retirement savings increased over twofold! This is

Table E.20 Phase 3, Freedom Worksheet—Ryan and Allison at Age 40

Goal/Bucket	Formula	A Balanced Path	Ryan & Allison	Gap
No oppressive debt (No debt at a rate over 10 percent)	0	$ 0	$ 0	$ 0
Cash reserve, checking + savings	Base unit × 1	$ 100,000	$ 115,000	$ 15,000
Other (jewelry, cars, furniture)	Base unit × 1	$ 100,000	$ 30,000	−$ 70,000
Long-term investments (after-tax)	Base unit × 3	$ 300,000	$ 0	−$300,000
Retirement savings	Base unit × 5	$ 500,000	$ 340,000	−$160,000
Total debt (mortgage)	Base unit × 8	($ 800,000)	($ 900,000)	($100,000)
Net worth	Base unit × 13	$1,300,000	$ 744,000	−$556,000
Total assets	Base unit × 21	$2,100,000	$1,644,000	−$456,000

Table E.21 Approximate Balance Sheet at Age 40

Assets	Amount	Liabilities	Amount
Checking account	$ 115,000	Oppressive debt	$ 0
Other (Jewelry/cars)	$ 30,000	Student debt	$ 0
Long-term investments	$ 0		
Retirement investments	$ 340,000		
Home	$1,159,000	Mortgage	$900,000
Total assets	**$1,644,000**	**Total liabilities**	**$900,000**
Net worth	**$ 744,000**		

the power of a base of assets plus savings. In fact, even though they only paid down a little bit of debt, Table E.21 shows their net worth increased over twofold as well in that five-year period.

While they should be feeling good about the short term, how does the long term look? The beacons are flashing brightest to build up their long-term investments and to build up their retirement investments. Since their debt ratio will fall as they build up assets, and since they like the tax benefits from debt, we will direct their investing and leave their debt constant. They know that they can always pay down debt any-time so they decide to focus first on building assets and to pay down debt later. They no longer have the cost of student debt. They calculate that they should be splitting their total savings 50/50 between retirement and long-term investments or $1,500 per month to each bucket.

Currently, they don't have an investment account so they decide to begin one with $40,000 from cash (leaving them with $75,000 in cash) and to save $1,500 per month to build up this bucket. The $40,000 plus $1,800 per month of savings for 27 years (324 months) would grow to $1,411,129, which I will round to $1.4 million.

Retirement savings would be calculated as follows: Existing assets of $340,000 plus $1,500 per month for 27 years at 6 percent = $2,920,950. They also have 27 employer matches of $7,200 (compounded at the same rate, annually) = $458,681. Total retirement savings = $2,920,950 + $458,681 = $3,379,631, which I will round to $3.4 million.

The house at 3-percent appreciation for 32 years would be worth about $2.575 million, which I round to $2.5 million. If cash grows at inflation, $75,000 would grow to $128,000, which I rounded to $125,000. "Other/stuff" does not impact the exercise and is just an estimate of their things. Table E.22 shows Ryan and Allison compared to the Equilibrium glide path at age 67 and Table E.23 illustrates their balance sheet at the same age.

Table E.22 Equilibrium Worksheet for Ryan and Allison at age 67

Goal/Bucket	Formula	A Balanced Path	Ryan & Allison	Gap
No oppressive debt (No debt at a rate over 10 percent)	0	$ 0	$ 0	$ 0
Approximate cash reserve (checking + savings)	Monthly income × 7	$ 140,000	$ 125,000	–$ 15,000
Approximate other (jewelry, cars, furniture)	Monthly income × 7	$ 140,000	$ 100,000	–$ 40,000
Approximate mortgage	Monthly income × 35	($ 700,000)	($ 900,000)	($ 200,000)
Approximate long-term investments (after-tax)	Monthly income × 56	$1,120,000	$1,400,000	$ 280,000
Approximate retirement savings	Monthly income × 91	$1,820,000	$3,400,000	$1,580,000
Approximate total investment assets	Monthly income × 147	$2,940,000	$4,800,000	$1,860,000

Table E.23 Approximate Balance Sheet for Ryan and Allison at Age 67

Assets	Amount	Liabilities	Amount
Checking account	$ 125,000	Oppressive debt	$ 0
Other (Jewelry/cars)	$ 100,000	Student debt	$ 0
Long-term investments	$1,400,000		
Retirement investments	$3,400,000		
Home	$2,500,000	Mortgage	$900,000
Total assets	**$7,525,000**	**Total liabilities**	**$900,000**
Net worth	**$6,625,000**		

Let's look at income in retirement. (The following is a brief highlight from the themes of the book *The Value of Debt in Retirement*, so for a comprehensive understanding I would refer you to that material.)

- Their investment assets are $4,800,000.
- A 6-percent return is $288,000 or $24,000 per month.
- Taxes would only be $5,000 per year, or $416 per month.[13]

- The mortgage would still be $36,000 or $3,000 per month.
- This would leave them with about $20,000 after taxes and mortgage.

What about their living expenses? They were spending $6,200 per month, about $8,500 including taxes and depreciation on the home. $8,500 at 2 percent for 27 years would be about $15,000 in future dollars. Even if their lifestyle does not scale back they have excess funds.

Importantly, Ryan and Allison have five secret weapons:

1. **Social Security:** At age 70, their Social Security benefit is estimated to be at $5,272 per month, or $63,273 per year. This would be excess income.[14]
2. **The ability to downsize:** They could move from their house to a $1.2 million property (the equivalent of about $500,000 in today's dollars) and own it outright and have no mortgage expense.
3. **The ability to work longer:** If things are not on track, they can work until 70, or beyond. Each year they work, they also have one less year of life expectancy.
4. **The ability to pay off their debt:** Any day they don't like this strategy, they can simply pay off their debt.
5. **The ability to borrow more money:** They can borrow against their house and they can borrow against their portfolio. They may not need to do this, but it gives them tremendous flexibility.

And herein lies the point: Any way you cut it, they are solidly on track for retirement. Ryan and Allison are a liquid, flexible force that is well on track for retirement by embracing the L.I.F.E. glide path. It may very well turn out that in their 50s they decide to pay off or pay down their house. However, until you break through the Equilibrium phase, if your after-tax cost of debt is less than your expected return on your portfolio, I would generally suggest not paying down any of your debt until you can pay down all of your debt. That is The Value of Debt in Building Wealth.[15]

Endnotes

1. This approach to calculating the future value of the home results in $551,848. The future value of $300,000 at 2 percent for 30 years is $546,362. The rounding avoids fractional months and makes the example easier to follow. To be

consistent across examples, I use the $551,848 value instead of the $546,362 value at year 30. This is not statistically significant: since they all own the exact same home for the exact same period of time has no impact on the illustration.

2. https://www.census.gov/housing/hvs/data/histtab11.xls.

3. http://www.adp.com/tools-and-resources/calculators-and-tools/payroll-calculators/salary-paycheck-calculator.aspx.

4. https://turbotax.intuit.com/tax-tools/calculators/taxcaster/. Married, 25, 25, $30,000 earnings each spouse, $2400 to IRA.

5. http://www.adp.com/tools-and-resources/calculators-and-tools/payroll-calculators/salary-paycheck-calculator.aspx.

6. https://turbotax.intuit.com/tax-tools/calculators/taxcaster/.

7. Tax laws are complex and subject to change. Tax information contained in this presentation is general and not exhaustive by nature. It is not intended or written to be used, and cannot be used, by any taxpayer for the purpose of avoiding U.S. federal tax laws. This material was not intended or written to be used for the purpose of avoiding tax penalties that may be imposed on the taxpayer. Individuals are encouraged to consult their tax and legal advisors (a) before establishing a retirement plan or account, and (b) regarding any potential tax, ERISA, and related consequences of any investments made under such plan or account. These materials and any statements contained herein should not be construed as tax or legal advice. Tax advice must come from your tax advisor.

8. "Social Security Calculator," http://www.bankrate.com/calculators/retirement/social-security-benefits-calculator.aspx. Married 67, 67 years old, $60,000 single earner ($29,860). Also see: https://www.ssa.gov/cgi-bin/benefit6.cgi.

9. http://www.nasra.org/files/Issue%20Briefs/NASRAInvReturnAssumptBrief.pdf.

10. Melissa S. Kearney, Benjamin H. Harris, Elisa Jácome, and Lucie Parker, "A Dozen Facts about America's Struggling Lower-Middle Class," The Hamilton Project (December 2, 2013), http://www.hamiltonproject.org/papers/a_dozen_facts_about_americas_struggling_lower-middle_class/.

11. "Salary Paycheck Calculator," http://www.adp.com/tools-and-resources/calculators-and-tools/payroll-calculators/salary-paycheck-calculator.aspx. $20,000 monthly gross pay, Federal taxes of $3,979.96, Medicare of $290.00 and FICA of $1,240.00. No federal allowances. Married. Texas is the state. $1,200 per month 401K deduction.

12. https://turbotax.intuit.com/tax-tools/calculators/taxcaster/. Married, joint, 35, $240,000 - $14,400 401K = $225,600 2015 taxable wages, $48,000 federal withholdings, 0 state withholdings, all income to one of the spouses, $36,000 mortgage interest, $15,000 real estate taxes, $2,000 in donations = $15,091 refund.

13. https://turbotax.intuit.com/tax-tools/calculators/taxcaster/. Married, joint, 67, 67 years old, $0 taxable wages (state or federal for either spouse), $36,000 mortgage interest payment, $15,000 real estate taxes, $2,000 donations,

$20,000 long-term gains, $10,000 taxable interest ($500K at 2%), $15K qualified dividends, 750K at 2%), $90,000 IRA distributions (4 percent), $4,931 taxes.

14. http://www.bankrate.com/calculators/retirement/social-security-benefits-calculator.aspx.

15. Author's note: The information in this chapter is to be considered in a holistic way as a part of the book and not to be considered on a stand-alone basis. This includes, but is not limited to, the discussion of the risks of each of these ideas as well as all of the disclaimers throughout the book. The material is presented with a goal of encouraging thoughtful conversation and rigorous debate on the risks and potential benefits of the concepts between you and your advisors based on your unique situation, risk tolerance, and goals.

Glossary

401(k): An employer-sponsored retirement savings plan that allows employees to save and invest a portion of their paycheck before taxes are taken out.

After-tax cost of debt: Some interest expense is tax deductible, some interest expense is not. If the interest expense is tax deductible then the after-tax cost of debt is the interest rate on debt multiplied by (100 percent minus the income tax rate).

Aggressive bucket: Investments that take a measured but higher level of risk while striving for increased returns.

Amortization: The process of paying off debt with a fixed repayment schedule over a period of time.

Asset allocation: The process and goal of allocating the assets in your investment portfolio in an attempt to balance risk and reward.

Asset class: A group of investments that have similar characteristics, behave similarly, and are subject to the same laws and regulations.

Balance sheet: A financial statement that summarizes your assets and liabilities at a particular point in time.

Capital gains: A profit from the sale of an asset where the sale price exceeds the purchase price.

Capital structure: The mix of various debt and equity capital maintained by a firm or individual.

Capture the spread: The process of earning a rate of return higher than your after-tax cost of debt.

Commodities: Any good traded on an exchange that traditionally includes agricultural products and raw materials (e.g., wheat, grain, oil, natural gas), but has expanded to include financial products such as foreign currencies and indexes.

Compounding: The process of an exponential increase in principal by creating a larger base that earns more principal and accumulated interest.

Correlation: A standardized statistical measure of the dependence of two random variables. Defined as the covariance divided by the standard deviations of the two variables.

Core bucket: Investments aimed at keeping money prudently invested and working for an individual investor over time. Ideally, it protects principal and grows it by inflation plus 4 percent on average.

Debt: Loan agreement that is a liability of the individual. An obligation to repay a specified amount at a particular time.

Debt ratio or debt-to-asset ratio: An indicator of financial leverage that is calculated by dividing your total liabilities by your total assets.

Debt service coverage ratio: The amount of cash available to pay current debt obligations.

Developed markets: Countries that are considered the most developed in terms of their economy and capital markets. Typically consists of 20 to 30 countries representing the largest economies in the world.

Diversification: Allocating your investments across a wide array of securities, from different industries and sectors to different countries in order to reduce risk. Not putting all your financial investment eggs in one basket.

Emerging markets: A nation's economy with low to middle per capita income that is progressing toward becoming advanced. Countries in this category make up approximately 80 percent of the world's population.

Enriching debt: Debt that may make you wealthier over time, such as a mortgage or debt borrowed through a securities-based line of credit at a low interest rate, that enables a careful investor to leverage that debt and capture the spread over time.

Equilibrium phase: Your net worth is greater than five times your gross annual pretax income. You have a healthy, accessible cushion of cash in reserve. You are saving and enjoying life. You're likely on track to retire with a comfortable amount of money to cover your expenses and enjoy life.

Equity: The difference between the value of an asset and the cost of the debt owed on that asset. Can also mean a security that represents an ownership interest.

Exchange-traded funds (ETFs): An investment fund that tracks an exchange like the S&P 500, Dow Jones, or NASDAQ, and holds assets such as stocks, bonds, or commodities.

Financing: The act of obtaining money for a purchase.

Freedom phase: Your net worth is between two and five times your gross annual pretax income. You are at the point where you can safely and confidently take advantage of the debt strategies I discuss here and reap the benefits of your financial decisions.

Glide path: A formula designed to guide you toward a desired outcome.

High-yield bonds: A high-paying bond with a lower credit rating than investment-grade corporate bonds. Often referred to as junk bonds.

Independence phase: You have a small nest egg and many people consider buying a home or taking on some working debt. Your net worth is between 50 percent and two times your gross annual pretax income.

Inflation: A fall in the buying power of a unit of currency.

Interest rate: The price paid for borrowing money.

Interest-only mortgage: A mortgage in which you pay only the interest on the mortgage through monthly payments for a set term.

Launch phase: In this phase, you are just starting to build your wealth with an emphasis on reducing oppressive debt and building up a savings reserve. Your net worth is less than 50 percent of your gross annual pretax income (if your income varies, use the most conservative estimate).

Leverage: The use of debt to increase the potential return of an investment.

Liabilities: Debts of the individual.

LIBOR: London Interbank Offered Rate. It is the rate the most credit-worthy banks charge one another for large loans of euros overnight in the London market.

Line of credit: An agreement that allows you to borrow up to a previously specified limit.

Liquidity: Refers to the ease and quickness of converting assets to cash. Also called marketability.

Long-term bonds: A bond typically with a maturity of more than 10 to 15 years.

Modern Portfolio Theory: A theory of financial investing from Nobel Prize–winning economist Harry Markowitz that attempts to maximize the return for any given level of risk, or minimize the risk for any given level of return.

Money market: An account that provides benefits of both savings and checking accounts by typically paying a higher interest rate than a savings account and offering the account holder limited ability to write checks.

Mortgage: A loan for the purchase of real estate that an individual is required to pay back with a predetermined set of payments.

Mortgage interest tax deduction: Allows taxpayers who own their homes to deduct the interest paid on their first and second mortgages up to approximately $1 million in principal.

Municipal bonds: Bonds issued by a municipality such as a city or state.

Negative correlation: A relationship between two variables in which one increases as the other decreases.

Net worth: Your assets minus your liabilities.

Opportunity cost: The value of the next best choice that is given up to pursue an alternative.

Oppressive debt: Low-quality debt that oppresses the debtor and makes them continually poorer, such as high-interest credit card debt.

Payday loan: A short-term form of borrowing small amounts that typically has a very high interest rate.

Position size: The amount of money bought or sold in an investment within a portfolio.

Positive correlation: A relationship between two variables in which both variables increase or decrease at the same time.

Preserve bucket: Easily accessible investments that preserve purchasing power.

Principal: The amount borrowed or still owed on a loan excluding interest.

Rate of return: The gain or loss of an investment over a period of time.

Rebalancing: Realigning the percentages or weightings of the assets in your portfolio, usually by selling certain assets that have done well over time, to return the portfolio to its original desired asset allocation.

Risk: A peril or danger; in financial matters, the chance the return on your investment will become worthless, or just worth less than it cost in the first place or than you expected it to be.

Securities: Tradable financial investments such as stocks, bonds, and derivatives.

Standard deviation: A measure of how spread out numbers are in a set of data from the mean. The more spread apart the data, the higher the deviation. Standard deviation is calculated as the square root of the variance.

Target date funds (TDF): Typically, a mutual fund or collective trust fund that automatically resets the asset mix in the portfolio to become more conservative as the target date approaches.

Tax-deferred: Investments in which taxes are paid at a later date, rather than in the period when the investment produces income.

Volatility: Refers to how likely it is for a security to move substantially up or down in any given time period. This is typically measured by standard deviation.

Working debt: Debt such as a mortgage, at a reasonable interest rate and with reasonable terms, that enables you to move forward with important life goals.

Resource Guide

This resource guide is designed to provide information to better understand certain concepts in the book. The following is a compilation of free online education videos from Khan Academy and Better Money Habits.

Khan Academy's mission is "to provide a free, world-class education for anyone, anywhere." Khan Academy is a not-for-profit entity; there are no ads and no subscriptions.

Better Money Habits is a partnership between Bank of America and Khan Academy. BetterMoneyHabits.com is "a free service that enables everyone to understand finances through objective and unbiased videos and tools."[1]

Basic Information

Introduction to Balance Sheets https://www.khanacademy.org/
economics-finance-domain/core-finance/housing/home-equity-
tutorial/v/introduction-to-balance-sheets

More on Balance Sheets and Equity https://www.khanacademy
.org/economics-finance-domain/core-finance/housing/home-
equity-tutorial/v/more-on-balance-sheets-and-equity

Inflation, Interest Rates, and Compound Interest

Inflation

Inflation Overview https://www.khanacademy.org/economics-
finance-domain/core-finance/inflation-tutorial/inflation-basics-
tutorial/v/inflation-overview

What Is Inflation? https://www.khanacademy.org/economics-
finance-domain/core-finance/inflation-tutorial/inflation-basics-
tutorial/v/what-is-inflation

Moderate Inflation in a Good Economy https://www
.khanacademy.org/economics-finance-domain/core-finance/
inflation-tutorial/inflation-scenarios-tutorial/v/moderate-
inflation-in-a-good-economy

Stagflation https://www.khanacademy.org/economics-finance-
domain/core-finance/inflation-tutorial/inflation-scenarios-
tutorial/v/stagflation

Hyperinflation https://www.khanacademy.org/economics-
finance-domain/core-finance/inflation-tutorial/inflation-
scenarios-tutorial/v/hyperinflation

Interest Rates

Real and Nominal Return https://www.khanacademy.org/
economics-finance-domain/core-finance/inflation-tutorial/real-
nominal-return-tut/v/real-and-nominal-return

Relations between Nominal and Real Returns and Inflation
https://www.khanacademy.org/economics-finance-domain/
core-finance/inflation-tutorial/real-nominal-return-tut/v/
relation-between-nominal-and-real-returns-and-inflation

Compound Interest

Compound Interest https://www.khanacademy.org/economics-
finance-domain/core-finance/interest-tutorial/compound-
interest-tutorial/v/introduction-to-compound-interest

The Time Value of Money https://www.bettermoneyhabits.com/
saving-budgeting/saving-for-future/time-value-money.html

Housing

Renting vs. Buying

Renting vs. Buying Overview https://www.khanacademy.org/
economics-finance-domain/core-finance/housing/renting-v-
buying/v/renting-versus-buying-a-home

Renting vs. Buying Part 2 https://www.khanacademy.org
/economics-finance-domain/core-finance/housing/renting-v-
buying/v/renting-vs-buying-a-home-part-2

Renting vs. Buying Detailed Analysis https://www.khanacademy
.org/economics-finance-domain/core-finance/housing/renting-
v-buying/v/renting-vs-buying-detailed-analysis

Deciding to Buy or Rent https://www.bettermoneyhabits.com
/home-buying-renting/deciding-to-buy-or-rent/should-i-rent-or-
buy.html

How Much Home You Can Afford

How Much Home Can You Comfortably Afford? https://www
.bettermoneyhabits.com/home-buying-renting/how-much-can-i-
afford/how-much-mortgage-can-i-afford.html

Buying a Home Comfortably and Affordably https://www
.bettermoneyhabits.com/home-buying-renting/how-much-can-i-
afford/buying-home-comfortably-affordably.html

Planning for Extra Costs When Buying a Home https://www
.bettermoneyhabits.com/home-buying-renting/how-much-can-i-
afford/additional-costs-of-buying-a-home.html

Mortgages

Introduction to Mortgages https://www.khanacademy.org/
economics-finance-domain/core-finance/housing/mortgages-
tutorial/v/introduction-to-mortgage-loans

What Makes Up a Mortgage Payment? https://www
.bettermoneyhabits.com/home-buying-renting/how-much-
can-i-afford/what-is-included-in-mortgage-payment.html

Mortgage Interest Rates https://www.khanacademy.org/
economics-finance-domain/core-finance/housing/mortgages-
tutorial/v/mortgage-interest-rates

Understanding Alternative Mortgage Options https://www
.bettermoneyhabits.com/home-buying-renting/your-mortgage-
options/different-types-of-mortgage-loans.html

Adjustable Rate Mortgages https://www.khanacademy.org/
economics-finance-domain/core-finance/housing/mortgages-
tutorial/v/adjustable-rate-mortgages-arms

Fixed vs. Adjustable Rate Mortgages https://www.bettermoney
habits.com/home-buying-renting/your-mortgage-options/fixed-
vs-adjustable-rate-mortgages-infographic.html
https://www.bettermoneyhabits.com/home-buying-renting/
your-mortgage-options/fixed-vs-adjustable-rate-mortgages.html

Corporate Debt vs. Traditional Mortgages https://www
.khanacademy.org/economics-finance-domain/core-finance/
stock-and-bonds/bonds-tutorial/v/corporate-debt-versus-
traditional-mortgages

Introduction to Stocks and Bonds

Introduction to Bonds https://www.khanacademy.org/
economics-finance-domain/core-finance/stock-and-bonds/
bonds-tutorial/v/introduction-to-bonds

The Relationship between Bond Prices and Interest Rates
https://www.khanacademy.org/economics-finance-domain/core-
finance/stock-and-bonds/bonds-tutorial/v/relationship-between-
bond-prices-and-interest-rates

What it Means to Buy a Company's Stock https://www
.khanacademy.org/economics-finance-domain/core-finance
/stock-and-bonds/stocks-intro-tutorial/v/what-it-means-to-buy-
a-company-s-stock

Bonds vs. Stocks https://www.khanacademy.org/economics-
finance-domain/core-finance/stock-and-bonds/stocks-intro-
tutorial/v/bonds-vs-stocks

Investment Vehicles

Traditional IRAs https://www.khanacademy.org/economics-finance-domain/core-finance/investment-vehicles-tutorial/ira-401ks/v/traditional-iras

Roth IRAs https://www.khanacademy.org/economics-finance-domain/core-finance/investment-vehicles-tutorial/ira-401ks/v/roth-iras

401(k)s https://www.khanacademy.org/economics-finance-domain/core-finance/investment-vehicles-tutorial/ira-401ks/v/401-k-s

Open-Ended Mutual Funds https://www.khanacademy.org/economics-finance-domain/core-finance/investment-vehicles-tutorial/mutual-funds/v/open-ended-mutual-fund-part-1

Exchange-Traded Funds (ETFs) https://www.khanacademy.org/economics-finance-domain/core-finance/investment-vehicles-tutorial/mutual-funds/v/exchange-traded-funds-etfs

Credit Score

What Is a Good Credit Score? https://www.bettermoneyhabits.com/credit/what-is-a-credit-score/good-credit-score.html

Your Credit Score: How It's Calculated https://www.bettermoneyhabits.com/credit/what-is-a-credit-score/how-credit-score-is-calculated.html

Ways to Boost Your Credit Score https://www.bettermoneyhabits.com/credit/what-is-a-credit-score/how-to-boost-credit.html

How Credit Scores Affect Interest Rates https://www.bettermoneyhabits.com/credit/what-is-a-credit-score/credit-score-impact-on-interest-rates.html

Calculators[2]

Rent vs. Buy https://www.google.com/#q=rent+versus+buy+markets+for+housing

Future Value Calculator http://www.CalculatorSoup.com

Social Security Estimator https://www.ssa.gov/cgi-bin/benefit6 .cgi

How Much Home Can I Afford? https://www.bettermoneyhabits .com/home-buying-renting/how-much-can-i-afford/how-much- house-can-i-afford-calculator.html

Endnotes

1. These resources are provided for your convenience. Neither Khan Academy nor Better Money Habits are affiliated with *The Value of Debt*, *The Value of Debt in Building Wealth*, Timber Wolf Publishing, Supernova Companies, or their affiliates. Accessing these resources, you are subject to their Terms of Use, Privacy Policies and copyrights. Neither the publisher, author, or Timber Wolf Publishing or its affiliated entities, including Supernova Companies, attests to the completeness or accuracy of information found in these resources. Content in these resources is subject to change without notice and therefore the applicability may change as well. The author neither agrees nor disagrees with the content of these resources. The resources identified herein are to foster and facilitate a better learning experience with respect to the content in *The Value of Debt in Building Wealth*.

2. These resources are provided for your convenience. These calculators are not affiliated with *The Value of Debt*, *The Value of Debt in Building Wealth*, Timber Wolf Publishing, Supernova Companies, or their affiliates. Accessing these resources, you are subject to their Terms of Use, Privacy Policies, and copyrights. Neither the publisher, author, or Timber Wolf Publishing or its affiliated entities, including Supernova Companies, attests to the completeness or accuracy of information found in these resources. Content in these resources is subject to change without notice and therefore the applicability may change as well. The author neither agrees nor disagrees with the content or results of these resources. The resources identified herein are to foster and facilitate a better learning experience with respect to the content in *The Value of Debt in Building Wealth*.

Bibliography

Books

Anderson, Thomas J. *The Value of Debt: How to Manage Both Sides of a Balance Sheet to Maximize Wealth.* Hoboken, NJ: John Wiley & Sons, 2013.
Anderson, Thomas J. *The Value of Debt in Retirement: Why Everything You Have Been Told Is Wrong.* Hoboken, NJ: John Wiley & Sons, 2015.
Bingham, Al. *The Road to 850: Proven Strategies for Increasing Your Credit Score.* Layton, UT: CP Publishing, 2007.
Covey, Stephen R. *The 7 Habits of Highly Effective People: Powerful Lessons in Personal Change.* New York: Free Press, 1989.

Text Books

Bodie, Ziv, Alex Kane, and Alan Marcus. *Investments.* 9th ed. New York: McGraw-Hill, 2011.
Ross, Stephen A., Randolph Westerfield, and Jeffrey Jaffe. *Corporate Finance.* 10th ed. New York: McGraw-Hill, 2013.

Nobel Prize–Winning Theories

Markowitz, H. "Portfolio Selection." *Journal of Finance* (1952), Modern Portfolio Theory.
Miller, Merton. "Debt and Taxes." *Journal of Finance* (May 1997).

Modigliani, F., and M. Miller. "The Cost of Capital, Corporation Finance and the Theory of Investment." *American Economic Review* 48, no. 3 (1958): 261–297.

Modigliani, F., and M. Miller. "Corporate Income Taxes and the Cost of Capital: A Correction." *American Economic Review* 53, no. 3 (1963): 433–443.

Articles

Bengan, William P. "Determining Withdrawal Rates Using Historical Data." *Journal of Financial Planning* (1994). Available at www.retailinvestor.org/pdf/ Bengen1.pdf.Thefourpercentrule.

Cooley, Philip L., Carl M. Hubbard, and Daniel T. Walz."Trinity Study." *Sustainable Withdrawal Rates from Your Retirement Portfolio.* www.afcpe.org/assets/pdf/ vol1014.pdf.

Trading Economics. www.tradingeconomics.com/united-states/gdp.

Ideas from the following papers are indirectly referenced through concepts in this book and directly referenced in the aforementioned textbooks. You are encouraged to read them as well:

Agrawal, Anup, and Nandu Nagarajan. "Corporate Capital Structure, Agency Costs, and Ownership Control: The Case of All Equity Firms." *Journal of Finance* 45 (September 1990).

Altman, E. I. "A Further Empirical Investigation of the Bankruptcy Cost Questions." *Journal of Finance*, September 1984.

Andrade, Gregor, and Steven N. Kaplan. "How Costly Is Financial (Not Economic) Distress? Evidence from Highly Leveraged Transactions That Became Distressed." *Journal of Finance*, October 1998.

Bar-Or, Yuval. "An Investigation of Expected Distress Costs." Unpublished paper, Wharton School, University of Pennsylvania, March 2000.

Barberis, Nicholas, and Richard Thaler. "A Survey of Behavioral Finance." In *The Handbook of the Economics of Finance*, ed. G. M. Constantinides, M. Harris, and R. Stulz (Amsterdam: Elsevier, 2003).

Bris, Auturo, Ivo Welch, and Ning Zhu. "The Costs of Bankruptcy: Chapter 7 Liquidation versus Chapter 11 Reorganization." *Journal of Finance*, June 2006.

Cutler, David M., and Lawrence H. Summers. "The Costs of Conflict Resolution and Financial Distress: Evidence from the Texaco—Penzoil Litigation." *Rand Journal of Economics*, Summer 1988.

Graham, John. "How Big Are the Tax Benefits of Debt?" *Journal of Finance*, 2000.

Graham, John, and Campbell Harvey. "The Theory and Practice of Corporate Finance." *Journal of Financial Economics*, May/June 2001.

Kahnerman, D., and A. Tversky. "Prospect Theory: An Analysis of Decision under Risk." *Econometrica* 47 (1979): 263–291.

Suggested Reading

Bernstein, William J. *The Investor's Manifesto: Preparing for Prosperity, Armageddon, and Everything in Between.* Hoboken, NJ: John Wiley & Sons, 2010.

Conrad, Edward. *Unintended Consequences: Why Everything You've Been Told about the Economy Is Wrong.* New York: Portfolio Penguin, 2012.

Ferguson, Niall. *The Ascent of Money: A Financial History of the World.* New York: The Penguin Press, 2008.

Graeber, David. *Debt: The First 5000 Years.* Brooklyn: Melville House, 2011.

Hanson, Jon. *Good Debt, Bad Debt—Knowing the Difference Can Save Your Financial Life.* New York: Portfolio Penguin, 2005.

Malkeil, Burton. *A Random Walk Down Wall Street,* 9th ed. New York: W.W. Norton & Co., 2007.

Reinhart, Carmen M., and Kenneth S. Rogoff. *This Time Is Different: Eight Centuries of Financial Folly.* Princeton, NJ: Princeton University Press, 2009.

Rickards, James. *Currency Wars: The Making of the Next Global Crisis.* New York: Portfolio Penguin, 2011.

Rickards, James. *The Death of Money: The Coming Collapse of the International Monetary System.* New York: Portfolio Penguin, 2014.

Thaler, Richard H., and Cass R. Sunstein. *Nudge: Improving Decisions about Health, Wealth, and Happiness,* revised and expanded edition. New York: Penguin Books, 2009.

Wessel, David. *Red Ink: Inside the High-Stakes Politics of the Federal Budget.* New York: Crown Business, 2012.

Wiedemer, David, Robert Wiedemer, and Cindy Spitzer. *Aftershock: Protect Yourself and Profit in the Next Global Financial Meltdown,* revised and updated, 3rd ed. Hoboken, NJ: John Wiley & Sons, 2014.

Whalen, Christopher. *Inflated: How Money and Debt Built the American Dream.* Hoboken, NJ: John Wiley & Sons, 2011.

Zingales, Luigi. *A Capitalism for the People: Recapturing the Lost Genius of American Prosperity.* New York: Basic Books, 2012.[1]

Endnotes

1. Author's note: The information in this chapter is to be considered in a holistic way as a part of the book and not to be considered on a stand-alone basis. This includes, but is not limited to, the discussion of the risks of each of these ideas as well as all of the disclaimers throughout the book. The material is presented with a goal of encouraging thoughtful conversation and rigorous debate on the risks and potential benefits of the concepts between you and your advisors based on your unique situation, risk tolerance, and goals.

Index

Page references followed by f indicate an illustrated figure; followed by t indicate a table.